STUDY GUIDE

AGE 11-14

KEY STAGE 3

MATHEMATICS

Ray Williams

- A clear introduction to the new National Curriculum

- Topic by topic coverage, with lots of diagrams and illustrations

- Investigations designed to encourage active learning

- Frequent questions to test your knowledge

- Index and glossary of terms

- Sample National Test questions and answers

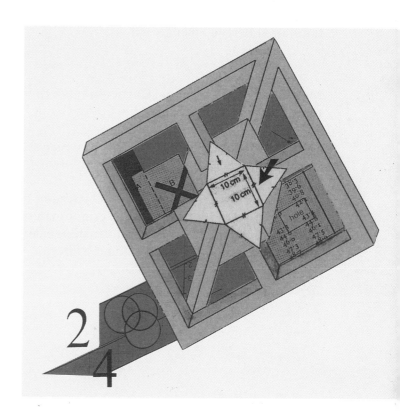

First published 1991
Reprinted 1991, 1992 (twice), 1993, 1994, 1996 (twice), 1998 (twice), 2000 (twice), 2001 (twice)
Revised 1995, 1998

Letts Educational
The Chiswick Centre
414 Chiswick High Road
London W4 5TF
Tel: 020 8996 3333

British Library Cataloguing in Publication Data
A CIP record for this book is available from the British Library

ISBN 1 85758 942 4

Acknowledgements
I have had considerable help from my family and friends in the
planning and writing of this book. I would like to thank them all.
I wish to give special mention to John Evans, my son Andrew and
the staff at Berry Hill High School.

Ray Williams

Material from the National Curriculum is Crown copyright and is
reproduced by permission of the Controller of HMSO.

Crown copyright material from the Key Stage 3 Mathematics
National Test is adapted by permission of the Controller of HMSO.

Every effort has been made to trace copyright holders and to obtain
their permission for the use of copyright material. The author and
publishers will gladly receive information enabling them to rectify
any error or omission in subsequent editions.

Printed and bound in Great Britain by Bath Press Colourbooks, Glasgow

Letts Educational Ltd, a division of Granada Learning Ltd.
Part of the Granada Media Group

www.letts.education.com

*C*ontents

CONTENTS

Shape, space and measures

Handling data

*I*ntroduction

SUCCESSFUL STUDYING AT KEY STAGE 3

During Key Stage 3 of the National Curriculum, you will have to study the following subjects:

English, Mathematics, Science, Technology, a modern foreign language (usually French or German), Geography and History. If you go to school in Wales, you will also be required to learn Welsh.

This stage of your education is very important because it lays the foundation which you will need to embark upon your GCSE courses. The National Curriculum requires you and all 11–14 year olds to follow the same programmes of study, which define the knowledge and skills you will need to learn and develop during your course.

At school, your teachers will be monitoring your progress. At the end of Key Stage 3, your performance will be assessed and you will be given a National Curriculum level. Most students should reach Level 5 or Level 6, some may reach Levels 7 or 8, or perhaps even higher. In English, Mathematics and Science, you will have to take a National Test towards the end of your last year at Key Stage 3. The results of your tests, also marked in levels, will be set alongside your teachers' assessment of your work to give an overall picture of how you have done.

How this book will help you

This book is designed for you to use at home to support the work you are doing at school. Think of it as a companion or study guide to help you prepare for class work, homework, and for the important National Tests. Inside the book, you will find the level descriptions which will be used to assess your performance. We have included them in the book so that, as you near the end of Key Stage 3, you will be able to check how well you are doing.

Also included at the end of the book is a bank of practice questions. These are of the same style and standard as the questions you will face in your National Tests. Attempting these questions in the months leading up to your tests should help you to do as well as you can.

Reading this book, and doing the questions and activities, will help you get to grips with the most important elements of the National Curriculum in mathematics. Before you begin to read the book itself, take a few moments to read the following sections on 'Maths in the National Curriculum' and 'How to use this book'.

MATHS IN THE NATIONAL CURRICULUM

At Key Stage 3 in mathematics, you are expected to make progress in four Attainment Targets:
- Attainment Target 1: Using and Applying Mathematics
- Attainment Target 2: Number and Algebra
- Attainment Target 3: Shape, Space and Measures
- Attainment Target 4: Handling Data

In each Attainment Target, the mathematics is taught at various levels from Level 1 to Level 8. Exceptional performances from the most able students may, on occasion, exceed Level 8. By the end of Key Stage 3, pupils should expect to be working within Levels 3 to 7. This book is intended to help you in all the Attainment Targets at whatever Level you might be working.

H OW TO USE THIS BOOK

The National Curriculum states what you should be taught in schools but not how it should be taught. This means that schools will have different approaches and may not follow the same path that this book follows. However, by the end of the book you will have covered the mathematics contained in the National Curriculum for Key Stage 3.

The book is written in sections linked with the Attainment Targets:

Section 1 Using and Applying Mathematics
Section 2 Number
Section 3 Algebra
Section 4 Shape, Space and Measures
Section 5 Handling Data

Each section is sub-divided into chapters, each tackling a different topic or topics. One approach to using this book might be:

1. Select a chapter or topic.
2. Each topic usually begins with a 'Can you ......?' statement. These are the skills that are going to be tested in this topic.
3. Try the 'Now test yourself' questions relating to the topic, checking your answers as you go along.
4. Keep working through the different topics until the maths becomes too difficult. (The questions are graded, starting easy but getting gradually harder.)
5. Note the point where you find the work too difficult. This is your 'sticking point'.
6. Tackle another chapter/topic in the same way.
7. Return to your 'sticking points' at a later date to see if you can get any further.
8. Test yourself using the Practice National Test Questions and see what National Curriculum level you can reach.

You can use this book to reinforce the work that you are doing with your maths teacher, picking out the topics that you are doing in class.

You can also use it as a revision book, preparing yourself for your class tests and Key Stage 3 National Tests.

Finally, you can use the Practice National Test Questions as preparation for the real thing to give you an idea of what to expect.

Calculators

 Questions designed to be done using a calculator will have this symbol in the margin

 Questions designed to be done without using a calculator will have this in the margin

Where there is no symbol then you can assume that the use of a calculator is optional.

CHAPTER 1

Using and applying maths skills

This part of the National Curriculum will be tested in the classroom by your own teacher. It will take place at any time but you should be told in advance.

You could be asked to do several different activities over a period of time and your teacher will mark the work.

There are certain skills that you can practise that will enable you to tackle a task of a practical nature or an investigation. Skills like:

(a) testing theories
(b) making generalizations
(c) breaking down tasks into smaller ones
(d) developing a line of thought
(e) conducting experiments
(f) interpreting diagrams.

These next few activities try to give you practice in developing those skills.

PRACTICAL MATHS

Can you solve practical problems using mathematics?

Now test yourself

You are going to invent a seating plan for a school pantomime using a system of co-ordinates for numbering the tickets.

1 Copy the seating plan shown or design one of your own.

2 Label each row by a letter.

3 Give each seat in every row a number.

4 Mark on your seating plan where these three ticket-holders would sit.

5 How would you mark the tickets that represent the two seats marked by crosses? ⊠ ⊠

Now test yourself

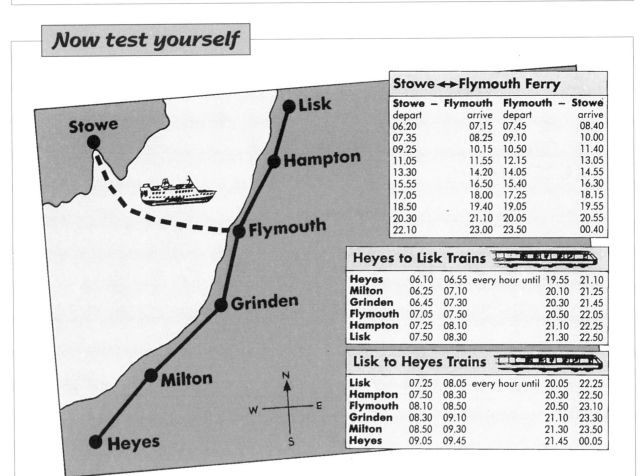

Stowe ↔ Flymouth Ferry

Stowe – Flymouth		Flymouth – Stowe	
depart	arrive	depart	arrive
06.20	07.15	07.45	08.40
07.35	08.25	09.10	10.00
09.25	10.15	10.50	11.40
11.05	11.55	12.15	13.05
13.30	14.20	14.05	14.55
15.55	16.50	15.40	16.30
17.05	18.00	17.25	18.15
18.50	19.40	19.05	19.55
20.30	21.10	20.05	20.55
22.10	23.00	23.50	00.40

Heyes to Lisk Trains

Heyes	06.10	06.55 every hour until 19.55	21.10
Milton	06.25	07.10	20.10	21.25
Grinden	06.45	07.30	20.30	21.45
Flymouth	07.05	07.50	20.50	22.05
Hampton	07.25	08.10	21.10	22.25
Lisk	07.50	08.30	21.30	22.50

Lisk to Heyes Trains

Lisk	07.25	08.05 every hour until 20.05	22.25
Hampton	07.50	08.30	20.30	22.50
Flymouth	08.10	08.50	20.50	23.10
Grinden	08.30	09.10	21.10	23.30
Milton	08.50	09.30	21.30	23.50
Heyes	09.05	09.45	21.45	00.05

Sally lives at Milton and wishes to visit her grannie who lives at Stowe. Her journey involves a train ride and a ferry to get across the water. She needs to use different timetables to plan her journey.

6 Plan a day visit giving the times of the trains and ferries she could catch. Whatever journeys you decide she should take, work out how long she could stay at her grannie's and how long she would have to wait to make the ferry and train connections.

SEARCHING FOR A PATTERN

Can you solve investigations by searching for a pattern?

Now test yourself

Explore the last digits of the multiples of various numbers;

<u>8</u>, 1<u>6</u>, 2<u>4</u>, 3<u>2</u>, 4<u>0</u>, 4<u>8</u> ... Multiples of 8

Record and present the results.

7   Write down the last digits in order for multiples of 2 to 10.

8   What types of numbers are they (e.g. odd, even, square, triangular, etc.)?

9   Can you spot any patterns?

10 Are there any similarities between the last digits of the multiples of one number and the last digits of the multiples of any other number?

Now test yourself

Investigate the statement for various examples.

If you add numbers of three consecutive houses you always get a multiple of 3

11 Investigate for three odd house numbers.
    (e.g. 5 + 7 + 9 = 21 = 7 × 3 and 21 is a multiple of 3).

12 Test for more odd house numbers.

13 Test for more even house numbers.

14 Is the statement true for houses that are numbered consecutively (e.g. 1, 2 and 3 or 7, 8 and 9)?
    Can you explain why in your own words?

Now test yourself

A mathematical milkman decided to multiply together the house numbers of adjacent houses. What did he find?

15 Work out several more. Don't forget numbers greater than a hundred!

16 What kind of numbers are your answers?

17 Are there any patterns?

18 Are there any numbers that cannot possibly be amongst your answers?
    Hint: Start with easy numbers and look for patterns in your answers.

INTERPRETING CHARTS, TABLES AND DIAGRAMS

Can you interpret charts, tables and diagrams by writing sentences about the information they try to convey?

This pictogram shows the amount of petrol sold at a supermarket petrol station for 1 week.

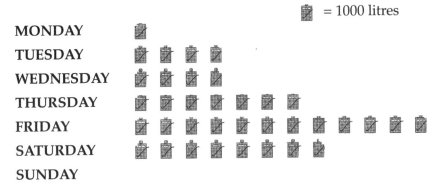

= 1000 litres

What information does this pictogram tell us?

(a) It was closed on Sunday.
(b) Least petrol was sold on Monday. Could this be when the supermarket had a half-day closing?
(c) Most petrol was sold on Thursday, Friday and Saturday. Could this be when there were late-night openings?
(d) There were equal sales on Tuesday and Wednesday. Was the shop equally busy on those days?
(e) Does the petrol station reflect how busy the store was? I think so!
(f) The average daily sales over the six days was 6000 litres.

This ability to read diagrams is something worth practising.

Now test yourself

What can you write about these mathematical charts?

19 On a long journey by car, I recorded the number of litres of petrol in the tank every 100 km. The graph shows this information.

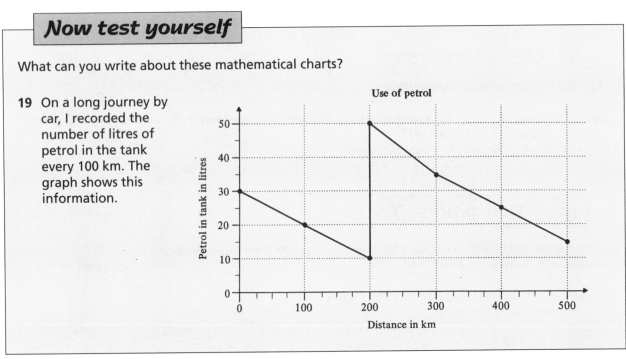

20 The sales in Fenton Music Store of CDs over a six-month period are represented in the following pictogram:

FENTON MUSIC STORE   represents 20 CDs

OCTOBER	🔘 🔘
NOVEMBER	🔘 🔘 ◔
DECEMBER	🔘 🔘 🔘 🔘 🔘
JANUARY	🔘 🔘 🔘 🔘 🔘 ◔
FEBRUARY	🔘 🔘 🔘 ◔
MARCH	🔘 ◔

21 The figures below show the output of Grafton Fireplaces last year.

MONTH	JAN.	FEB.	MAR.	APR.	MAY
SALES	30	45	70	60	50

22 Last season my football team scored 100 goals. This pie chart shows when the goals were scored during the match.

TESTING BY EXAMPLE

Can you check for yourself whether your theory/rule/generalization is correct by trying out and testing it with a few examples?

Fiona was trying to answer the question:

'$5^2 - 4^2$: Is there a quick way to work out the difference between two squares?'

Fiona's work begins:

Problem: You have $5^2 - 4^2$.   Do the sum and try to find a rule.

$$5^2 - 4^2$$
$$= 25 - 16$$ 5 add 4 = $\underline{9}$ which is the answer to the sum.
$$= \underline{9}$$

Try $7^2 - 6^2$ 7 + 6 = $\underline{13}$
$$= 49 - 36$$ This rule works.
$$= \underline{13}$$

Rule: The difference between 2 squares is equal to the sum of the two numbers!

Fiona has made a generalization by stating a rule.
What she must now do is to test her rule by **trying a few more examples!**

23 Continue with Fiona's work. **Hint:** Try $6^2 - 4^2$; then $6^2 - 3^2$; then $5^2 - 2^2$.
Is she right or wrong?
If she is wrong, can you find another rule?
Test this rule by trying some more examples.

TESTING A THEORY

If you take a theory of your own, then can you use your own evidence to put together a good, clear explanation of what you have found out?

Suppose you have a theory that:
'When you roll 2 dice and add the scores together, you get more 7s than any other number!'
This can be tested by performing a simple **experiment**. Don't forget to roll the dice at least 100 times.

Another theory might be:
'Red is the most popular colour for a car.'
This can be tested by performing a simple **survey** of at least 500 cars.

Or how about:
'The taller you are, the wider your arm-span!'
This can be tested by measuring people's heights and arm-spans and plotting a **scattergraph** to see if there is any positive correlation.

Always be on the lookout for evidence of mathematics in all walks of life that you can use in this way.

24 Make a hypothesis about children's weight in relation to their height and test it by reference to a scattergraph.

25 Make a hypothesis about the number of people living in the houses in your street and test it by reference to a frequency table and subsequent bar chart and pie chart.

B REAKING DOWN PROBLEMS

Can you solve quite complex problems by breaking them down into smaller, more manageable tasks?

Suppose you wanted to find out how many sugar cubes 1 cm by 1 cm by 1 cm would fit into a box measuring 5 cm by 5 cm by 8 cm.

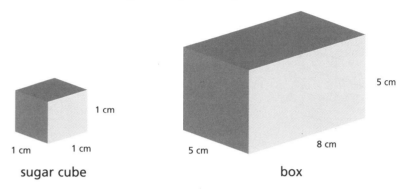

sugar cube

box

To solve the problem, consider the box to be made up of 5 layers of sugar cubes on top of each other.

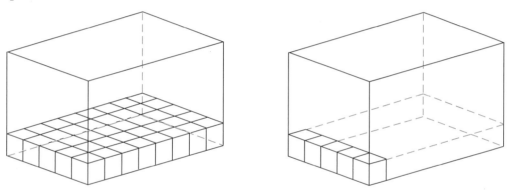

This could be broken down even further as a layer could be considered as 8 rows of 5 sugar cubes.

By breaking the problem down like this, you can see that the total number of sugar cubes is:

     5 layers of   8 rows of   5 sugar cubes
= 5   ×   8 ×   5
= 200 sugar cubes.

Many problems can be tackled in this way!

Now test yourself

26 You cannot see some of the windows in these buildings. How many windows are there?

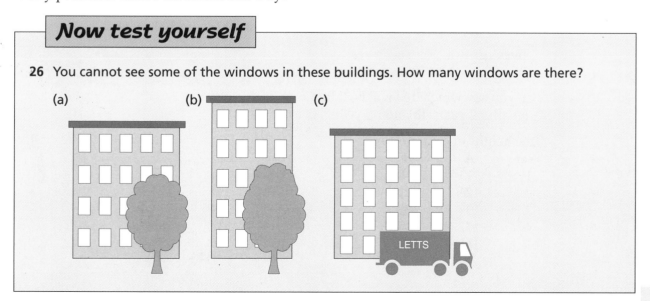

(a)   (b)   (c)

27 (a) How many 1 cm sugar cubes can be put into a box 20 cm long, 15 cm wide and 10 cm high?

   (b) How many match boxes 2 cm by 5 cm by 8 cm can be put into a bigger box 40 cm long, 20 cm wide and 10 cm high?

28 How many boxes are in these piles?

(a)

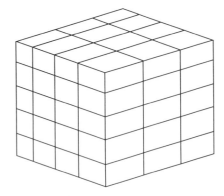

(b)

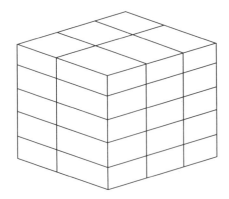

29 How many boxes will these trolleys hold?

(a)

(b)

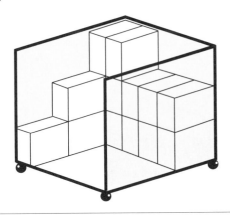

A SKING QUESTIONS

If you are presented with a problem together with some information, can you ask yourself questions to arrive at a solution and even suggest related tasks?

Greenacres Nurseries plant two trees, both of which are 100 cm tall.

Tree A grows 13 cm each year.
Tree B grows by 10% each year.

Can you say which tree will be taller:
   (a) after 2 years; (b) after 5 years; (c) after 10 years?

Tree height in centimetres

Year	A	B	Year	A	B
1	113	110	6	178	177.2
2	126	121	7	191	194.9
3	139	133.1	8	204	214.4
4	152	146.4	9	217	235.8
5	165	161	10	230	259.4

This table could lead to a graph:

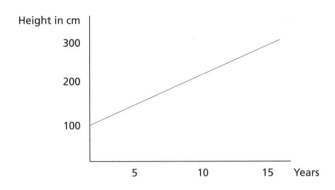

Copy the graph axes. I have plotted the heights of tree A. On your axes, copy my graph and then plot the heights of tree B.

(a) After how many years are the trees the same size?
(b) How much taller is Tree B than Tree A after 10 years?
(c) Extend the graphs. Roughly when will Tree B be twice as tall as Tree A?

Now test yourself

Now use the solution to the Tree problem to help you solve these related problems.

30 The world's population in 1994 was 6.0 billion (i.e. 6 000 000 000) people. The world's population is increasing at 3% per year.
   (a) In what year will the world's population be around 10 billion?
   (b) If this increase was reduced to only 1%, in what year would the world's population be 10 billion?

31 If you invest your money in a bank or building society your money will grow.
   (a) What will £100 be worth after 10 years if it grows at 10% per year?
   (b) After how many years will you double your money with this annual increase?
   (c) After how many years will you double your money with an annual increase of 5%?

T HEORY AND EXPERIMENT

Can you see the difference between what is expected and what actually happens when performing a mathematical experiment?
   In theory, the probability of an event happening can be worked out as a fraction. We say:

$$\text{Probability of an event } = \frac{\text{Total no. of favourable outcomes}}{\text{Total no. of possible outcomes}}$$

So:

(a) the probability of tossing a coin
 and it lands on 'heads' = $\frac{1}{2}$

(b) the probability of rolling a die
 and it lands on a '6' = $\frac{1}{6}$

(c) the probability of spinning a spinner
 and it falls on a '2' = $\frac{1}{5}$

(d) the probability of cutting a pack of
 cards and getting a 'spade' = $\frac{1}{4}$

Now test yourself

Remembering this, try to answer these questions.

32 How many heads would you expect if you tossed a coin 20 times?

33 How many 6s would you expect if you rolled a die 30 times?

34 How many scores of 2 would you expect if the spinner is spun 40 times?

35 How many spades would you expect if you cut a pack of playing cards 60 times?

Now perform each of the four experiments outlined above.
Are your results what you expected?
Don't worry, they are not always the same! That is what this exercise sets out to prove!

*U*sing and Applying Mathematics

At the start of Key Stage 3 the majority of pupils will have reached at least Level 4 in Mathematics. By the end of Key Stage 3 most pupils should be within the range of Levels 4–7. Levels 5–6 are the target for 14-year-olds. Level 8 is the standard reached by very able pupils.

Use our checklist to assess the Level reached, by ticking the skills that have been mastered.

Level 4

- ☐ Develop strategies for solving problems and use these strategies both in working within mathematics and in applying mathematics to practical contexts.
- ☐ Present information and results in a clear and organized way, explaining the reasons for the presentation.
- ☐ Search for a pattern by trying out ideas.

Level 5

- ☐ In order to carry through tasks and solve mathematical problems, identify and obtain necessary information; check results, considering whether these are sensible.
- ☐ Show understanding of situations by describing them mathematically using symbols, words and diagrams.
- ☐ Make general statements, based on the evidence produced, and give an explanation of the reasoning.

Level 6

- ☐ Carry through substantial tasks and solve quite complex problems by breaking them down into smaller, more manageable tasks.
- ☐ Interpret, discuss and synthesize information presented in a variety of mathematical forms.
- ☐ Write explanations of diagrams.
- ☐ Begin to give a mathematical justification for generalizations; testing by checking particular cases.

Level 7

- ☐ Starting from problems or contexts that have been presented, introduce own questions which generate fuller solutions.
- ☐ Examine critically and justify choice of mathematical presentation, considering alternative approaches and explaining improvements.
- ☐ Justify generalizations or solutions, showing some insight into the mathematical structure of the situation being investigated.
- ☐ Appreciate the difference between mathematical explanation and experimental evidence.

Level 8

- ☐ Develop and follow alternative approaches.
- ☐ Reflect on own lines of enquiry when exploring mathematical tasks; in doing so, introduce and use a range of mathematical techniques.
- ☐ Convey mathematical meaning through consistent use of symbols.
- ☐ Examine generalizations or solutions reached in an activity, commenting constructively on the reasoning and logic employed, and make further progress in the activity as a result.

Exceptional performance

- ☐ Give reasons for the choices made when investigating within mathematics itself or when using mathematics to analyse tasks; these reasons explain why particular lines of enquiry are followed and others rejected.
- ☐ Apply known mathematics in familiar and unfamiliar contexts.
- ☐ Use mathematical language and symbols effectively in presenting a convincing reasoned argument.
- ☐ Include mathematical justifications in reports, explaining solutions to problems involving a number of features or variables.

CHAPTER 2

P lace value and the number system

You should by now have mastered the ability to count reliably.

You should be able to read and write numbers like 164 and two hundred and sixteen. You should be able to write a series of numbers in ascending order with the smallest first. Try putting this set in order:

75, 835, 285, 582, 358

You should also be able to tell whether a digit is a unit, a ten or a hundred according to its position on the number line, in such numbers as 735, 259 and 867.

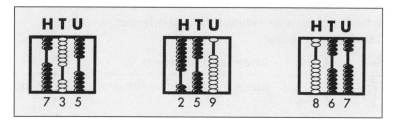

The decimal point should be familiar to you in an amount of money such as: three £1 coins, six 10p pieces and three 2p pieces represent £3.66

and that when you share £4 equally between five people each person gets £0.80.

When you think about the temperature in winter when it is below freezing you should think NEGATIVE NUMBERS. You should have seen a negative number on a calculator display.

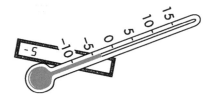

Just think about all these things that you already know.

H UNDREDS AND THOUSANDS

Can you read, write and put whole numbers in order according to size?

Large whole numbers are written with the digits in groups of three to help you to read them more easily.

For instance:

(a) Thousands	H T U	(b) Millions	Thousands	H T U
67	5 9 2	2	640	1 5 0
67 thousand	five hundred and ninety-two	2 million	640 thousand	one hundred and fifty

Now test yourself

1   Copy and complete the table below which shows the attendances at various football grounds one Saturday last season:

	Thousands	H T U	Attendance in words
Port Vale	7	5 4 9 ·	seven thousand five hundred and forty-nine
Stoke City	1 2	4 7 5	
Man. Utd			thirty-seven thousand one hundred and eleven
Leek Town	1	0 9 2	
Leeds Utd	2 6	9 0 7	
Halifax Town			two thousand seven hundred and sixty-five
Enfield			eight hundred and fifty-five
Man. City	3 0	4 6 1	

2   Copy and complete this table for the population of certain areas:

	Millions	Thousands	H T U	Population in words
Ainslie	2	6 4 0	1 5 0	
Bramble	3	2 4 5	6 2 5	
Chire				one million seven hundred and sixty-five thousand eight hundred and fifty-seven
Dodds		4 8 7	6 5 0	
Efflick				nine hundred and forty-three thousand four hundred and fifty
Fromhead		3 5 0	0 0 0	
Gatcombe				two hundred and seventeen thousand nine hundred

3   Copy and complete these cheques for three pools winners. Place the wins in order of 'biggest win first'.

(a)   (b)   (c)

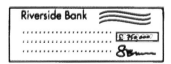

PLACE VALUE IN WHOLE NUMBERS

Can you understand and use the relationship between place values in whole numbers?

We all know that the figure 5 followed by three noughts is five thousand.
5000 = five thousand.

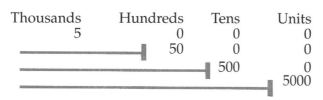

	Thousands	Hundreds	Tens	Units
	5	0	0	0
First push to the right		50	0	0
Second push to the right			500	0
Third push to the right				5000

We can see that 5000 is 5 thousands or 50 hundreds or 500 tens or 5000 units.

Remember: Large numbers are grouped in threes to help you to read them (e.g. in 62 734, the sixty-two is in the thousands group).

Now test yourself

4   What is the value of each digit that is underlined:
    (a) 2346; (b) 27 562; (c) 275 419; (d) 61 247?

5   What is the difference in the values of the digit 5 in these:
    (a) 525; (b) 5245; (c) 512 563; (d) 4550?

6   Complete the statements:

(a) 3000 is   3   [thousands]
    3000 is   30 [   ]
    3000 is   [   ]   tens
    3000 is   [   ]   units

(b) 7000 is   [   ]   thousands
    7000 is   [   ]   hundreds
    7000 is   700   [   ]
    7000 is   [   ]   units

7   Describe the number 80 000 in different ways.

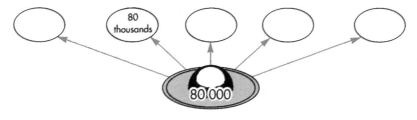

8   Describe the number 600 000 in different ways.

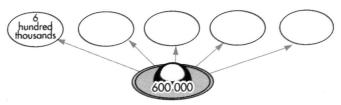

9   Fill in the spaces
    (a)   (b)

MULTIPLYING BY 10 OR 100

Can you see the effect of multiplying a whole number by 10 or 100?

When you multiply 27 by 10 the '2 tens' become '2 hundreds' and the '7 units' become '7 tens'. You then put a '0' in the units space.

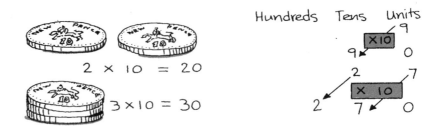

Hint: when you multiply a number by 10, every figure moves **one** place to the left.

Now test yourself

10 (a) $7 \times 10 =$
  (b) $16 \times 10 =$
  (c) $25 \times 10 =$
  (d) $98 \times 10 =$
  (e) A shirt costs £13. What will the cost of ten shirts be?
  (f) A tile is 22 cm long. How long will a line of ten tiles be?

Hint: when you multiply a number by 100, every figure moves **two** places to the left.

Now test yourself

11 Draw a diagram to show these:
  (a) 36×100; (b) 317×100; (c) 95×100
  (d) A box contains 12 golf-balls. How many in:
    (i) 10 boxes; (ii) 100 boxes?
  (e) How far would 100 pipes, each measuring 25 metres long, stretch if they were placed end to end?

MULTIPLICATION UP TO 10 × 10

Can you remember multiplication facts up to 10 × 10 and use them in multiplication and division problems?

 When you have not got a calculator handy, you will need to be able to multiply two numbers together from memory. To be able to do this you must memorize this table.

X	2	3	4	5	6	7	8	9	10
2	4	6	8	10	12	14	16	18	20
3	6	9	12	15	18	21	24	27	30
4	8	12	16	20	24	28	32	36	40
5	10	15	20	25	30	35	40	45	50
6	12	18	24	30	36	42	48	54	60
7	14	21	28	35	42	49	56	63	70
8	16	24	32	40	48	56	64	72	80
9	18	27	36	45	54	63	72	81	90
10	20	30	40	50	60	70	80	90	100

Now test yourself

12 Complete these multiplication grids, without referring to the large one above:

X	3	4	9
2	6		
5		20	
7			63

X	2		6
7		35	
3			
	16		

X	8	5	3	6
5		25		
2	16			
10			30	
7		35		

X	3			8
4		24		
			42	
2			10	
9				

13 What will the middle 'magic square' become when we multiply it by: (a) 7; (b) 4?

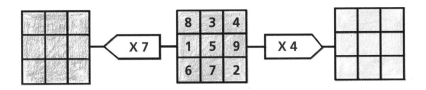

14 How many days are there in nine full weeks?

15 Share 48 sweets equally between eight children. How many does each child get?

16 Mrs Steele has four pints of milk every day of the week. How many pints is that for one week altogether?

17 What is the total cost of seven theatre tickets at £3.00 each?

18 Mr Williams pays £15 altogether to send his three children on a train journey. How much does each ticket cost?

19 In the school hall there are nine rows of seats with nine chairs in each row. How many seats are there in the hall?

20 A supermarket sells cans of coke in a six-pack. How many cans are there altogether in five packs?

21 A machine can paint a bike frame in seven minutes. How long will it take the machine to paint seven frames?

MENTAL MATHEMATICS

Can you add or subtract 2 two-digit numbers, or add a short list of single-digit numbers in your head?

On paper, without using a calculator, can you add or subtract 2 three-digit numbers?

Can you also multiply and divide a two-digit number by a single-digit number without the aid of a calculator?

When adding numbers look for pairs that will make up a ten.
You might even look for 3 numbers that will make up a ten or a twenty.

 Ask a parent or a friend to read these out to you.

Mental test A
1 23 plus 44
2 48 minus 25
3 Subtract 36 from 73
4 Add together 44 and 77
5 What is 2 + 3 + 6 + 9?
6 John has 24 records, Joan has 29. How many records do they have altogether?
7 Joe starts off with 72 nails but uses 17. How many does he have left?
8 I buy four items costing 4p, 7p, 8p and 5p. How much do I spend alogether?

Mental test B
1 52 plus 37
2 76 minus 32
3 Subtract 25 from 81
4 Add together 56 and 68
5 What is 3 + 7 + 2 + 4?
6 A line 35 mm long is joined to a line 58 mm long. How long is the line now?
7 Sarah has 86p in her pocket. She spends 28p. How much does she have left?
8 In snooker Sid makes a break of 1, 5, 1, 7, 1, 3. What is his score for potting these six balls?

Now test yourself

 Without a calculator do these:

22 How much longer is 742 mm than 495 mm?

23 If I walk 736 metres and jog a further 465 m how far have I travelled altogether?

24 One TV costs £450 and another costs £299. What is the difference in price?

25 Share a pools win of £95 equally between five people. How much does each person get?

26 I pay eight monthly payments of £27 per month. How much do I pay altogether?

27 Mrs Smith can save £55 per month out of her wages. How much can she save in six months?

28 If I share 78 sweets between three people how many sweets does each person get?

29 Cut a piece of string 84 cm long into six equal pieces. How long is each piece of string?

LONG MULTIPLICATION AND LONG DIVISION

Can you solve long multiplication and long division problems without the aid of a calculator using simple whole numbers?

```
    136
  × 35
    680   ← This is 136 × 5.
  4080   ← This is 136 × 30.
  4760   ← Adding the two answers together gives 136 × 35.
```

Now test yourself

30 Try these:
(a) 147 × 15; (b) 236 × 23; (c) 158 × 32; (d) 362 × 45; (e) 475 × 66

31 A builder earns £278 per week. How much will he earn over a 52-week year?

32 A car can be bought for 24 monthly payments of £255.
How much does the car cost altogether?

33 A fishing club has 65 members. They each pay £108 in membership fees. How much is raised by the club altogether through membership fees?

```
        19
  15 ⌐ 285
       15↓
       135
       135
       000
```

Method:

1 15s into 2 – won't go.
2 15s into 28 will go once with a remainder of 13.
3 Move the digit 5 down to the remainder of 13.
4 15s into 135 – try 9 (since 15 × 10 = 150 – too big).
5 15 × 9 is exactly 135 thus giving no remainder.
6 You can always check back by multiplying 15 by 19 to see if you arrive at an answer of 285.

Now test yourself

34 Try these (there are no remainders):
(a) $621 \div 23$; (b) $840 \div 35$; (c) $988 \div 26$; (d) $935 \div 17$

35 A group of 16 men share a pools win of £592 equally between themselves. How much does each man get?

36 A car travels 448 km on 32 litres of petrol. How many kilometres will the car travel on 1 litre?

POWERS OF 10

Can you multiply and divide, in your head, single-digit multiples of powers of 10 to get whole number answers?

Examples:
$$7 \times 5 = 35$$
$$7 \times 50 = 7 \times 5 \times 10 = 350$$
$$7 \times 500 = 7 \times 5 \times 100 = 3500$$
$$70 \times 50 = 7 \times 10 \times 5 \times 10 = 3500$$
$$70 \times 500 = 7 \times 10 \times 5 \times 100 = 35\,000$$
$$700 \times 500 = 7 \times 100 \times 5 \times 100 = 350\,000$$

What you have to do is multiply the digits (7×5 in this case) and then work out how many tens you are also multiplying. Add a 'nought' for each ten.

For instance:
$$4^{1}0^{2}0 \times 3^{3}0^{4}0^{5}0 = 4 \times 3 \times 1^{1}0 \times 1^{2}0 \times 1^{3}0 \times 1^{4}0 \times 1^{5}0 = 12 \times 1^{1}0^{2}0^{3}0^{4}0^{5}0 = 12^{1}0^{2}0^{3}0^{4}0^{5}0$$

Now test yourself

37 Work out the answer to these without a calculator:

(a) 80×30 (e) 2000×70
(b) 60×40 (f) 400×800
(c) 90×500 (g) 700×3000
(d) 300×700 (h) 5000×3000

When you are dividing, the method is similar. In this case, you divide the digits and then divide the 'tens'.

For instance: $800 \div 20 = (8 \div 2) \times (100 \div 10) = 4 \times 10 = 40$;
or $9000 \div 30 = (9 \div 3) \times (1000 \div 10) = 3 \times 100 = 300$.

Another method is to write the division as a fraction and then cancel down.

For instance: $6000 \div 300 = \dfrac{6000}{300} = 20$

Now test yourself

38 Without a calculator, use either method to work out the value of:

(a) $8000 \div 40$ (e) $180\,000 \div 600$
(b) $1500 \div 30$ (f) $900 \div 30$
(c) $45\,000 \div 900$ (g) $14\,000 \div 70$
(d) $1200 \div 60$ (h) $1\,600\,000 \div 4000$

MORE MENTAL MATHEMATICS

Can you multiply or divide in your head single-digit multiples of any power of 10?
   Do you also realise the effect of multiplying and dividing any number by a number between 0 and 1?

Multiplying:
$80 \times 200 = 16000$
$80 \times 20 = 1600$
$80 \times 2 = 160$
$80 \times 0.2 = 16$
$80 \times 0.02 = 1.6$

Dividing:
$80 \div 200 = 0.4$
$80 \div 20 = 4$
$80 \div 2 = 40$
$80 \div 0.2 = 400$
$80 \div 0.02 = 4000$

If you look at the pattern of numbers you should be able to see that multiplying by a number less than 1 has a 'decreasing effect'.

Also you should be able to see that dividing by a number less than 1 has an 'increasing effect'.

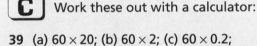

Now test yourself

C Work these out with a calculator:

39 (a) 60×20; (b) 60×2; (c) 60×0.2; (d) 60×0.02

40 (a) $90 \div 30$; (b) $90 \div 3$; (c) $90 \div 0.3$; (d) $90 \div 0.03$

41 (a) 70×40; (b) 70×4; (c) 70×0.4; (d) 70×0.04

42 (a) $150 \div 50$; (b) $150 \div 5$; (c) $150 \div 0.5$; (d) $150 \div 0.05$

43 (a) $12 \div 0.6$; (b) 12×0.6

44 (a) $160 \div 0.8$; (b) 160×0.8

45 (a) $400 \div 0.5$; (b) 400×0.5

46 (a) $80 \div 0.4$; (b) 80×0.4

MULTIPLICATION AND DIVISION IN PRACTICE

Can you solve multiplication and division problems involving numbers of any size?

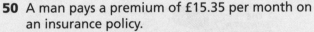

Now test yourself

47 What is the total weekly wage bill for a factory employing 126 people each earning £189.50?

48 A rocket travels at 3250 km/h. How far will it travel in four days?

49 There are 32 people in a pools syndicate at work. They win £750 000 one week. How much will each person receive?

50 A man pays a premium of £15.35 per month on an insurance policy.
   (a) How much does he pay in a year?
   (b) How much does he pay over 25 years?

51 It costs £26.40 to print 240 leaflets for an advertising campaign. What will it cost to print a further 750 leaflets at the same rate?

52 On average there are 480 words to a page in a novel. How many words are there in the novel if the book has 225 pages?

53 The cost of a seat at the cinema is £2.80. What will the total takings be if all 444 seats are sold?

54 Through how many degrees does the minute hand of a clock turn in one week?

55 A multi-storey block of flats has 4050 panes of glass. There are 18 storeys each with the same number of panes of glass. How many does each storey have?

56 A bus travels 239 miles every day for a year. How many miles is that altogether?

57 1120 athletes pay £4760 in entrance fees for a 'fun run'. What is the entrance fee per runner?

58 What is the area of a rectangle measuring 1.25 m long and 1.05 m wide?

59 1425 kg of potatoes are put into 15 kg bags. How many bags are needed?

60 Stamps are put into packets of 14. How many packets are needed for 6090 stamps?

61 Boxes used to pack tins of beans will hold 24 tins. How many boxes can be filled from 3800 tins of beans. How many tins will be left over?

62 If 4.5 metres of material cost £17.91, find the cost of 3.5 metres of the same material.

63 One tin of yellow paint will paint a 'no parking' line 13.5 m long. How many tins of paint will be needed to paint 378 m?

64 A box of chocolates contains 26 chocolates. How many chocolates will be needed to fill 10 500 boxes?

65 Stamps are in sheets of 120. How many stamps will there be in 450 sheets?

66 What is the product of 12.25 and 0.75?

NEGATIVE NUMBERS

Can you use negative numbers in everyday situations?
   The most common use of **negative numbers** is when we talk about the temperature.

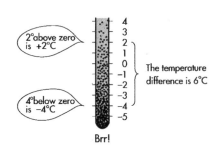

Now test yourself

67 (a) Put these temperatures in order (lowest first):

   (i)   2°C, –2°C, –5°C
   (ii) –7°C, –4°C, –10°C
(b) What is the difference in temperature between these:
   (i)   3°C and –4°C;   (ii) 12°C and –5°C;
   (iii) –1°C and –13°C; (iv) 1°C and –7°C

68 The table below shows the temperature for five cities on a certain day:

Write the name of each city next to its temperature on the thermometer.

City	Temperature
London	4°C
Moscow	–5°C
Lisbon	7°C
Chicago	–1°C
Rome	2°C

Rome

(a) What is the difference in temperature between Moscow and Chicago?
(b) If the temperature in London fell by 7°C, what would the new temperature be?
(c) What is the temperature difference between Moscow and Rome?
(d) What would be the new temperature in Chicago if it rose by 6°C?
(e) What is the temperature difference between the highest and lowest values?

69 Study the graph (below) of the temperatures recorded every three hours at Glasgow Airport.
(a) What was the temperature at 6.00 a.m.?
(b) What was the lowest temperature recorded?
(c) What was the highest temperature recorded?
(d) At what time was this recording made?
(e) By how many degrees did the temperature go up betwen 3.00 a.m. and 9.00 a.m.?

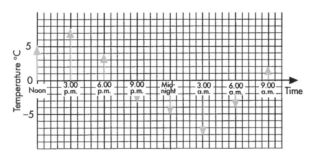

70 Write in the missing numbers for these patterns:
(a) 20, 15, 10, 5, ☐ ☐ ☐; (b) 11, 7, 3, ☐ ☐ ☐

MULTIPLYING AND DIVIDING DIRECTED NUMBERS

Can you multiply and divide one negative number by another?
   Follow the number patterns in this series of multiplications:

$$3 \times 4 = 12$$
$$2 \times 4 = 8$$
$$1 \times 4 = 4$$
$$0 \times 4 = 0$$
$$-1 \times 4 = -4$$
$$-2 \times 4 = -8$$

You can see that when you multiply a negative number by a positive number, the answer is a NEGATIVE number.

Now let's continue with the number pattern for the '–3 times table':

$$3 \times -3 = -9$$
$$2 \times -3 = -6$$
$$1 \times -3 = -3$$
$$0 \times -3 = 0$$
$$-1 \times -3 = 3$$
$$-2 \times -3 = 6$$

You can see that a negative number times another negative is a POSITIVE number.

The rules are the same for division:

(A negative number) ÷ (A positive number) = A negative answer
(A positive number) ÷ (A negative number) = A negative answer

BUT

(A negative number) ÷ (A negative number) = A positive answer

Now test yourself

71 $5 \times (-6) =$

72 $(-5) \times 7 =$

73 $(-3) \times (-5) =$

74 $(-10) \times (-7) =$

75 $(-24) \div 6 =$

76 $(-55) \div (-11) =$

77 $27 \div (-9) =$

78 $(-100) \div (-20) =$

REMEMBER
+ × + = +ve answer
+ × − = −ve answer
− × + = −ve answer
− × − = +ve answer

ALSO
+ ÷ + = +ve answer
+ ÷ − = −ve answer
− ÷ + = −ve answer
− ÷ − = +ve answer

INDEX NOTATION

Can you use index notation to show powers of whole numbers? For instance $10^2 = 100$.

Paul is putting slabs down to make a patio. He started by making a square in each corner.

(a) How many slabs has he laid in the top left corner?
(b) How many has he laid in the top right corner?
(c) How many has he laid in the bottom left corner?
(d) How many has he laid in the bottom right corner?
(e) How many has he got to put down altogether?

When we multiply a number by itself, we say that we are **squaring** the number. The square of 4 is the same as $4 \times 4 = 16$.

When you square 5 you get 25. We write 5 **squared** like this: 5^2. This is called the index number.

The index number tells us how many 5s to multiply together. So:

$5^3 = 5 \times 5 \times 5$; $3^4 = 3 \times 3 \times 3 \times 3$; $2^5 = 2 \times 2 \times 2 \times 2 \times 2$ ... and so on

Now test yourself

79 Write these in index form (the first is done for you):
(a) $3 \times 3 = 3^2$; (b) $5 \times 5 \times 5 \times 5 =$ (c) $7 \times 7 \times 7 =$
(d) $10 \times 10 \times 10 \times 10 \times 10 \times 10 =$ (e) $2 \times 2 \times 2 =$
(f) $4 \times 4 \times 4 =$

80 Write these out **in full** and then work out the numerical value (the first is done for you):
(a) $6^3 = 6 \times 6 \times 6 = 216$;   (d) $10^4 =$
(b) $5^2 = 5 \times 5 =$ (e) $2^5 =$
(c) $8^3 =$ (f) $12^2 =$

81 Work these out to find the larger number:
(a) 5^3 or 3^5; (b) 2^5 or 5^2; (c) 5^4 or 4^5

When you write 5^2 you say '5 squared'
When you write 5^3 you say '5 cubed'
When you write 5^4 you say '5 to the power of 4'
When you write 5^5 you say '5 to the power of 5'
When you write 5^6 you say '5 to the power of 6'
When you write 5^{10} you say '5 to the power of 10'
... and so on.

CHAPTER 3

*D*ecimals/fractions/percentages/ratio

You should already be able to recognize simple fractions like halves and quarters. You should also understand that a fraction can be written as a decimal and that the decimal point separates the whole number from the fraction.

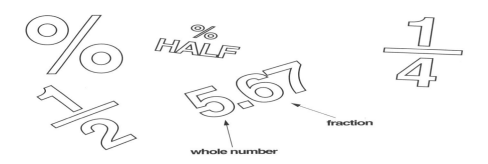

Most of this chapter may be new to you, so take special care.

D ECIMAL DISTANCES: NOTATION

Can you measure distances using decimals and write them down to two decimal places where necessary?

Now test yourself

1 Paul was 1 metre and 68 centimetres tall in 1995. This can be written as 1.68 m.

In 1994 he was 1.64 m tall.
How tall was he in:
(a) 1993;
(b) 1992;
(c) 1991;
(d) 1990?

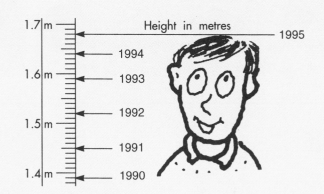

2 Use a decimal point to write these distances in metres:
(a) 4 m 45 cm; (b) 3 m 22 cm; (c) 10 m 38 cm; (d) 25 m 75 cm

3 Write these measurements in centimetres:
(a) 3.25 m; (b) 9.24 m; (c) 32.88 m; (d) 0.83 m

4 A joiner is measuring shelves using a builder's tape. Write down the length of each shelf (in metres only).

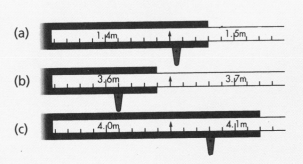

5   Study the lengths in this picture.
    (a) What is the gap from the top
        of the door to the ceiling?
    (b) How tall is the bookcase?
    (c) How tall is the teacher?
    (d) What is the height of the
        blackboard?

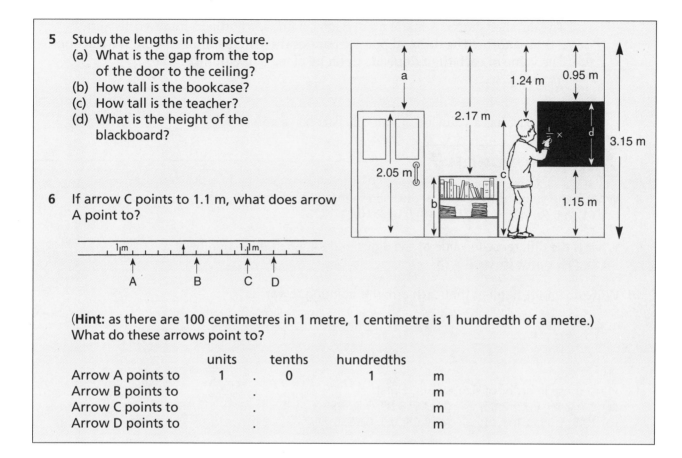

6   If arrow C points to 1.1 m, what does arrow
    A point to?

(**Hint:** as there are 100 centimetres in 1 metre, 1 centimetre is 1 hundredth of a metre.)
What do these arrows point to?

	units	tenths	hundredths	
Arrow A points to	1	. 0	1	m
Arrow B points to		.		m
Arrow C points to		.		m
Arrow D points to		.		m

O RDERING DECIMALS

Can you read, write and put into order of size, decimal numbers?
  Can you also understand the relationship between place values?

Although we say 'Two pounds **forty** five', we never say 'Two point **forty** five
metres'. We always say 'Two point **four** five metres'.

Now test yourself

7   How would you say these:
    (a) £4.95; (b) 4.95 m; (c) 7.64 km; (d) 0.045 km; (e) 1.39 s;
    (f) £1.39; (g) 2.23 h; (h) 11.11 mph?

The number shown is made up of 5 tens, 5 units, 5 tenths, 5 hundredths and 5 thousandths. The decimal point separates the whole numbers from the fractions. The value of each digit depends upon its place in the number line.

Also,   55.5̲5̲5̲   55.55̲5̲
         ↑   ↑
This part has a value of $\frac{55}{100}$ This part has a value of $\frac{55}{1000}$

Now test yourself

8   What is the value of the digits underlined in these numbers:
    (a) 61.3̲54; (b) 2.95̲; (c) 107.6̲2̲; (d) 0.04̲35; (e) 17.725̲?

9   What is the difference in value of the digits underlined in these numbers:
    (a) 25̲.35̲4; (b) 1.6̲76̲; (c) 2̲43.25̲?

10 Write down the number that each arrow is pointing towards.

11 Place these in order of size, smallest first:
    (a) 2.7; 2.55; 0.25; 2.05;   (c) 3.9; 3.89; 3.8; 3.98;
    (b) 10.5; 1.05; 1.1; 1.11;   (d) 0.05; 0.5; 0.15; 0.1

PROBLEMS USING DECIMALS

Can you solve problems that involve the decimal point?

For instance: 2.7 + 3.9 + 14.65
                              ↑

2.70   This is the
3.90   ←   same number
14.65
―――――
21.25
―――――
 1 2

You must remember when adding or subtracting decimals,
KEEP THE DECIMAL POINTS IN LINE.

But what happens when there is **no decimal point**?

For instance: 2.95 + 3.7 + 13   2.95
You could write 13 as 13.00   3.70
but make sure the 3 goes   1③.00
in the units column.   ―――――
                                  19.65

Now test yourself

12 Calculate the following:
    (a) 1.75 + 2.6 = ; (b) 2.9 + 3.14 + 7 = ; (c) 95.2 + 1.59 = ;
    (d) 7.6 − 1.9 = ; (e) 17.11 − 5.84 = ; (f) 1.7 − 0.64 =
    (**Hint:** You may find it easier to add or subtract if you write the numbers underneath each other.)

13 A plumber has 8 m of copper tubing. For a repair, he needs one piece of length 2.45 m and another of length 3.62 m.
   (a) What length does he need altogether to do the repair?
   (b) What length of copper tubing will he have left?

14 A woman spends £11.65, £15.95 and £9.32 at three different shops.
   (a) How much does she spend altogether?
   (b) What change will she have left from a £50 note?

15 Last year Susie was 1.5 m tall. This year she is 1.63 m tall. How much has she grown in the last year?
   (Leave your answer in metres.)

Multiplying example

$$3.64 \times 5 = 18.20$$
$$\begin{array}{r} 3.64 \\ \times\ \ \ \ 5 \\ \hline 18.20 \end{array}$$

Dividing example

$$\begin{array}{r} 1.34 \\ 4\overline{)5.\overset{1}{3}\overset{1}{6}} \end{array}$$

This is the same as ordinary multiplication and division. Remember to put a decimal point in your answer in the most sensible place.

Now test yourself

16 Work out:
   (a) $2.75 \times 9 = $; (b) $16.96 \div 4 = $; (c) $37.6 \times 6 = $;
   (d) $36 \div 8 = $; (e) $0.74 \times 7 = $; (f) $1.62 \div 6 = $

17 The weight of 1 metre of piping is 1.65 kg. What is the weight of 6 metres of piping?

18 A pile of nine exercise books is 10.8 cm high. How thick is each exercise book?

19 If five cakes can be made from 1.25 kg of flour, how much flour is used for each cake?

20 A wooden fence panel is 1.85 m wide. What will be the total length of eight panels, placed side by side?

Take extra care with these because your calculator answers will be more accurate than you need.

For instance: how many 17p stamps can I buy for £1.00?

£1.00 = 100p   100p ÷ 17p = 5.8823529 stamps

This means that I can buy five stamps. They would cost 5 × 17p = 85p. I would have 15p change.

21 How many 19p stamps can I buy for £5.00?
What change will I get?

22 Eggs are packed in boxes of six.
How many boxes can I fill if I have 92 eggs?
How many eggs will I have left over?

23 I need to take 50 people to the theatre.
My car holds four passengers besides myself.
How many journeys will I need to make?
How many spaces will there be in the last journey?

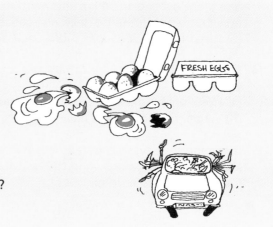

E VERYDAY FRACTIONS

Can you recognize and understand simple everyday fractions?

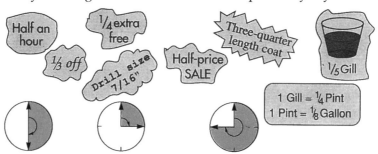

Half an hour	Quarter of an hour	Three-quarters of an hour
$\frac{1}{2}$ an hour	$\frac{1}{4}$ of an hour	$\frac{3}{4}$ of an hour
30 minutes	15 minutes	45 minutes

24 Estimate what fraction of the jugs are full.
(a)   (b)   (c)   (d)

25 Here is John's hand of cards:

(a) What fraction of the hand is black?
(b) What fraction of the hand is red?
(c) What fraction of the hand is diamonds?
(d) What fraction of the hand is spades?
(e) What fraction of the red cards are hearts?

26 What fraction of the hour is shaded? How many minutes are there in each part?

27 Some rulers measure in **inches**. What fraction of an inch are the small divisions on these rulers?

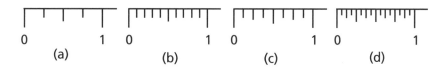

   (a)   (b)   (c)   (d)

28 What fraction of the flags are shaded blue?

29

Make out these butcher's bills:

(a)   £   p

$1\frac{1}{2}$ lb of cheese   =

$2\frac{1}{2}$ lb of sausage   =

$\frac{3}{4}$ lb of boiled ham   = _____

        Total   _____

(b)   £   p

$\frac{1}{2}$ lb of cheese   =

$\frac{3}{4}$ lb of sausage   =

$\frac{1}{2}$ lb of boiled ham   = _____

        Total   _____

30

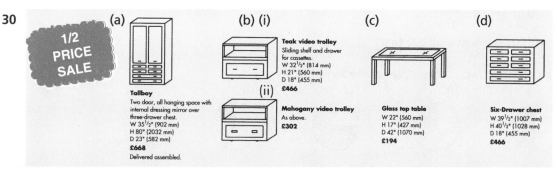

What is the sale price for these items?

31 At 'Sid's Electrical Store' there is a sale.

(a) How much discount does Sid give you for each of the above items in the sale?
(b) Work out the sale price for each item.

PROBLEMS USING PERCENTAGES

Can you recognize and understand simple percentages?

Now test yourself

32 Write these marks as percentages:
(a) John 70 out of 100; (b) Joan 46 out of 100; (c) Ranjit 92 out of 100

33 Can you convert these marks to percentages?

(**Hint:** put them out of 100 first)

34 What percentage of the circle is shaded here?
(a)   (b)   (c)   (d)

(**Hint:** imagine the circle to be worth 100.)

35 What percentage of these storage tanks are full?

(a)   (b)   (c)   (d)

  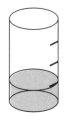 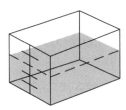

36 A storage tank holds 120 litres when full. How many litres are in the tank when it is:
(a) 50% full; (b) 25% full; (c) 75% full?

37 Jim gets £5 pocket money. On his birthday he gets a 50% increase.
(a) How much extra does he get?
(b) How much pocket money does he get after the rise?

38 In a maths test at school there were 20 questions. The top girl got 75% correct.
(a) How many questions did she get correct?
(b) How many did she get wrong?
(c) What percentage did she get wrong?

39 John's examination results were: maths 50%; English 75%; science 60%.
(a) How many questions did he get correct in maths if there were 40 questions altogether?
(b) The English exam was out of 20.
How many did he get correct?
(c) The science exam was out of 50.
How many did he get correct in this exam?

40 Mrs Khan and Mr Smith bake a cake each.
These charts show the ingredients of each
cake.
Write in **roughly** the percentage of the
whole cake that each ingredient represents.

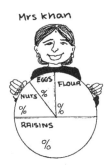 

41

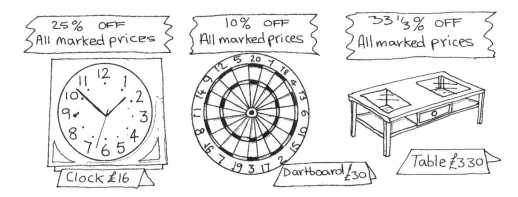

(a) How much will they take off each of these items?
(b) How much will each item cost in the sale?

CALCULATING DISCOUNTS

Can you work out fractional and percentage changes?

In the sale 'Beagood Sports' will give you a discount of 10% (i.e. they will reduce the selling price by 10%).

What is the discount price of the ball?

10% of £40 = $\frac{10}{100} \times 40$ = £4

Discount price = £40 − £4 = £36

C This calculation could be done in one step on a **basic** calculator:

$\boxed{4}\boxed{0}\boxed{-}\boxed{1}\boxed{0}\boxed{\%}$

Now test yourself

42 What will the discount price be for these items in the Beagood Sports sale?

43 Calculate the new weekly wage for these workers once their pay rise has been added:

44 Work out the new price for each item at the two stores:

(a) Junior Snooker table £55

(b) Dart board £15

(c) Track Suit £45

Old pay £280 per week pay rise 12%

Old pay £210 per week pay rise 8%

Old pay £195 per week Pay rise 9%

D.I.Y. STORE CLOSING DOWN SALE
2/3 OFF LISTED PRICES
WALLPAPER..... £4.95 A ROLL
CARPETS FROM £90
2½ LITRES PAINT.... £7.50
CURTAINS FROM £9.90

SUPER STORE ½ PRICE SALE
EACH ITEM SOLD FOR HALF THE MARKED PRICE
THREE PIECE SUITE... £880
WARDROBE........... £324
DRESSING TABLE.....£125
CHEST OF DRAWERS....£68

EQUIVALENT FRACTIONS

Can you see the connection between fractions, decimals and percentages?

As you can see from the diagrams on the next page, fractions, decimals, percentages and ratios are all related to one another. It is an excellent skill to learn to be able to convert from one to another, e.g. $\frac{1}{2}$ = 0.5 = 50%.

The most common should be remembered, just like you learn your multiplication tables.

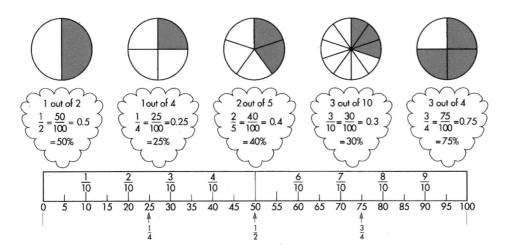

Now test yourself

45 Copy, complete and learn the following table.

Fraction	Decimal	Percentage
$\frac{1}{2}$	0.5	50%
$\frac{1}{10}$	0.1	10%
$\frac{3}{10}$	?	?
?	0.25	?
?	?	75%
$\frac{1}{5}$	?	?
?	0.6	?
?	?	80%
?	0.9	?
$\frac{1}{3}$	?	?
$\frac{2}{3}$	?	?

46 If you were asked to compare the two lines shown here, what would you say?

         3 cm   Line A

         4 cm   Line B

Using your knowledge of ratios, fractions and percentages you could say:

(i) The ratio of line A to line B is 3:4;

(ii) Line A is 75% of line B; (iii) Line A is $\frac{3}{4}$ the length of line B.

Compare each of the following lines as in the example:

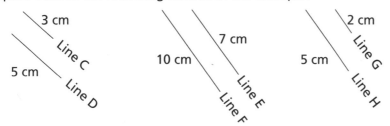

F RACTIONS, DECIMALS AND PERCENTAGES

Can you convert fractions to decimals and percentages and write one number as a percentage of another?

To convert fractions (and decimals) to percentages, **multiply** by 100.

For instance: $\frac{7}{10} = (\frac{7}{10} \times 100)\% = 70\%$.

To convert fractions to decimals, **divide** the numerator by the denominator.

For instance: $\frac{5}{8} = 5 \div 8$. Write 5 as 5.000 before you do the division.

$$\begin{array}{r} 0.6\,2\,5 \\ \hline 8\,\big|\,5.0^{2}0^{4}0 \end{array}$$

C You will find it easier using a calculator. Key in $\boxed{5}\,\boxed{\div}\,\boxed{8}\,\boxed{=}$ $\boxed{0.625}$

To convert percentages to fractions or decimals, **divide** by 100.

For instance: $45\% = \frac{45}{100} = \frac{9}{20} = 0.45$.

Now test yourself

47 Copy and complete the table:

	Fraction	Decimal	Percentage
a	$\frac{3}{4}$		
b	$\frac{1}{5}$		
c			36%
d		0.35	
e	$1\frac{1}{10}$		
f		1.70	
g			250%

To write one thing as a percentage of another, firstly write it as a **fraction**, then convert it to a **percentage** by multiplying the fraction by 100.

For instance: write £5 as a percentage of £25:

(a) write it as a fraction $\frac{5}{25}$;

(b) convert to a percentage $\frac{5}{\underset{1}{25}} \times \frac{\overset{4}{100}}{1} = 20\%$

Now test yourself

48 A shopkeeper buys a TV for £200 and sells it for £250.
(a) What is his profit?
(b) Write the profit as a fraction of the cost price.
(c) Now write this profit as a percentage of the cost price.

49 A man buys a car for £2000 and sells it two years later for £1200.
(a) What was his loss?
(b) Write this loss as a percentage of the cost price.

50 Express a profit of £12 as a percentage return on an investment of £180.

C ALCULATING FRACTIONS AND PERCENTAGES

Can you calculate fractions and percentages of quantities using a calculator where necessary?

Calculating fractions

Although $\frac{1}{2}$ is a larger fraction than $\frac{1}{3}$ and $\frac{1}{2}$ of an amount is greater than $\frac{1}{3}$ of the **same** amount, it is possible for $\frac{1}{3}$ of a **different** amount to be greater.

To find $\frac{1}{2}$ of an amount you divide by 2.

To find $\frac{1}{3}$ of an amount you divide by 3.

To find $\frac{1}{4}$ of an amount you divide by 4.

To find $\frac{1}{5}$ of an amount you divide by 5.

To find $\frac{1}{10}$ of an amount you divide by 10, and so on …

Now test yourself

51 Find these:
(a) $\frac{1}{4}$ of 36; (b) $\frac{1}{3}$ of 66; (c) $\frac{1}{5}$ of £40; (d) $\frac{1}{10}$ of £250; (e) $\frac{1}{8}$ of £64

To find $\frac{3}{4}$ of a number, you find $\frac{1}{4}$, then multiply by 3.

To find $\frac{4}{5}$ of a number, you find $\frac{1}{5}$, then multiply by 4.

Now test yourself

52 Find these:
(a) $\frac{3}{4}$ of £96; (b) $\frac{2}{3}$ of £600; (c) $\frac{2}{5}$ of £20; (d) $\frac{3}{10}$ of £300; (e) $\frac{7}{8}$ of £56

To find $\frac{3}{4}$ of 60 on your calculator you would press $\boxed{6}\,\boxed{0}\,\boxed{\div}\,\boxed{4}\,\boxed{\times}\,\boxed{3}\,\boxed{=}$

Calculating percentages

A coat has been reduced by 25% in a sale. The old price was £40.
How much reduction is there?
We have to find 25% of £40.

Method 1: Use fractions

$25\% = \frac{1}{4}$; $\frac{1}{4}$ of £40 = £10

You can only use this method when percentages can be changed into fractions easily.

Method 2: Work with 10%

10% of £40 = £4

10% of £40 = £4

5% of £40 = £2

_____

25% of £40 = £10

This method can only be used when finding 10%, 15%, 20%, 25%, 30%, 35%, etc.

Method 3: Use hundredths

$25\% = \frac{25}{100}$

so 25% of £40 = $\frac{25}{100} \times$ £40 = £10

or $\frac{25}{100} = 0.25$; $0.25 \times 40 = $ £10

This method can be used for any percentages.

 On a calculator you would press: $\boxed{2}\,\boxed{5}\,\boxed{\times}\,\boxed{4}\,\boxed{0}\,\boxed{\div}\,\boxed{1}\,\boxed{0}\,\boxed{0}\,\boxed{=}$

or $\boxed{0}\,\boxed{\cdot}\,\boxed{2}\,\boxed{5}\,\boxed{\times}\,\boxed{4}\,\boxed{0}\,\boxed{=}$ or $\boxed{2}\,\boxed{5}\,\boxed{\times}\,\boxed{4}\,\boxed{0}\,\boxed{\%}$

When you are dealing with money, you can use another method.
e.g. 15% = 15 per hundred = 15p in every £.
For instance: 15% of £9 = 9 × 15p = £1.35.

Now test yourself

53 Use any method to find these:
   (a) 15% of £60   (e) 40% of £40
   (b) 25% of 44 cm   (f) 50% of 900
   (c) 75% of 120 kg   (g) 5% of 80p
   (d) 38% of £11   (h) 16% of £6

54 Work out:
   (a) 15% of £17;   (c) 8% of £25;
   (b) 24% of £16;   (d) 12% of £50

U NITARY RATIOS

Can you use and understand unitary ratios? For instance 1:x or x:1.
Mortar is made by mixing cement and sand in the ratio 1:3 (one to three).

It could be one shovelful of cement to three shovelfuls of sand,

or one bucketful of cement to three bucketfuls of sand.

In fact, it doesn't matter what you use to measure the cement and sand, so long as they are in the same **ratio** of 1:3.

If the ratio of cement to sand is 1:3 then the ratio of sand to cement is 3:1. **The order of the objects is very important**. Remember that the ratios are numbered in the same order as they are written.

Now test yourself

55 In a recipe, the ratio of flour to currants is 5:1.
(a) What is the ratio of currants to flour?
(b) If you need 10 ounces of flour, how many ounces of currants will you need?

56 The ratio of Peter's pocket money to Susan's pocket money is 1:3. Peter gets £2. How much does Susan get?

57 I spend £5 on my cousin and £25 on my mum for Christmas.
(a) What is the ratio of the cost of my cousin's present to my mother's present?
(b) What is the ratio of the cost of my mother's to my cousin's present?

58 The ratio of my age to my father's age is 1:4.
My father is 44 years old. How old am I?

C ALCULATING RATIOS

Can you calculate using ratios in a variety of situations?

Mrs Smith has a recipe to make an apple pie for eight people. She wants to make an apple pie large enough to serve six people.

She divides the amounts by 8 to find out how much is needed for one person. She then multiplies by 6.

The ingredients are:			**To make an apple pie for six:**
160 g margarine	⟶	$160 \div 8 \times 6 =$ ⟶	120 g margarine
320 g flour	⟶	$320 \div 8 \times 6 =$ ⟶	240 g flour
4 tablespoons of water	⟶	$4 \div 8 \times 6 =$ ⟶	3 tablespoons of water
2.4 kg cooking apples	⟶	$2.4 \div 8 \times 6 =$ ⟶	1.8 kg cooking apples
120 g sugar	⟶	$120 \div 8 \times 6 =$ ⟶	90 g sugar

Now test yourself

59 What are the ingredients to make an apple pie large enough to serve:
   (a) 10 people?
   (b) 5 people?

60 Shirts and blouses are often made from a mixture of cotton and
   a man-made fibre called polyester.
   Write these ratios in their simplest form:
   (a) cotton 70%; polyester 30%   (c) cotton 65%; polyester 35%
   (b) cotton 60%; polyester 40%   (d) cotton 45%; polyester 55%

61 'Three parts of sand to one part cement for this brick wall',
   thought the builder.
   (a) What is the total number of parts?
   (b) What fraction of the mixture is:
       (i) sand; (ii) cement?
   (c) How much of each is needed for 8 cubic metres of the mixture?
   (d) How much cement will the builder need for 20 cubic metres of the mixture?

62 Concrete is made by mixing gravel, sand and cement in the ratio 3:2:1.
   (a) What fraction of the mixture is: (i) sand; (ii) gravel; (iii) cement?
   (b) How much sand is needed to mix with 6 cubic metres of gravel?
   (c) How much gravel will be used for 12 cubic metres of concrete?

63 The length and width of a room is in the ratio of 5:4.
   (a) What is the width of a room 5.5 m long?
   (b) What is the length of a room 8.4 m wide?

64 Miss Jones and Mrs Cooper share an inheritance of
   £32 000 in the ratio 3:2.
   How much does each person get?

65 Mrs Green and Mrs White share a pools win in
   the ratio of 2:3. Mrs Green won £16 000.
   (a) How much did they win altogether?
   (b) How much did Mrs White win?

66 The ingredients for rice pudding for 50 servings are given below:
   (a) 150 schoolchildren eat rice pudding one lunchtime.
       Write down a list of ingredients for the cook.
   (b) Suppose you are making rice pudding for 10 people.
       How many pints of milk would you need?
   (c) Suppose you were making rice pudding for 20 people.
       How much sugar would you need?

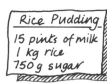

Rice Pudding
15 pints of milk
1 kg rice
750 g sugar

67 A DIY shop mixes red and white paint to make three different shades of pink.
   (a) To make 'Rose White', how many tins of white do you mix with
       6 tins of red?
   (b) To make 'Pale Pink', how many tins of red do you mix with
       10 tins of white?
   (c) To make 'Dusky Pink', how many tins of white do you mix with
       12 tins of red?
   (d) If you mix 12 tins of red and 20 tins of white, which shade of
       pink are you mixing?
   (e) If you mix 4 tins of each colour, how many extra tins of white do
       you need to make 'Rose White'?

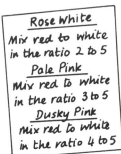

Rose White
Mix red to white
in the ratio 2 to 5

Pale Pink
Mix red to white
in the ratio 3 to 5

Dusky Pink
Mix red to white
in the ratio 4 to 5

Tom is 18 years old and Ray is 9 years old.

Tom is **twice** as old as Ray.

The ratio of Tom's age to Ray's age is 18:9 or much simpler: the ratio of Tom's age to Ray's age is 2:1.

The ratio of Tom's height to Ray's height is 160:120 or much simpler: the ratio of Tom's height to Ray's height is 4:3.

Now test yourself

68 John is the oldest (aged 15 years). Sue is 12 years old and little sister Jo is 9 years old.

   (a) What is the ratio of John's age to Jo's?
   (b) What is the ratio of Sue's age to John's?
   (c) What is the ratio of Jo's height to John's?
   (d) What is the ratio of Sue's height to Jo's?
   (e) What is the ratio of all three ages, in the order of oldest first?

Scale models and scale drawings

A model boat might be made to a scale of 1 to 10.

This means that for every 1 cm on the model the real boat is 10 cm. If the model is 1 metre long then the real boat is 10 metres long. If the model is 40 cm wide then the real boat is 400 cm wide (or 4 metres wide).

Now test yourself

69 This model racing-car is built to a scale of 1:20. The model is 9 cm wide.
   (a) How wide is the actual car?
   (b) The real car is 320 cm long. How long will the model be?

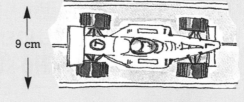

9 cm

70 This model of a bus is built to a scale of 1:50. The real bus is 3 metres wide.
   (a) The model is 9 cm high. How high will the bus be, in metres?
   (b) How wide is the model?

71 Here is a sketch of the plan of a bungalow.
   An architect wants to draw an accurate plan using a ratio 1:50.
   (a) What are the dimensions of the lounge on the plan?
   (b) Draw an accurate plan of the bungalow.
   (c) On the far right is the plan of an extension.

   Measure it and work out the real length and width.

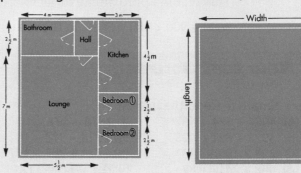

CHAPTER 4

Approximations and your calculator

You should have learned by now about rounding numbers up or down to the nearest 10 or 100. Let's see if you can remember:

Approximate 37 to the nearest 10.

Approximate 537 to the nearest 100.

What is 816 to the nearest 100?

You will also know about remainders! If eggs are packed in boxes of 6, how many boxes can be filled with 40 eggs and how many eggs will be left over?

Your calculator is your most valuable friend. Learn how to use it and take care of it!

MAKING INTELLIGENT GUESSES: ADDITION AND SUBTRACTION

Can you use estimation and approximation to check your answers to addition and subtraction problems?

For addition and subtraction calculations it is a good idea to check your answers by estimating what they should be.

Consider the addition:

7645 + 887 + 92

This would approximate to:

7600 + 900 + 100 = 8600, to the nearest 100.

You can estimate an answer to check a calculation quite quickly.

Now test yourself

Now estimate these to the nearest 100:

1 (a) 4624 + 624 + 587   (f) 1678 – 497
   (b) 4922 + 821 + 408   (g) 2318 + 978 – 1614
   (c) 228 + 195 + 1131   (h) 5624 + 987 – 1472
   (d) 968 + 2412 + 87   (i) 284 + 921 – 1121
   (e) 628 – 415   (j) 719 – 322 + 2197

In all the questions you have just done, the approximation was to the nearest 100.
You could just as easily approximate to the nearest 10 or nearest 1000.

Now test yourself

2   Choose a suitable approximation for these:
    (a) 78 + 121 + 62
    (b) 1898 + 2101
    (c) 789 – 281
    (d) 19 216 + 1789
    (e) At three successive football matches the attendances were 27 175, 36 895 and 29 144.
        What was the approximate total attendance for all three matches?

3   Can you spot the obvious mistakes? Some of the calculations below are wrong.
    Without actually doing them on paper can you tell which are incorrect?
    (a) 735 + 1943 – 298 = 2380
    (b) 596 + 8384 – 182 = 8118
    (c) 705 + 1923 + 289 = 2917
    (d) £2987 – £1712 = £1015
    (e) A new car is priced at £7995 + £1199 VAT. That is £9294 altogether.

MAKING INTELLIGENT GUESSES: MULTIPLICATION AND DIVISION

Can you now make use of estimation and approximation to check your answers to
multiplication and division problems?

Always make sure that the answers are sensible. This can be done by rounding
off the numbers and doing a rough check.

For instance: What is the cost of 29 stamps at 21p each?

First make a rough estimate and then calculate accurately:

Rough estimate: **Accurate calculation:**
30 x 20p = £6.00   29 x 21p = £6.09

Now test yourself

4   Find the total weight of 90 nails at 19 g each.

5   What is the cost of 22 pencils at 9p each?

6   A length of wire is 418 cm long. If it is cut into 19 equal pieces, what will
    be the length of each piece?

7   How heavy are 205 pencils each weighing 31 g?

8   A line of coins laid end to end stretches 3045 mm.
    If each coin has a diameter of 29 mm, how many
    coins are there?

Here is another example: $\dfrac{29 \times 81}{11}$

Rough estimate:
$\dfrac{30 \times 80}{10}$
$= 240$

Accurate calculation:
$29 \times 81 = 2349$

$2349 \div 11 = 213.54545$

Now test yourself

Choose the best approximate answer for the following calculations:

9 $\dfrac{504 \times 31}{48}$ = (a) about 30; (b) about 300; (c) about 150

10 $485 \div 31$ = (a) about 170; (b) about 17; (c) about 1.7

11 $278 \div 39$ = (a) about 5; (b) about 6; (c) about 7

12 $5021 \div 49$ = (a) about 10; (b) about 50; (c) about 100

13 $\dfrac{2011 \times 18}{503}$ = (a) about 80; (b) about 800; (c) about 8

APPROXIMATION: SIGNIFICANT FIGURES

Can you approximate to an agreed number of significant figures or decimal places?

The distance of the Earth from the Sun is taken as 93 000 000 miles. This is not the exact distance since it varies throughout the year. Only the first two figures are said to be **significant**. The zeros are there to give the correct place value to the 9 and the 3.

The distance from the Earth to the Sun correct to one significant figure (s.f.) would be 90 000 000 miles.

Here is another example:

The attendance at the recent international match was 72 532.
Write this number correct to: (a) 3 s.f.; (b) 2 s.f.; (c) 1 s.f.

Answers: (a) 72 500 (to 3 s.f.)
           (b) 73 000 (to 2 s.f.)
           (c) 70 000 (to 1 s.f.)

Now test yourself

14 Round these numbers to: (i) three significant figures; (ii) two significant figures.
Don't forget to put the zeros in the correct positions!
(a) 4247; (b) 86 519; (c) 1724.5 (d) 23.84; (e) 15.499

When a zero appears in the middle of other numbers, it counts as a **significant** figure. For instance: 70 175 = 70 200 (to 3 s.f.).

Now test yourself

15 Write these to three significant figures:
(a) 20 168; (b) 0.004 579; (c) 0.1077; (d) 10 984

R EADING YOUR CALCULATOR

Can you read your calculator to the nearest whole number?
Can you make sense of a result on a calculator that has a rounding error?

C Suppose a book contained 40 000 words on 140 pages.
Approximately how many words per page is this?

40 000 ÷ 140 = 285.71429 words.
↑

In order to round the number to the nearest whole number we consider the figure immediately after the decimal point.

Is it equal to 5 or more?

If the answer is **no** the previous figure is left unchanged

MATHS

In this case the answer is **yes** and so you round the figure up to make 286 words.
285.7 is nearer to 286 than 285

Now test yourself

16 Round each of the following to the nearest whole number:
(a) 37.2; (b) 46.8; (c) 39.7; (d) 123.49; (e) 27.55

17 Give the answer to these to the nearest whole number:
(a) 300 ÷ 8; (b) 27.15 × 7; (c) 2.66 × 1.88; (d) 32.5 ÷ 5.95

Now test yourself

18 (a) A rally driver covers 1430 miles in a 24 hour non-stop race. How many miles is this per hour approximately?
(b) Roughly how many matches are there per box if 2900 matches are used to fill 60 boxes?

Rounding up on your calculator

 Divide the number 20 by 3 on your calculator. What is your answer?

6.6666666

Now divide the number 20 by 7 on your calculator. What is the answer?

2.8571428

Divide the number 20 by every number up to 20. Which numbers give an answer that fills the display on your calculator like the ones above?

This time divide the number 20 by 7, then multiply your answer by 7. See what happens.

When you divide 20 by 7 and then multiply by 7 you get back where you started from – at 20.

No you don't! 20 ÷ 7 = 2.8571428 when you multiply this by 7 you get 19.999999

This is called a **rounding error**. The answer is really 20 and should always be 20 and never 19.999999.

Now test yourself

19 Try a few for yourself.

(a) Divide 7 by 3 and then multiply by 3. What does your calculator say? What is the correct answer?
(b) (15 ÷ 4) × 4 Why does this behave differently?
(c) (15 ÷ 3) × 3 Why does this behave differently?
(d) (16 ÷ 9) × 9 =

Now test yourself

20 Does this rounding error happen with **all** calculators? Try a few out.
(Some calculators, especially the scientific calculators, have a much larger memory and do not have these rounding errors.)

STANDARD FORM

Can you understand your calculator when you have done a multiplication of two large numbers and your answer seems wrong?

Try these on your calculator and check your answers with mine. You will need to use a scientific calculator.

300 × 400   =   120000

3000 × 4000   =   12000000

But 30 000 × 40 000   =   1.2   09   What does this mean?

is the calculator's way of saying $1.2 \times 10^9 = 1\,200\,000\,000$.

This is how very large numbers are written in standard form

Now test yourself

21 6.2 08 $= 6.2 \times 10^8 =$ 25 $400\,000 \times 70\,000 = \underline{\hspace{2cm}} =$

22 1.7 11 $=\qquad=$ 26 $60\,000 \times 300\,000 = \underline{\hspace{2cm}} =$

23 2.5 07 $=\qquad=$

24 2.25 12 $=\qquad=$

TRIAL AND IMPROVEMENT METHODS

Can you adapt 'trial and improvement' methods to solve problems?

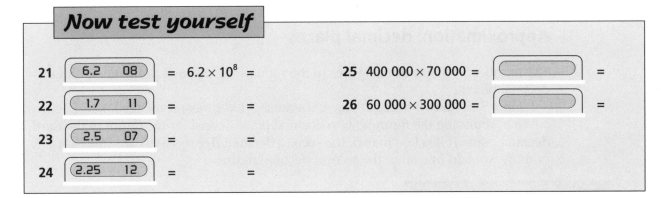

Suppose I wanted to find the edge of a square whose area was 20 cm²

Follow the flow chart

Begin

Try $4^2 = 16$

Now $5^2 = 25$

This side is more than 4 cm but less than 5 cm

$4.5^2 = 20.25$ (just too much)

$4.4^2 = 19.36$ (just too small)

A more accurate guess would be 4.45 cm

Now test yourself

27 Use this method to find the side length of a square whose area is:
(a) 40 cm^2; (b) 70 cm^2; (c) 54 cm^2

Suppose I wanted to find the edge of a cube whose volume was 100 cm³

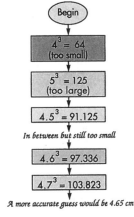

Follow the flow chart

Begin

$4^3 = 64$ (too small)

$5^3 = 125$ (too large)

$4.5^3 = 91.125$

In between but still too small

$4.6^3 = 97.336$

$4.7^3 = 103.823$

A more accurate guess would be 4.65 cm

Now test yourself

28 Use this method to find the edge of a cube whose volume is:
(a) 40 cm³; (b) 84 cm³; (c) 200 cm³

Approximation: decimal places

The number 5.<u>148</u> has three figures to the right of the decimal point, i.e. to three decimal places.

5.148 = 5.15 (to two decimal places) because 5.148 is nearer to 5.150 than 5.140.

When rounding the figure to two decimal places, consider the figure in the third decimal place. If it is less than 5, the second decimal figure stays the same. If it is 5 or more, we add one on to the second decimal figure.

Now test yourself

29 Round each of the following to: (i) one decimal place; (ii) two decimal places.
(a) 0.572; (b) 0.529; (c) 7.626; (d) 23.108; (e) 7.598

APPROXIMATING IN PRACTICAL SITUATIONS

Can you use the skills you have learned to make good approximations in everyday situations?

Now test yourself

30 Here is a diagram of the four walls of a bedroom.

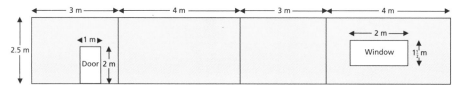

(a) If one tin of emulsion covers 10 m², how many tins will it take to paint all four walls?
(b) A painter uses one tin of paint every 45 minutes. Approximately how long will it take him to paint the four walls?

31 At a football match the total attendance was 8978. Of these 2015 were season ticket holders and did not pay at the gate. The rest paid £7 to watch the match. Estimate how much money was taken at the turnstiles to the nearest hundred pounds.

32 An aircraft flying at 248 km/h is making a journey of 4010 km. Approximately how long will the journey take?

33 A woman spends an average of £58.20 per week on food. Roughly how much does she spend in a whole year?

34 A garden contains 40 shrubs ranging in price from £2.50 to £8.00. What do you think is a rough estimate of the total cost of the shrubs?

35 A large city has a population of 250 000. Make a guess at how many cars are owned by the people who live in the city.

36 Give the following estimations as percentages:
   (a) how many houses have a television?
   (b) how many houses have a garage?
   (c) how many people wear spectacles?
   (d) how many schools have their own swimming pool?
   (e) how many houses have double-glazing?

37 A man pays a premium of £48.95 per month for 25 years to an insurance company. Approximately how much does he pay altogether?

38 Estimate the petrol costs for a year if a driver travels 15 000 miles in a car that does 30 miles to the gallon and petrol costs around £2 per gallon.

U SING THE MEMORY

Can you use the memory and bracket facility of a calculator to plan a calculation and work out expressions?

 You should familiarize yourself with the use of the memory keys on your calculator so that you will have the confidence to use them in your calculations. Remember also that different models have different memory keys.
   Follow these instructions carefully:

1 Put the number 5 in your calculator and press the memory key.

Depending on the model press:
[Min] or [x→M] or [STO]

A letter 'M' should appear somewhere in the display screen.

2 Clear the display.

The letter 'M' should remain.

3 Recall the number in the memory.

Press [MR] or [RM] or [RCL]

Your number 5 should re-appear.

4 Add 7 to the contents of the memory.

Press [7] [M+]

5 Recall the memory.

Press [MR] or [RM] or [RCL]
Display should now show 12.

6 Subtract 3 from the memory.

Press [3] [M–]

7 Recall memory.

Display should now show 9.

8 To multiply the memory by another number.

Press [5] [×] [RM] (or [MR] or [RCL]) [=]
Display should now show 45.

9 To divide the memory by another number.

Press [RM] (or [MR] or [RCL]) [÷] [3] [=]
Display should now show 15.

10 To clear the memory.

Press [CE] or [C] (this should display 0)

then press [x→M] (or [Min] or [STO])

The letter 'M' should disappear.

Now test yourself

39 Try these calculations using the memory key:

C
(a) Put the number 540 into the memory of your calculator. Then find out which of the following numbers are factors of 540:
3, 4, 12, 15, 22, 28, 32, 35, 72, 81

(b) Put the number 16 into the memory of your calculator. Add together the results of multiplying the memory by the numbers 1 to 10, one number at a time.
Divide your final answer by the number 16.
What is your answer?
How else could you arrive at this answer using only the numbers 1 to 10?

Using the brackets

C It is important that you know how your calculator works. Some work from left to right (LTR) and some use scientific logic.
If you do the calculation $4 + 2 \times 5$ you will get:

LTR $(4 + 2) \times 5 = 30$
Scientific $4 + (2 \times 5) = 14$

Due to this fact, you need to use brackets to make sure that you do exactly what you mean to do.
Consider the calculation: $8 + 2 \times 3$
By using brackets the final answer can be changed.

$(8 + 2) \times 3 = 30$
$8 + (2 \times 3) = 14$

By using brackets you are giving priority to a certain part of the calculation. For instance:

Work out $\dfrac{10}{2 + 3}$. A very common mistake is to press the following keys:

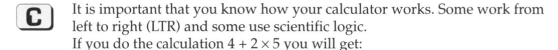

$\boxed{1}\,\boxed{0}\,\boxed{\div}\,\boxed{2}\,\boxed{+}\,\boxed{3}\,\boxed{=}$ $\boxed{\qquad 8}$ which is incorrect

You should use the brackets and press: $\boxed{1}\,\boxed{0}\,\boxed{\div}\,\boxed{(}\,\boxed{2}\,\boxed{+}\,\boxed{3}\,\boxed{)}\,\boxed{=}$ $\boxed{\qquad 2}$

Now test yourself

C Use your calculator for the following:

40 (a) $\dfrac{54}{11 + 7}$; (b) $\dfrac{5 \times 28}{22 + 18}$; (c) $\dfrac{13.6 - 5.1}{7 - 2}$; (d) $(3.2 - 1.5) \times (4.1 - 1.6)$

41 Write down what keys you would press on your calculator to work out:
$\dfrac{5 + 7}{6 - 2}$ using (a) the memory
(b) brackets

LEVEL DESCRIPTIONS: NUMBER

In this book, the level descriptions for Number are given together with the level descriptions for Algebra, just as they are in the National Curriculum. These can be found at the end of the Algebra section on page 87.

CHAPTER 5

Number patterns and algebra

PATTERNS, SEQUENCES AND FINDING NUMBER RELATIONSHIPS

You should already know how to explain patterns and to discover the next numbers in a sequence. Try these: 5, 10, 15, 20, __; or even 14, 24, 34, __! You should be able to do sums like 27 + 31 without writing it down. This is how: 27 + 31 = 20 + 7 + 30 + 1 = 50 + 8 = 58. Easy, when you know how!

You should also be able to recognize if a number can be divided by 2, 5 or 10; even if the numbers are very large. Which of the following numbers is the odd one out: 2, 14, 17, 28, 30, 66?

Now read on!

DOUBLING AND HALVING

Can you recognize and understand number patterns?

In Marskool, they can only multiply by 2 (double) or divide by 2 (halve) when they do a maths sum. How can they work out 23 × 8?

      23 × 8
  =   46 × 4
  =   92 × 2
  =   184

What about 120 ÷ 8?
120 ÷ 8 = 60 ÷ 4 = 30 ÷ 2 = 15 (not so easy)

Now test yourself

1 In Lunarskool, they can only multiply by 2 or 3 and divide by 2 or 3.
   Show how they can work out:
   (a) 15 × 6; (b) 21 × 9; (c) 13 × 12
   Be careful with these:
   (d) 72 ÷ 6; (e) 60 ÷ 12

Now test yourself

2   Continue these fraction patterns:

(a) $\frac{1}{2} = \frac{2}{4} = \frac{3}{6} = \frac{4}{8} = \frac{5}{\Box} = \frac{6}{\Box} = \frac{\Box}{14} = \frac{\Box}{16}$

(b) $\frac{2}{3} = \frac{4}{6} = \frac{6}{9} = \frac{8}{\Box} = \frac{\Box}{15} = \frac{\Box}{18} = \frac{\Box}{21}$

(c) $\frac{3}{5} = \frac{6}{10} = \frac{\Box}{15} = \frac{12}{\Box} = \frac{\Box}{\Box} = \frac{18}{\Box} = \frac{\Box}{\Box}$

$\frac{1}{2} =$ $\frac{2}{4} =$ $\frac{3}{6} =$ $\frac{4}{8} =$

3   Can you make up a pattern of equivalent fractions for these:

(a) $\frac{3}{4}$; (b) $\frac{2}{5}$; (c) $\frac{3}{8}$?

GENERALIZING IN WORDS

Can you explain in words the number patterns that you have recognized?

If I said 11, 14, 17, 20 What comes next?

Easy, the difference between the numbers is 3 so the next number is 23 then 26 and so on.

What about 1, 5, 13, 29 What comes next?

Not so easy. The differences change, so you are not just adding or multiplying. You are multiplying by 2 then adding 3......the next number is 61.

Now test yourself

4   Write the next number in the sequence and describe the pattern in words:

(a) 15, 19, 23, 27 ...
(b) 29, 24, 19, 14 ...
(c) 3, 6, 12, 24 ...
(d) 48, 24, 12, 6 ...

(e) 2, 3, 5, 9, 17 ...
(f) 2, 10, 34, 106 ...
(g) 2, 5, 9, 14, 20 ...
(h) 1, 1, 2, 3, 5, 8, 13 ...

Look at this match-stick pattern. How many matches will be used in the next stage? Spot the pattern in the numbers.

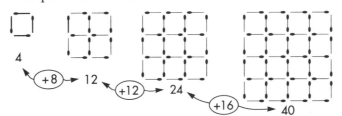

Add an **extra** 4 on each time.

Stage 5 will be 40 + 20 = 60

60 matches for stage 5

Now test yourself

5 Draw the next two stages in this match-stick diagram.
Write down the numbers used in each stage.
Try to predict how many matches will be used in the
next stage after that (i.e. do not draw this one).
Use your own words to describe the pattern of numbers.

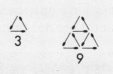

6 Describe the patterns of numbers in the following diagrams.

(a)

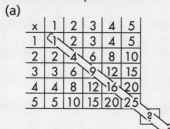

(b)

These two sets of numbers should be remembered along with their names. They are
used all the time in mathematics.

THE LANGUAGE OF NUMBERS

Can you understand and use terms such as prime, square, cube, square root, cube
root, multiples and factors?

How many different numbers multiply together to make 12?

$$1 \times 12 = 12 \quad 2 \times 6 = 12 \quad 3 \times 4 = 12$$

We call all these numbers **factors of 12**.

Now test yourself

Write down all the factors of:

7 (a) 8; (b) 15; (c) 30; (d) 16; (e) 54

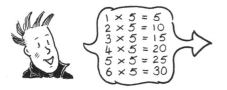

These are **multiples** of 5. When you
multiply 5 by any other number, the
answer you get will be a multiple of 5.

Now test yourself

8 (a) Write down the multiples of 8 less than 50.
   (b) Write down the multiples of 6 that lie between 20 and 50.

Every number is **divisible by 1**.
Every number is **divisible by itself**.

Some numbers, like 11, are not divisible by any other numbers.
They have **only two** factors and are called **prime numbers**.
0 and 1 are **not** prime numbers. 2 is the only **even** prime number.

Now test yourself

9 (a) Continue the pattern of prime numbers up to 50:
       2, 3, 5, 7, 11, 13, 17...
   (b) Make a 10 by 10 grid and put in numbers from 1 to 100. Circle each prime number. Is
        there a pattern to these prime numbers?

10 With the help of a diagram like the one below, find out the **prime factors** of:
    (a) 42; (b) 40; (c) 80
    Try to draw a different diagram for 80.

```
            60
           /  \
          6    10
         / \   / \
        2   3 2   5
        _____/
```

These are the **prime factors** of 60

A **square number** is formed when you multiply any number by **itself**.

For instance: $5 \times 5 = $ (25)
                    ↑
This is a square number $1 \times 1 = 1$

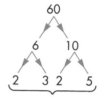

$2 \times 2 = 4$

$3 \times 3 = 9$

$4 \times 4 = 16$

Square numbers can be shown as a **dot diagram**.

Now test yourself

11 On your 10 by 10 grid that you used in question 9(b) put a square around all the **square**
    numbers. Is there a pattern?
    Could a square number also be a prime number?

12 This dot diagram gives you **triangular numbers**.

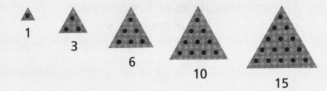

Put a triangle around the triangular numbers on your grid. Can you spot the pattern? What
are the next three triangular numbers?

Cube numbers go like this:

$$1 \times 1 \times 1 = 1$$

$$2 \times 2 \times 2 = 8$$

$$3 \times 3 \times 3 = 27$$

$1^3 = 1 \times 1 \times 1 = 1$
$2^3 = 2 \times 2 \times 2 = 8$ These are cube numbers
$3^3 = 3 \times 3 \times 3 = 27$

Now test yourself

13 Can you write down the cube numbers up to 1000?

C **14** Look carefully at your calculator. Can you see a button like this? This is called a **square root** button.

If $5 \times 5 = 25$

then $\sqrt{25} = 5$

and $\sqrt{36} = 6$; $\sqrt{100} = 10$

Work these out without a calculator:

(a) $\sqrt{49}$; (b) $\sqrt{81}$; (c) $\sqrt{144}$; (d) $\sqrt{225}$; (e) $\sqrt{400}$

C Work these out using a calculator:

(f) $\sqrt{6.25}$; (g) $\sqrt{56.25}$; (h) $\sqrt{625}$; (i) $\sqrt{1600}$; (j) $\sqrt{9801}$

15 A **cube root** button looks like this: If $5 \times 5 \times 5 = 125$ then $\sqrt[3]{125} = 5$

(Some calculators do not have this button.)

Work these out without a calculator:

(a) $\sqrt[3]{8}$; (b) $\sqrt[3]{27}$; (c) $\sqrt[3]{64}$

C Work these out with the help of your calculator:

(d) $\sqrt[3]{15.625}$; (e) $\sqrt[3]{1331}$; (f) $\sqrt[3]{3375}$

16 Use words that describe numbers to fill in the gaps about the number 25.

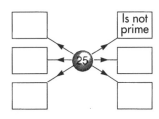

Is not prime

PRIME FACTORS

Can you see how whole numbers can be broken down and shown as a multiplication of their prime factors?

A **prime number** is one with only **two** factors, 1 and itself. Any other number can be made by multiplying prime numbers together. Follow the diagrams below to find out how a number can be written as a product of its **prime factors**.

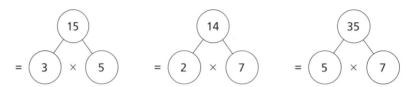

Now test yourself

17 Copy and complete these diagrams:

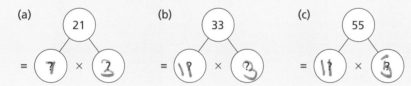

18 What are the prime factors of: (a) 6; (b) 77; (c) 121?
Check your answers by multiplying the prime factors together.

Sometimes there are more than two prime factors.
Look at the examples below:

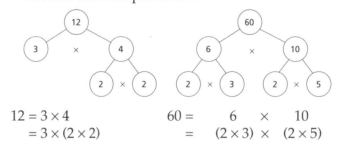

$12 = 3 \times 4$
$\quad = 3 \times (2 \times 2)$

$60 = \quad 6 \quad \times \quad 10$
$\quad = \quad (2 \times 3) \times (2 \times 5)$

NUMBER PATTERNS

Number patterns can arise through patterns in diagrams. Can you spot them?

Now test yourself

19 Instead of making up triangular numbers using equilateral triangles, copy and complete the pattern using right-angled triangles.

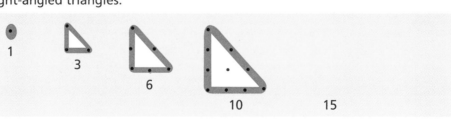

If we now take two successive triangular numbers and join them together, what do you notice about the result?

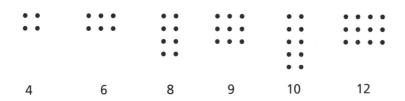

$$3 + 1 = 4$$

$$6 + 3 = 9 \qquad 10 + 6 =$$

Check your findings by combining 6 and 10. What number do you get by combining them?
What **type** of number is this?
State this result in your own words.
Divide these dot diagrams into triangular numbers:

(a)

(b)

20

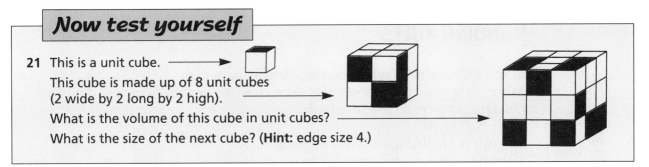

4   6   8   9   10   12

These numbers are called **rectangular numbers**. Can you see why? Draw a dot diagram to show the next three rectangular numbers.
Look carefully at the numbers that are missing. What **type** of numbers are they?
Can you describe your findings in your own words?

Cubes

Now test yourself

21 This is a unit cube.
This cube is made up of 8 unit cubes (2 wide by 2 long by 2 high).
What is the volume of this cube in unit cubes?
What is the size of the next cube? (**Hint:** edge size 4.)

NUMBER SEQUENCES

Can you form any number patterns of your own?
    When we arrange numbers in order, according to a **rule**, the numbers form a
sequence. Each number in a sequence is called a **term**. An everyday example of a sequence of numbers is shown here.

The rule is   +2

22 Starting at the number 1, write down the next six terms in the sequence for the following rules (the first one is started for you):

(a) Rule [+5 ⟩ Sequence: 1 ⟍(5)⟋ 6 ⟍(5)⟋ 11

(b) Rule [+3 ⟩ Sequence: 1 . . . .

(c) Rule [×2 ⟩ Sequence: 1 . . . .

(d) Rule [×3 ⟩ Sequence: 1 . . . .

Some sequences are generated by a combination of rules. Write down the next six terms in the sequence for the following rules:

(e) Rule [×2 + 3 ⟩ Sequence: 1 ⟍(×2 + 3)⟋ 5 ⟍(×2 + 3)⟋ 13 ⟍(×2 + 3)⟋

(f) Rule [×3 – 1 ⟩ Sequence: 1 . . . .

(g) Rule [×5 – 3 ⟩ Sequence: 1 . . . .

(h) Rule [÷2 ⟩ Sequence: 128 . . . .

(i) Rule [–2 × 2 ⟩ Sequence: 5 . . . .

23 In this special sequence, the next number is the sum of the two numbers before it. Can you continue the sequence for a further three terms?
1, 1, 2, 3, 5, 8, 13, …
Write down the next four terms in these sequences:
(a) 3, 4, 7, 11, ? ? ? ?
(b) 2, 4, 6, 10, ? ? ? ?

F INDING RULES

Can you spot any rules when forming number patterns?

When a sequence of numbers gets larger, the rule usually involves adding or multiplying or a combination of both.

e.g. 1, 3, 7, 15, 31 …

The rule is 'double the number and add 1'.

If the rule is not obvious you might try the **difference method**.

For instance: explore the following sequence. Write down the next two terms.

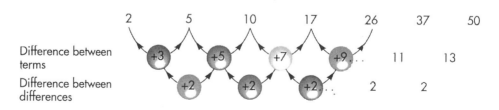

	2		5		10		17		26	37	50
Difference between terms		+3		+5		+7		+9	. .	11	13	
Difference between differences			+2		+2		+2	. .	2	2		

Now test yourself

24 Explore these and write down the next two terms.
(a) 1, 2, 4, 7, 11, 16 … (b) 1, 4, 9, 16, 25, 36 … (c) 2, 7, 14, 23, 34 …
(d) 1, 5, 11, 19, 29 …   (e) 2, 4, 8, 14, 22 …

If you are only given the first three terms of a sequence, there could be more than one possibility.
   For instance: 1, 2, 4 … may be part of 1, 2, 4, 8, 16 (doubling)
                 or could be part of 1, 2, 4, 7, 11 (as in 24(a) above)

Now test yourself

25 Explore these to see if there is more than one alternative.
(a) 1, 2, 3 … (b) 1, 2, 5 … (c) 1, 3, 7 … (d) 1, 4, 10 … (e) 2, 5, 11 …

U SING SYMBOLS

Can you use symbols (or letters) to show these rules of number patterns?
   Each number in a sequence of numbers is called a **term**. The numbers in a sequence could go on for a long time so it is usual to generalize, and use algebra, with the introduction of the nth term.

For example:

term	1st	2nd	3rd	4th	5th	....	n^{th}
sequence	2	4	6	8	10	....	$2n$

In this example the sequence is generated by doubling each term.

Now test yourself

26 Write down the nth term in each of these sequences:

(a)

term	1st	2nd	3rd	4th	5th	....	n^{th}
sequence	3	6	9	12	15	....	?

(b)

term	1st	2nd	3rd	4th	5th	....	n^{th}
sequence	1	3	5	7	9	....	?

(c)

term	1st	2nd	3rd	4th	5th	....	n^{th}
sequence	1	4	9	16	25	....	?

(d)

term	1st	2nd	3rd	4th	5th	....	n^{th}
sequence	4	7	10	13	16	....	?

(e)

term	1st	2nd	3rd	4th	5th	....	n^{th}
sequence	$\frac{1}{2}$	$\frac{2}{3}$	$\frac{3}{4}$	$\frac{4}{5}$	$\frac{5}{6}$	....	?

Hints:
1 Look at the difference between consecutive values. If they are the same this will give you the multiple.
2 Adjust this by adding or taking away.

If you are given the nth term, can you write down the sequence? This is quite simple. All you have to do is let $n = 1$, then 2, then 3, and so on …
For instance: write down the sequence if the nth term is $3n - 1$:

If $n = 1$ then $3n - 1 = 2$
If $n = 2$ then $3n - 1 = 5$
If $n = 3$ then $3n - 1 = 8$ The sequence is 2, 5, 8, 11, … $(3n - 1)$
If $n = 4$ then $3n - 1 = 11$

Now test yourself

27 Write down the sequences if the nth term is:

(a) $2n + 3$; (b) $5n - 2$; (c) $\frac{n^2}{2}$; (d) $n(n - 1)$; (e) $\dfrac{2n}{n + 2}$

R ECIPROCALS

Can you understand the meaning of 'reciprocal' and its place in number patterns?
If the product of two numbers is 1 then each number is called the **reciprocal** of the other.

You know that $2 \times \frac{1}{2} = 1$

so you can say 2 is the reciprocal of $\frac{1}{2}$ and $\frac{1}{2}$ is the reciprocal of 2.

Similarly, $\frac{1}{3}$ is the reciprocal of 3 and $\frac{1}{5}$ is the reciprocal of 5.

Now test yourself

28 Write down the reciprocals of these:

(a) 8; (b) $\frac{1}{7}$; (c) 20; (d) $\frac{1}{10}$; (e) 50

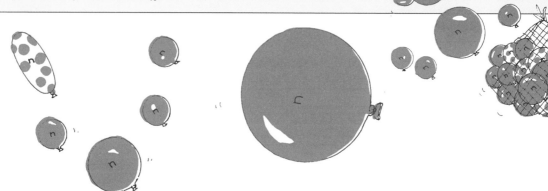

Another way of looking at reciprocals is to say:
The reciprocal of a number is 1 divided by that number.

C A reciprocal can also be written as a decimal and can therefore be worked out using a calculator.
For instance: what is the reciprocal of $\frac{3}{4}$?

You can say $\frac{3}{4} \times \frac{4}{3} = 1$ or $1 \div \frac{3}{4} = \frac{4}{3}$

In all cases the reciprocal of a fraction is obtained by turning the fraction upside down.

Now test yourself

29 Work out the reciprocals of these:

(a) $\frac{2}{3}$; (b) $\frac{4}{5}$; (c) $\frac{7}{10}$; (d) $\frac{5}{8}$

C What is the reciprocal of 2.5?

(a) Press keys: $\boxed{1}\boxed{\div}\boxed{2}\boxed{.}\boxed{5}\boxed{=}$ $\boxed{\quad 0.4\quad}$

(b) Scientific calculators will have a key $\boxed{1/x}$

To use it press $\boxed{2}\boxed{.}\boxed{5}\boxed{1/x}$ $\boxed{\quad 0.4\quad}$ no need to press $\boxed{=}$

Now test yourself

30 Use your calculator to work out the reciprocals of these:

C (a) 1.25; (b) 0.2; (c) 6.25; (d) 12.5 (e) 25

CHAPTER 6

*F*ormulae, functions and equations

It is more than likely that you have never heard of number machines before.

Take a look at this! Follow the set of numbers from start to finish as they pass through the number machine.

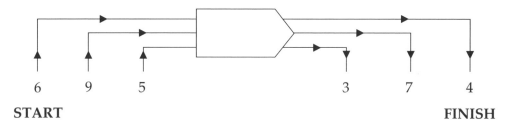

| 6 | 9 | 5 | | 3 | 7 | 4 |

START   **FINISH**

Can you describe what is happening to the left-hand numbers once they pass through the number machine and appear on the right-hand side? Of course you can!

Now, if you think hard enough you also know what number machine will undo what you have just done. In other words, to get back to the numbers that you first started with:

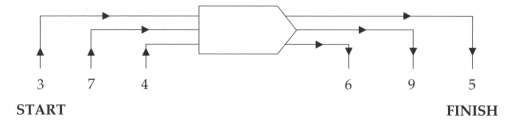

| 3 | 7 | 4 | | 6 | 9 | 5 |

START   **FINISH**

S IMPLE FORMULAE

Can you understand and use simple formulae expressed in words?

These are function machines.
The rule for this function
machine mapping is: × 3

This mapping or relationship
could be described as: × 10 + 1

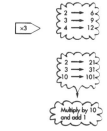

Now test yourself

1 Describe these mappings in words:

(a) 3 → 12   (b) 3 → 11   (c) 2 → 7
      4 → 16   4 → 14   5 → 13
      6 → 24   10 → 32   8 → 19

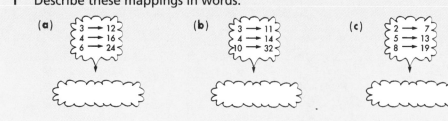

Now test yourself

2   Now solve these:
    (a) If I double a number, then add 5 and the result is 21, what is the number?
        (**Hint:** undo the formula.)
    (b) If I treble a number, then add 4 and the result is 19, what is the number?
    (c) If I multiply a number by 10 then subtract 3 and the result is 57, what is the number?
    (d) If I multiply a number by 6 then take away 10 and the result is 32, what is the number?
    (e) If I halve a number, then add 9 and the result is 15, what is the number?

INVERSE OPERATIONS

Can you check your calculations by working backwards from your answer?

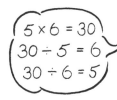

Now test yourself

3   Link together the following sets of numbers. Use multiplication and division.
    (a) 7, 10, 70; (b) 8, 9, 72

4   Work out on your calculator 25×32.
    (a) Divide your answer by 25. What answer do you expect?
        Work out 25×32 again on your calculator.
    (b) Now divide your answer by 32. You should know the answer without doing a calculation.

5   Work out on your calculator $270 \div 15$.
    What do you expect if you multiply your answer by 15? Check your prediction.

Now test yourself

6   Which of the following are wrong? You should be able to spot the incorrect ones without calculation.

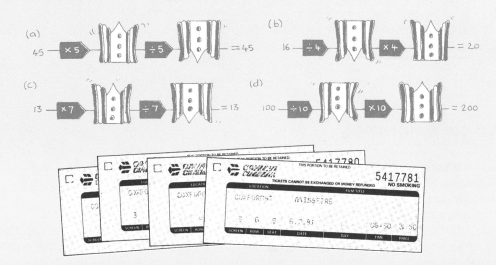

7   If you bought four tickets for the cinema at £3.50 each, the total cost would be:
$4 \times £3.50 = £14$
Looking at it another way, you could say 'I have just paid £14 for four cinema tickets.'
That's $£14 \div 4 = £3.50$ each.
Write the inverse of these statements:
(a) 'I've just spent 45 minutes doing 9 problems. That's 5 minutes per problem.'
(b) 'I've just bought 4 L.P.s at £5.95 each. The total cost came to £23.80.'
(c) Six children share 66 marbles equally. Each child gets 11 marbles.

MORE SIMPLE FORMULAE

Can you understand and use simple formulae using letters instead of words?

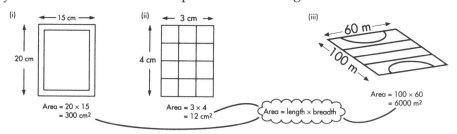

Choose a suitable letter for each quantity (say Area = A; length = L; breadth = B).
   We can now say $A = L \times B$
   In algebra we try not to use the multiplication sign.
   Letters next to each other are being multiplied.
   So we can say $A = LB$.
   This is now the formula $A = LB$ for the area of a rectangle. The formula can be used to find the area of any rectangle.

Now test yourself

8 (a) Calculate the perimeter of each of the rectangles shown on the previous page.
(b) If we let the perimeter of the rectangle be *P*, the length *L* and the breadth *B*, write down a formula for calculating the perimeter.

9 Use the formulae that you have written to find: (a) the area, and
(b) the perimeter of a rectangle measuring 5 cm by 12 cm.

10 To work out the speed of a car you divide the distance it travels by the time taken to travel the distance.

(a) Using suitable letters, write down a formula for the speed of the car.
(b) Can you change the formula to find the distance it travels if you know the speed of the car and the time taken to make the journey?
(c) Use your formula from part (a) to work out the speed of a car that travels 100 miles in 2 hours.

11 The formula for converting temperature from Celsius to Fahrenheit is:

$$F = \frac{9}{5}C + 32$$

What is 15° Celsius in °Fahrenheit?

ALGEBRAIC FUNCTIONS

When we shop and do not have the correct money we usually hand over an amount and wait for the change.

The rule is:

Change wanted = money given minus the cost of the item

A formula is: $C = M - P$
where C = change
M = money given
P = price of item

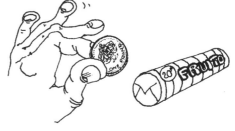

Now test yourself

12 Test the formula out for these:
(a) (b)

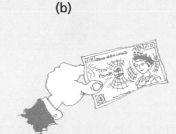

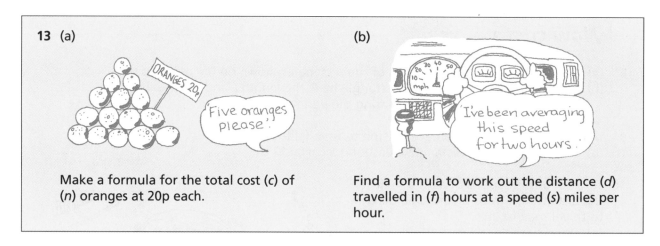

13 (a) Make a formula for the total cost (c) of (n) oranges at 20p each.

(b) Find a formula to work out the distance (d) travelled in (f) hours at a speed (s) miles per hour.

At 'Benny's Car Hire' cars cost £15 plus 10p per mile.
   The rule is:
   Cost = 1500 + number of miles × 10

The formula is: $C = 1500 + 10n$
where C is the symbol used for the cost, in pence, and n is the number of miles.

Now test yourself

14 Find a formula for each of these hire firms:

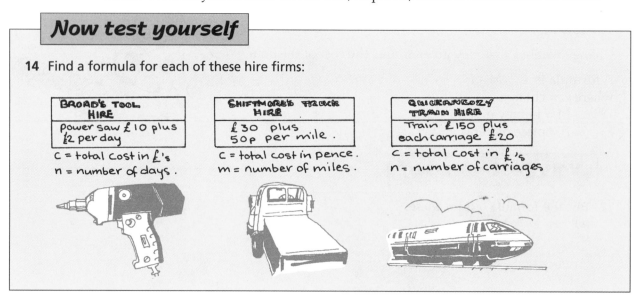

S OLVING LINEAR EQUATIONS

Can you solve simple equations?
   $4 + 5 = 9$ is called an **arithmetic equation**.
   $x + 5 = 9$ is called an **algebraic equation**, where x has a value of 4.
   Most equations are not this easy to solve so you need to know some rules. For instance: consider the equation $2x + 4 = 10$.

An equation is like a pair of scales pivoting on the equals sign. You have to maintain the balance, which means that whatever you do to the left-hand side of the equation you must also do to the right-hand side.

Follow these steps:
(i) subtract 4 from both sides $\quad 2x + 4 - 4 = 10 - 4$
$$2x = 6$$
(ii) divide both sides by 2 $\quad \dfrac{2x}{2} = \dfrac{6}{2}$
$$x = 3$$

Now test yourself

15 Solve these equations. (**Remember** to balance the equations.)
(a) $3x + 5 = 11$; (b) $2x + 7 = 15$; (c) $5x + 1 = 16$;
(d) $2x - 3 = 7$; (e) $2x - 6 = 12$; (f) $3x - 2 = 19$
(**Hint:** with the last three examples you have to add to both sides, not subtract.)

Now consider the equation $5x - 1 = 2x + 11$.

Follow these steps:
(i) add 1 to both sides $\quad 5x - 1 + 1 = 2x + 11 + 1$
$$5x = 2x + 12$$
(ii) subtract $2x$ from both sides $\quad 5x - 2x = 2x + 12 - 2x$
$$3x = 12$$
(iii) divide both sides by 3 $\quad \dfrac{3x}{3} = \dfrac{12}{3}$
$$x = 4$$

I don't understand this!

Help me please!

Now test yourself

16 Solve these equations:
(a) $3x + 2 = x + 6$; (b) $4x - 5 = x + 1$; (c) $7x - 4 = 3x + 12$;
(d) $5x - 12 = 3x$; (e) $2x + 5 + x = x - 1$. (**Hint:** not all of the answers are positive.)

Sometimes it is easier to collect the numbers on the left-hand side and the x's on the right-hand side.
Now consider the equation $2x - 5 = 5x - 11$

Follow these steps:
(i) Add 11 to both sides $\quad 2x - 5 + 11 = 5x - 11 + 11$
$$2x + 6 = 5x$$
(ii) subtract $2x$ from both sides $\quad 2x + 6 - 2x = 5x - 2x$
$$6 = 3x$$
(iii) divide both sides by 3 $\quad \dfrac{6}{3} = \dfrac{3x}{3}$
$$2 = x$$
which is the same as $x = 2$

Now test yourself

17 Solve the following equations (try to spot the ones where it is easier to collect the x's on the right-hand side):
(a) $2x - 1 = 4x - 7$ $\qquad$ (d) $3x - 4 = x + 2$
(b) $5x + 1 = 4x - 9$ $\qquad$ (e) $x - 3 = 2x + 1$
(c) $4x + 7 = 5x - 4$ $\qquad$ (f) $2x - 7 = 4x + 11$

TRIAL AND IMPROVEMENT

Can you find x by trial and improvement?

 Solve $x^2 = 5$ (using a calculator – but not the key)

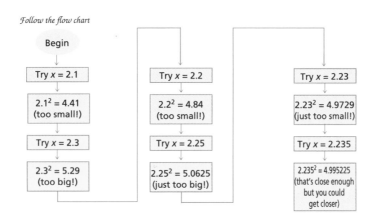

Follow the flow chart

Try $x = 2.1$ $2.1^2 = 4.41$ too small!
Try $x = 2.3$ $2.3^2 = 5.29$ too big!
Try $x = 2.2$ $2.2^2 = 4.84$ too small!
Try $x = 2.25$ $2.25^2 = 5.0625$ just too big!
Try $x = 2.23$ $2.23^2 = 4.9729$ just too small!
Try $x = 2.235$ $2.235^2 = 4.995225$ that's close enough (but you could get closer!)

Now test yourself

C Use this method of trial and improvement to solve the following to 3 decimal places:

18 (a) $x^2 = 12$; (b) $x^2 = 60$; (c) $x^2 = 200$

19 (a) $x^3 = 20$; (b) $x^3 = 50$; (c) $x^3 = 100$

20 (a) $x^4 = 100$; (b) $x^5 = 200$; (c) $x^{10} = 500$

INDICES

Can you understand and use indices?
   Indices have the same meaning in algebra as in arithmetic.
   For example: $a^3 = a \times a \times a$

To understand the basic rules of indices, it is easier if you write each term in full.
For instance: (a) Simplify $a^2 \times a^3$

$$(a \times a) \times (a \times a \times a) = a \times a \times a \times a \times a = a^5$$

Another way of simplifying $a^2 \times a^3$ is to say $a^2 \times a^3 = a^{2+3} = a^5$

(b) $2y^3 \times 3y^4 = 2 \times (y \times y \times y) \times 3 \times (y \times y \times y \times y) = 6y^7$
   or $2y^3 \times 3y^4 = 2 \times 3 \times y^{3+4} = 6y^7$

Now test yourself

21 Simplify the following expressions:
   (a) $5a^3 \times 3a^2$; (b) $4a^7 \times 5a^2$; (c) $3m^2 \times 7m^5$; (d) $2n^4 \times 5n^5$

In terms such as $3ab^3$, only the b is 'to the power of 3'.
   So $3ab^3 = 3 \times a \times b \times b \times b$
   If the power of all of the term is needed you have to use brackets.

For instance:
   Simplify $(2a^2)^3$
   $(2a^2)^3 = (2a^2) \times (2a^2) \times (2a^2) = (2 \times a \times a) \times (2 \times a \times a) \times (2 \times a \times a)$
   $\qquad\ = 8a^6$

Now test yourself

22 Simplify the following expressions:
   (a) $(5x^3)^2$; (b) $(2a^2)^5$; (c) $(3x^3)^3$; (d) $(4a^2)^4$

Addition of indices

Only **like** indices can be added to make a single index. This is referred to as collecting **like terms**. For example: $3x^2 + 2x^2 + 5x^2 = 10x^2$
   $\qquad\qquad\qquad\ \text{or}: 7y^3 + 8y^3 + y^3\ = 16y^3$
   Unlike terms cannot be added together and written as a single term.
   For example: $3x + 5x^2 + 4x^3$ cannot be simplified.

Simplify, by collecting like terms:
   (a) $2x^3 + 3x^3$ (b) $2x^2 + 5x^3 + 3x^2 + 6x^3$
   $\quad = 5x^3 \qquad\quad = 5x^2 + 11x^3$

Now test yourself

23 Simplify the following expressions by collecting like terms where possible:
   (a) $5a^3 + 7a^3$; (b) $3a^2 + 4a^2 + 5a^3$; (c) $2x^3 + 3y^2 + 2x^3 + 4y^2$

INEQUALITIES

Can you solve inequalities using a number line?
   An inequality is a statement that one quantity is greater than or less than another. For example: $x > 3$ is an inequality (as opposed to $x = 3$ which is an equality or equation).
   In this case, the inequality is true when x stands for any number greater than 3. The inequality can be shown on a number line.

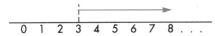

The line at $x = 3$ is dotted because it is **not** in the range of values for which the inequality is true. It is the boundary of the inequality.

Look carefully at these expressions and what they mean:

$x < 3$ $x \leqslant 3$ $x > 3$
x is less than 3 x less than or equal to 3 x is greater than 3

Now test yourself

24 Use a number line to show the range of values of x for which the following inequalities are true:
(a) $x < 6$; (b) $x > -3$; (c) $x > 7$; (d) $x < -1$

Consider an inequality $5 > 2$ true
Add 2 to both sides $7 > 4$ still true
Subtract 3 from both sides $4 > 1$ still true
Multiply both sides by 4 $16 > 4$ still true
Divide both sides by 2 $8 > 2$ still true

From this simple exercise you can see that the inequality holds true if both sides of the inequality are treated exactly the same.

Now consider the inequality $x - 3 > 4$.

You can solve this inequality by finding the range of values of x for which $x - 3 > 4$ is true.

Add 3 to both sides $x - 3 + 3 > 4 + 3$
                           $x > 7$ is the range of values for x

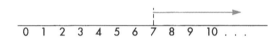

Now test yourself

25 Solve the following inequalities and illustrate your answers on a number line:
(a) $x + 2 > 7$; (b) $x - 5 < -2$; (c) $x + 3 < -4$; (d) $x - 3 > 5$

Now solve the inequation $2x - 5 < 3$ and show the answer on a number line.
                             $2x - 5 < 3$
Add 5 to both sides $2x < 8$
Divide both sides by 2 $x < 4$

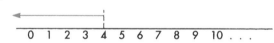

Now test yourself

26 Solve the following inequalities and illustrate your solutions on a number line:
(a) $3x - 5 < 7$; (b) $2x + 8 > 2$; (c) $4x - 3 > 9$; (d) $5x + 4 > -1$

Now find the range of values of x which satisfy both of the inequalities $2x - 1 > 5$ and $2x - 1 < 13$.

Illustrate both inequalities on a number line.

(The two inequalities can be written like this: $5 < 2x - 1 < 13$)

Treat the inequalities separately:
                       $2x - 1 > 5$ $2x - 1 < 13$
Add 1 to both sides $2x > 6$ $2x < 14$
Divide both sides by 2 $x > 3$ $x < 7$

Now test yourself

27 Solve the following inequalities and illustrate your solutions on a number line:
(a) $-3 < 2x + 1 < 5$; (b) $-5 < 3x - 2 < 7$

28 List the values of n where n is a **whole number** such that:
(a) $-10 < 2n \leq 20$;　(c) $-7 \leq 2n + 1 \leq 5$;
(b) $12 \leq 3n \leq 30$;　(d) $-11 < 3n - 2 \leq 10$

FURTHER TRIAL AND IMPROVEMENT

C Can you solve harder equations by trial and improvement?
Solve $x^2 + x = 5$ (using a calculator)

Try $x = 2$ 　　　　　$2^2 + 2 = 6$ 　too big!

Try $x = 1.8$ 　　　　$1.8^2 + 1.8 = 5.04$ 　just too big!

Try $x = 1.79$ 　　　$1.79^2 + 1.79 = 4.9941$ 　just too small!

Try $x = 1.791$ 　$1.791^2 + 1.791 = 4.998\,681$ 　excellent!

Follow the flow chart

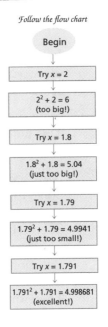

Now test yourself

C Use this method of trial and improvement to solve the following to 3 decimal places:

29 (a) $x^2 - x = 50$; (b) $b^2 + b = 10$

30 (a) $x^3 + x = 20$; (b) $x^3 - x = 50$

31 (a) $x^3 + x^2 = 50$; (b) $x^3 - x^2 = 10$

32 (a) $x^3 + x^2 + x = 100$; (b) $x^3 - x^2 - x = 15$

33 (a) $2x^2 + 3x = 15$; (b) $3x^2 - 2x = 100$

SIMULTANEOUS EQUATIONS

Can you solve simultaneous equations (e.g. equations with x and y)?
Up to now all the equations you have solved have had only one unknown quantity.
There can be more than one!

A simple equation like $x + y = 5$ could have solutions $x = 1$ and $y = 4$

or $x = 2$ and $y = 3$

or $x = 3$ and $y = 2$ and so on.

Supposing you are told that $2x + y = 7$ as well as $x + y = 5$

Solutions for $2x + y = 7$ could be $x = 1$ and $y = 5$

or $x = 2$ and $y = 3$

or $x = 3$ and $y = 1$

These two form a set of **simultaneous equations** and are both satisfied by the same values of x and y. In this case you can see that $x = 2$ and $y = 3$ are the solutions.

The easiest method of solving simultaneous equations is to eliminate one of the two unknowns.

For instance:

$2x + y = 7 \ldots$ **A**

$x + y = 5 \ldots$ **B**

In this case, try subtracting the second equation from the first. The y term disappears leaving you with:

A – **B** $x = 2$

Now substitute 2 for x in equation **B**

This will give you $2 + y = 5$ so $y = 3$

You can now check your answers to see if $x = 2$ and $y = 3$ satisfy equation **A**.

Now try this problem:

Solve the equations $4x + y = 14 \ldots$ **C**

$x + y = 5 \ldots$ **D**

Subtracting **C** – **D** $3x = 9$

$x = 3$

Put $x = 3$ into equation **D** $3 + y = 5$ so $y = 2$

Check in equation **C** $12 + 2 = 14$

Therefore the solution is $x = 3$ and $y = 2$

Now test yourself

34 Solve the following pairs of simultaneous equations:

(a) $2x + y = 12$;   (b) $4x + 2y = 10$;   (c) $5a + 3b = 25$;   (d) $2x + 3y = 7$

     $x + y = 7$ $2x + 2y = 8$ $2a + 3b = 19$ $2x + \ y = 5$

Not all simultaneous equations can be solved by subtracting one equation from the other.

Sometimes it is possible to eliminate one of the unknowns by adding them together.

For instance:

$2x + y = 12 \ldots$ **E**

$x - y = 3 \ldots$ **F**

E + **F** gives $3x = 15$ so $x = 5$

Put $x = 5$ into equation **F** $5 - y = 3$ so $y = 2$

Check in equation **E** $10 + 2 = 12$

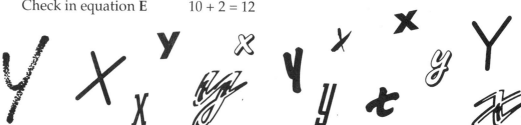

Now test yourself

35 Solve the following pairs of simultaneous equations:
  (a) $3x + y = 7$;   (b) $5a - 2b = 6$;   (c) $4x + 3y = 23$;   (d) $7x + 2y = 25$
        $2x - y = -2$ $3a + 2b = 10$ $x - 3y = 2$ $3x - 2y = 5$

You should have noticed certain similarities about the ones you have done so far.

If the signs in front of the letter to be eliminated are the same you should **subtract**; if they are different you should **add**.

Now test yourself

36 Try to solve these harder equations:
  (a) $2x - y = 7$;   (b) $4a + 3b = 8$;   (c) $5x - 2y = 5$;   (d) $3x + 2y = 5$
        $2x - 5y = 3$ $7a - 3b = 14$ $3x - 2y = -1$ $3x - y = 2$

Solving simultaneous equations is not always this simple. So far, it has been easy to eliminate one of the unknowns by either adding or subtracting them. This will only happen if there are the same number of x's or the same number of y's in each equation.

For instance:
  $2x - y = 9 \dots$ **G**
  $x + 3y = 8 \dots$ **H**

Adding or **subtracting** will not eliminate any of the letters.
Equation **G** $\times 3$ gives $6x - 3y = 27 \ \dots$ **I**
                                      $x + 3y = 8 \ \ \dots$ **H**
Now **I** + **H** gives $7x = 35$ so $x = 5$
Put $x = 5$ into equation **G** $10 - y = 9$ so $y = 1$
Check in equation **H** $5 + 3 = 8$
Therefore the solution is $x = 5$ and $y = 1$

Now test yourself

37 Solve the following pairs of simultaneous equations:
  (a) $2x - 3y = 13$;   (b) $2x + y = 7$;   (c) $4a - 3b = 18$;   (d) $2x - 3y = 5$
        $x + y = 9$ $3x + 2y = 11$ $a + b = 8$ $6x - y = 55$

CHAPTER 7

*G*raphs

In this chapter you are doing work that is new to you.

Graphs are a way of showing algebraic functions as if they are pictures. This makes it easier to compare different functions and to find out information directly from the graph.

Now find out more by reading on!

C O-ORDINATES

Can you find a point in the first quadrant using co-ordinates?

This is a graph with letters on it.

The letter F is at (2, 3).

(2,3) are called the co-ordinates of F.

Can you see how to use the co-ordinates to locate a position on the axes?

You should always read along the *x* axis first and then along the *y* axis.

For example: (0,1) (2,1) (3,2) gives the code PET.

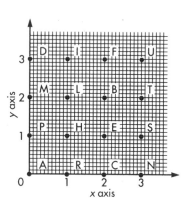

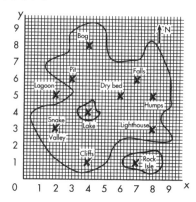

Now test yourself

1 Decode this message:
(1,1) (0,0) (3,0) (0,3)
(0,2) (2,1)
(3,2) (1,1) (0,0) (3,2)
(0,1) (2,1) (3,0)

2 Write down the codes for these words:
(a) HEALTH
(b) MATHS
(c) HINDER

3 Study the map of Devil's Island.
Which places on the map are given by the co-ordinates:
(a) (4,8)   (b) (3,6)   (c) (7,6)   (d) (8,3)?

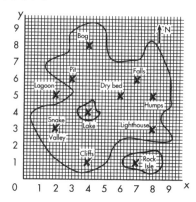

Now give the co-ordinates which locate the following places:
(e) Lagoon;   (f) Lake;   (g) Humps;   (h) Cliffs
Give the name and co-ordinates of the following places:
(i)   somewhere directly south of the falls
(j)   somewhere directly west of the lighthouse

4 Draw a set of axes as shown.

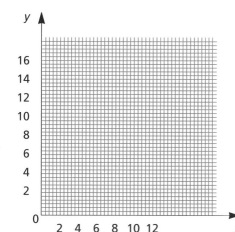

Use a suitable scale, say 1 cm to
1 unit on both axes.
Label the x-axis from 0 to 12
Label the y-axis from 0 to 16.
Draw the shapes given by the
co-ordinates below on the same set
of axes. You only need to draw
the set of axes once.

When you have drawn each shape
try to identify them by writing
its name inside the shape you
have drawn.

For each question, plot the points in the given order and join them likewise.
(a) (1,13) (1,15) (4,15) (1,13)
(b) (5,8) (5,12) (7,12) (9,8) (5,8)
(c) (9,11) (12,12) (12,10) (9,11)
(d) (5,13) (5,15) (9,15) (9,13) (5,13)
(e) (0,9) (2,9) (4,13) (2,13) (0,9)

(f) (9,1) (9,3) (11,3) (11,1) (9,1)
(g) (2,0) (7.2) (2,4) (0,2) (2,0)
(h) (3,8) (1,7) (2,5) (4,5) (5,7) (3,8)
(i) (8,4) (9,4) (10,5) (10,6) (9,7)
       (8,7) (7,6) (7,5) (8,4)

NEGATIVE CO-ORDINATES

Can you understand and use co-ordinates in all four quadrants?

By using negative numbers we can extend the diagram
(graph). We extend the x axis towards the left and the y axis
downward, marking the numbers with a negative sign as shown
in the diagram which is now divided into four quadrants as
shown.

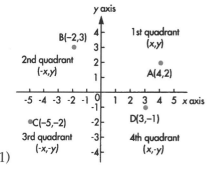

The point (0,0) on any graph is known as the **origin**.

We can now identify a few points on our graph. For instance,
point A has co-ordinates (4,2). Point B has co-ordinates (–2,3),
point C has co-ordinates (–5,–2) and point D has co-ordinates (3,–1)

Now test yourself

5 List the co-ordinates of all the points in the diagram shown by the letters.

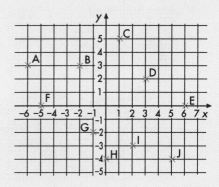

6 Draw a set of axes and scale each one from –5 to 5. The gaps between the numbers must be the same.
Plot the points A(–1,5) B(0,5) C(0,4) D(1,2) E(1,–1) F(2,–1) G(2,–4) H(0,–4) I(0,–2) J(–1,–2) K(–1,–4) L(–3,–4) M(–3,–1), N(–2,–1) P(–2,2) Q(–1,4). Join the points in alphabetical order and join Q to A.

7 (a) Draw a set of axes and label each one from –6 to 6. Using the same set of axes plot these points and join them up in the given order:
   (i)   (–6,2) (–6,5) (–4,5) (–4,2) (–6,2)
   (ii)   (–3,3) (–2,5) (2,5) (1,3) (–3,3)
   (iii) (–3,0) (–3,2) (–1,2) (–1,0) (–3,0)
   (iv)   (1,1) (1,2) (2,3) (3,3) (4,2) (4,1) (3,0) (2,0), (1,1)
   (v)   (–5,1) (–4,–4) (–5,–6) (–6,–4) (–5,1)
   (vi)   (–3,–1) (0,–2) (–3,–3) (–3,–1)
   (vii) (–3,–4) (–1,–4) (0,–6) (–4,–6) (–3,–4)
   (viii) (0,–4) (3,–4) (3,–6) (0,–4)
   (ix)   (4,0) (5,–3) (4,–6), (3,–3) (0,4)
   (b) Can you name each shape accurately?
   (c) Draw in the diagonals of shape (iii). What are the co-ordinates of the point of intersection (where they cross) of these diagonals?
   (d) What are the co-ordinates of the points of intersection of the diagonals in shapes (v) and (ix)?

8 Draw another set of axes and label each one from –6 to 6.
   (a) Plot the points (–5,–1) (0,2) (5,5) and join them up.
   (b) Plot the points (–5,–6) (0,–3) (5,0) and join them up. What do you notice about the two lines that you have drawn?
   (c) Can you draw another line, parallel to these two, that passes through the origin?

USING CO-ORDINATES TO SHOW MAPPINGS

Can you plot points using co-ordinates to show mappings?
Consider the mapping:

$$1 \rightarrow 2 \quad (1,2)$$
$$2 \rightarrow 3 \quad (2,3)$$
$$3 \rightarrow 4 \quad (3,4)$$
$$4 \rightarrow 5 \quad (4,5)$$

The general case is: $x \rightarrow x + 1$

This mapping can be shown on a set of Cartesian axes. The points can be joined together to form a straight line.
Sometimes the mapping is written in a different way.

Instead of saying $x \rightarrow x + 1$
you can say $y = x + 1$

$y = x + 1$ is the equation of the line joining up the points.

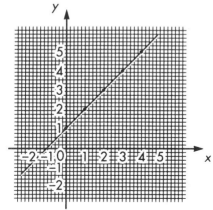

9 On the diagram draw the line to represent this mapping:
1 → 3
2 → 4
3 → 5
4 → 6

(a) What is the general case?
(b) What is the equation of the line?

10 Show on Cartesian axes the lines representing:
(a) $y = x - 1$; (b) $y = 2x + 1$; (c) $y = 3x - 2$

The mapping may not always be represented by a straight line. Suppose $x \rightarrow x^2$

Under this function:
−3 → 9 (−3,9)
−2 → 4 (−2,4)
−1 → 1 (−1,1)
  0 → 0 (0,0)
  1 → 1 (1,1)
  2 → 4 (2,4)
  3 → 9 (3,9)

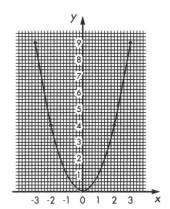

11 Taking x values between −3 and +3 plot on Cartesian axes the graphs of:
(a) $y = x^2 + 1$

(b) $y = 2x^2 - 3$
Remember to square before you multiply by the 2.

SIMULTANEOUS EQUATIONS

Can you use graphs to solve simultaneous linear equations?
The simultaneous equations $y = 2x - 1$ and $y = x + 2$ can be plotted as straight lines. The co-ordinates of the point of intersection of the two lines are the solutions of the equations.
Check the answers by substituting them into the equations.
Point of intersection = (3,5)
$x = 3$ and $y = 5$ are the solutions.
Therefore: $5 = (2 \times 3) - 1$ which is correct.
Check that this works for the second equation.

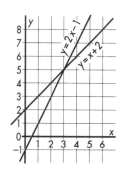

12 What are the solutions to the following simultaneous equations:

(a)

$y = 3x - 1$
$y = x + 3$

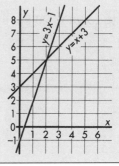

(b)

$y = x + 1$
$y = 5 - x$

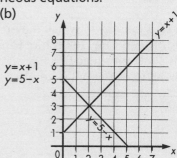

13 (i) and (ii) are two pairs of simultaneous equations:

(i) $y = 2x + 1$
    $y = x + 2$

x	0	1	2	3	4
y = 2x + 1					
y = x + 2					

(ii) $y = x - 1$
     $y = 2x - 3$

x	0	1	2	3	4
y = x − 1					
y = 2x − 3					

(a) Draw and label both axes from − 2 to +5.
(b) Copy and complete the table.
    (It is a good idea to look for patterns in the values of each graph.)
(c) Plot the graphs.
(d) Write down the solutions.

Once you have solutions, check them by substituting your answers back into the equations.

STRAIGHT LINE GRAPHS

Can you draw and read straight line graphs?
    The following graph shows the distance in km travelled by a car on the motorway at a constant speed.

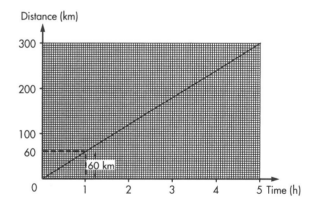

To find the gradient of this line you work out the increase in distance in one hour. What does this tell us? What are the units?

Gradient $= \dfrac{60}{1} = 60$ km per hour, which is the speed of the car.

Now test yourself

14 Draw a graph of a journey in which a man travels from town A to town B, 20 km away, at a constant speed. The journey takes him four hours.
(a) What is his constant speed?
(b) How far away from town B is he after three hours?

15 Draw a graph of a journey in which a woman rides a bicycle from home to work, a distance of 15 km, at a constant speed of 10 km per hour.
   (a) How long does the journey take?
   (b) How far from work is she after an hour?

The following graph shows charges made by a car hire firm.

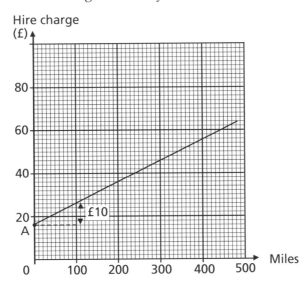

Point A tells you how much the car hire firm charges you just for borrowing the car: i.e. £16.

The gradient is the increase in charge per 100 miles: i.e. £10 per 100 miles or 10p per mile.

How much would you be charged if you travelled 300 miles?

From the graph: 300 miles would cost £46, made up of £16 standard charge plus 300 miles at 10p per mile.

Now test yourself

16 What would the hire charge be for journeys of:
   (a) 50 miles; (b) 250 miles; (c) 400 miles?
   (Check your answers by calculation.)

17 Draw a graph that shows the cost of hiring a minibus, if the hire firm make a standard charge of £20 plus 5p per mile travelled.
   Use your graph to work out the cost of hiring the van to travel:
   (a) 200 miles; (b) 300 miles; (c) 450 miles.

CONVERSION GRAPHS

Can you understand 'real-life' graphs?

One way of changing English money (£) into American dollars ($) is to use a **conversion graph**.

Look at this graph.
You can see that: $5 = £3
and that: £6 = $10

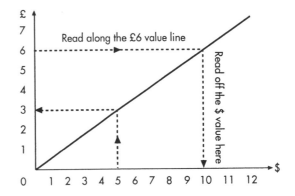

Look at the smaller graph.
$3 is just under £2 (say £1.80).

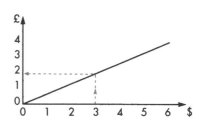

Now test yourself

18 (a) Use the graphs to say how much in British money is:
        (i) $4; (ii) $6; (iii) $9
    (b) Roughly how many $ is:
        (i) £2; (ii) £5; (iii) £7?

19 The exchange rate for France is
    £1 = 9.5 francs. Draw a conversion graph to change
    £ to francs on a set of axes as in the diagram.
    (a) Use your graph to convert these to francs:
        (i) £3; (ii) £4; (iii) £6.50
    (b) **Roughly** what is the value of these in £:
        (i) 6 francs; (ii) 24 francs; (iii) 30 francs?
    (c) Use your graph to find the approximate
        prices for these items bought on the ferry:

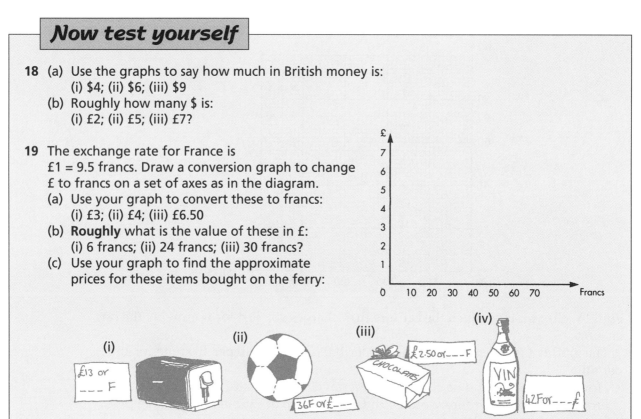

Conversion graphs are not only used for money. They can be used to convert
temperatures from °Fahrenheit to °Celsius.

Now test yourself

20 Here are some conversions done for you to help you to plot the graph:

Fahrenheit (°F)	32	41	68	176
Celsius (°C)	0	5	20	80

Use these conversions to plot a larger graph and then use the 'dotted line' method to convert
these to °Celsius: (a) 50°F; (b) 86°F; (c) 140°F
Now convert these to °Fahrenheit: (d) 15°C; (e) 25°C; (f) 50°C

Number and Algebra

At the start of Key Stage 3 the majority of pupils will have reached at least Level 4 in Mathematics. By the end of Key Stage 3 most pupils should be within the range of Levels 4–7. Levels 5–6 are the target for 14-year-olds. Level 8 is the standard reached by very able pupils.

Use our checklist to assess the Level reached, by ticking the skills that have been mastered.

Level 4

- [ ] Use understanding of place value to multiply and divide whole numbers by 10 or 100.
- [ ] In solving number problems, use a range of mental and written methods of computation with the four operations, including mental recall of multiplication facts up to 10×10.
- [ ] Add and subtract decimals to two places.
- [ ] In solving problems with or without a calculator, check the reasonableness of results by reference to knowledge of the context or to the size of the numbers.
- [ ] Recognize approximate proportions of a whole and use simple fractions and percentages to describe these.
- [ ] Explore and describe number patterns, and relationships including multiple, factor and square.
- [ ] Begin to use simple formulae expressed in words.
- [ ] Use and interpret co-ordinates in the first quadrant.

Level 5

- [ ] Use understanding of place value to multiply and divide whole numbers and decimals by 10, 100 and 1000.
- [ ] Order, add and subtract negative numbers in context.
- [ ] Use all four operations with decimals to two places.
- [ ] Calculate fractional or percentage parts of quantities and measurements, using a calculator where appropriate.
- [ ] Understand and use an appropriate non-calculator method for solving problems that involve multiplying and dividing any three-digit by any two-digit number.
- [ ] Check solutions by applying inverse operations or estimating using approximations.
- [ ] Construct, express in symbolic form, and use simple formulae involving one or two operations.

Level 6

- [ ] Order and approximate decimals when solving numerical problems and equations such as $x^2 = 20$, using trial-and-improvement methods.
- [ ] Be aware of which number to consider as 100 per cent, or a whole, in problems involving comparisons, and use this to evaluate one number as a fraction or percentage of another.
- [ ] Understand and use the equivalences between fractions, decimals and percentages, and calculate using ratios in appropriate situations.

- [ ] When exploring number patterns, find and describe in words the rule for the next term or nth term of a sequence where the rule is linear.
- [ ] Formulate and solve linear equations with whole number coefficients.
- [ ] Represent mappings expressed algebraically, interpreting general features and using graphical representation in four quadrants where appropriate.

Level 7

- [ ] In making estimates, round to one significant figure and multiply and divide mentally.
- [ ] Understand the effects of multiplying and dividing by numbers between 0 and 1.
- [ ] Solve numerical problems involving multiplication and division with numbers of any size, using a calculator efficiently and appropriately.
- [ ] Understand and use proportional changes.
- [ ] Find and describe in symbols the next term or nth term of a sequence where the rule is quadratic.
- [ ] Use algebraic and graphical methods to solve simultaneous linear equations in two variables.
- [ ] Solve simple inequalities.

Level 8

- [ ] Solve problems involving calculating with powers, roots and numbers expressed in standard form, checking for correct order of magnitude.
- [ ] Choose to use fractions or percentages to solve problems involving repeated proportional changes.
- [ ] Choose to use fractions or percentages to calculate the original quantity given the result of a proportional change.
- [ ] Evaluate algebraic formulae, substituting fractions, decimals, and negative numbers.
- [ ] Calculate one variable, given the others, in formulae such as $V = \pi r^2 h$.
- [ ] Manipulate algebraic formulae, equations and expressions, finding common factors and multiplying two linear expressions.
- [ ] Solve inequalities in two variables.
- [ ] Sketch and interpret graphs of linear, quadratic, cubic and reciprocal functions.
- [ ] Sketch and interpret graphs that model real situations.

Exceptional performance

- [ ] Understand and use rational and irrational numbers.
- [ ] Determine the bounds of intervals.
- [ ] Understand and use direct and inverse proportion.
- [ ] In simplifying algebraic expressions, use rules of indices for negative and fractional values.
- [ ] In finding formulae that approximately connect data, express general laws in symbolic form.
- [ ] Solve problems using intersections and gradients of graphs.

CHAPTER 8

*E*stimating and measuring

You should already be familiar with metric units and recognize words such as kilometre, metre, centimetre and millimetre; litre and millilitre; kilogram and gram.

Try to measure the length, width and weight of this book. Which metric units will you use?

There are many types of measuring instruments which you can use. Think about these. Tape measures and clocks are two examples to start you off!

You should be skilful at estimating measures. Have you ever tried to guess the length of a car, how much milk a milk bottle holds, or how long the adverts last between two television programmes?

METRIC UNITS

Can you understand the units of measurement?

Length

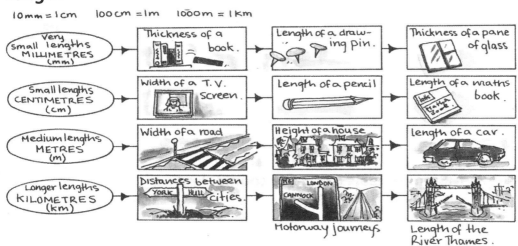

Capacity (and volume)

1000 ml = 1 litre   100 cl = 1 litre

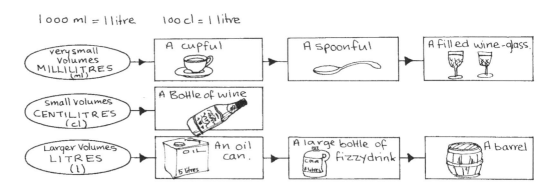

Weight

1000 grams = 1 kilogram   1000 kilograms = 1 tonne

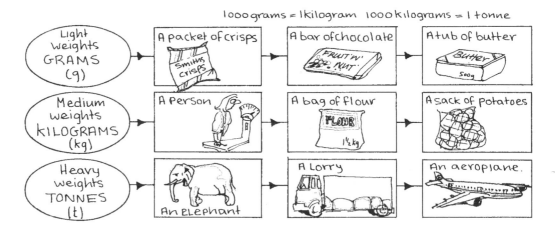

Now test yourself

1   Which units would you use to measure these:
    (a) The length of a football pitch?
    (b) The thickness of your exercise book?
    (c) The diameter of an LP record?
    (d) The capacity of a large carton of fruit juice?
    (e) The capacity of a bottle of perfume?
    (f) The weight of a bag of coal?
    (g) The weight of a bus?
    (h) The weight of a baby?
    (i) The weight of an exercise book?

2   Sometimes you could have a choice of units to measure
    things. Which units could you use to measure these:
    (a) The depth of your bathwater?
    (b) The height of an adult?
    (c) The weight of a bag of sugar?
    (d) The volume of a tub of ice-cream?
    (e) The length of a hair from your head?
    (f) The capacity of a beer glass?
    (g) The height of Mount Everest?

E STIMATING

Are you good at estimating?
Estimates can be made by direct comparison with a known distance.

Now test yourself

3 If the van is 2 m high:
   (a) how high is the lamp
       post?
   (b) how tall is the man?
   (c) what about the dog?
   (d) how high is the bus?

4 In the picture below, the width of the canal is 7 m. Can you estimate:
   (a) the length of the lorry?
   (b) the width of the barge?
   (c) the width of the opening of the bridge?
   (d) the length of the bridge?

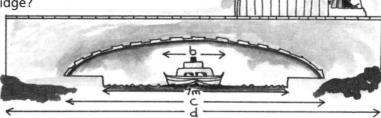

5 Now try some everyday objects in the home or classroom (**remember:** a school ruler is usually
   30 cm long):

   (a) the height of your   (b) the height of   (c) the width and height
       desk or table.   your chair seat.   of your TV set.

6 Can you make a sensible estimate for these:
   (a) the width of a railway carriage in metres?
   (b) the length of a family saloon car in metres?
   (c) the length of a new pencil in centimetres?
   (d) your handspan in centimetres?
   (e) the width of a hockey pitch in metres?
   (f) the height of your front door?
   (g) the thickness of a glass window pane?
   (h) the width of a set of goals in soccer?

Estimates do not always involve distances.

Now test yourself

7 Ask a friend to time you to see how close you can get to an interval of:
   (a) 1 minute
   (b) 40 seconds
   (c) 2 minutes
   (d) 5 minutes

8 Guess the weight of these:
   (a) a school exercise book in grams
   (b) a packet of crisps in grams
   (c) a sports bag containing football boots, shirt, socks, shorts and towel
   (d) a video recorder

9 Guess the capacity of these using metric units of litres, centilitres or millilitres:
   (a) a teacup
   (b) a wine glass
   (c) the petrol tank on a 50 cc motor bike
   (d) a milk bottle
   (e) a washing up bowl

10 How long would you think it would take to make these journeys:
   (a) a steady 10 mile hike?
   (b) a 10 mile cycle ride?
   (c) a 60 mile car journey along the motorway?
   (d) a 60 mile car journey along country roads?
   (e) a 4 mile drive to the station at peak rush hour traffic time?

11 Examine this timetable.
   (a) Approximately how long does the journey from Stoke-on-Trent to London take on Mondays to Saturdays?
   (b) Approximately how long does the same journey take on Sundays?
   (c) If I have a 5.00 p.m. Monday appointment in London, what is the latest train I can catch from Stoke-on-Trent?
   (d) The 15.15 Sunday train is half an hour late leaving Stoke. Approximately what time should it arrive in London?

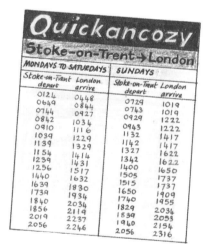

Quickancozy
Stoke-on-Trent → London

MONDAYS TO SATURDAYS		SUNDAYS	
Stoke-on-Trent depart	London arrive	Stoke-on-Trent depart	London arrive
0124	0448	0729	1019
0649	0844	0743	1019
0744	0927	0929	1222
0842	1034	0943	1222
0910	1116	1132	1417
1039	1229	1142	1417
1139	1329	1327	1622
1154	1414	1342	1622
1239	1431	1400	1650
1256	1517	1505	1737
1440	1632	1515	1737
1639	1830	1650	1909
1739	1934	1740	1955
1840	2034	1829	2034
1856	2114	1839	2053
2019	2237	1940	2154
2056	2246	2056	2316

Changing Units

Can you change one metric unit to another?

In Britain, we use both imperial units and metric units but most countries of the world use a **metric** system of measuring length.

This nail is 3 centimetres long or 30 millimetres since 1 cm = 10 mm.

Now test yourself

12 Use a ruler and measure these in:
(a) cm; (b) mm
(**Remember** to start at 0)

(i)   (ii)   (iii)

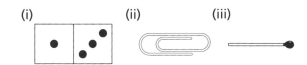

1 metre = 100 centimetres   1 kilometre = 100 metres

1 m = 100 cm   1 km = 1000 m

Remember:
changing to a larger unit means fewer of them – therefore divide by 10, 100 or 1000; changing to a smaller unit means more of them – therefore multiply by 10, 100 or 1000.

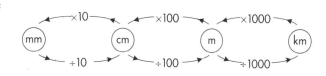

13 Change these metric units by filling in the box:

(a) 15 mm = ☐ cm   (f) $\frac{1}{2}$ m = ☐ cm   (k) 3000 m = ☐ km

(b) 90 mm = ☐ cm   (g) 275 cm = ☐ m   (l) 1500 m = ☐ km

(c) $\frac{1}{2}$ cm = ☐ mm   (h) 25 cm = ☐ m   (m) $3\frac{1}{2}$ km = ☐ m

(d) 11 cm = ☐ mm   (i) 15 m = ☐ cm   (n) $5\frac{1}{4}$ km = ☐ m

(e) 250 cm = ☐ m   (j) 200 cm = ☐ m   (o) 750 m = ☐ km

14 Best St is $1\frac{1}{4}$ km long, Elm St is 800 m long and New Road is 700 m long.

(a) How long is Best St in metres?
(b) How far does Sue have to walk to school and back in a day:
(i) in metres? (ii) in kilometres?

15 How tall is the unit:
(a) in cm?
(b) in metres?

Capacity is like volume. How much can containers hold?
 Here we measure capacity in litres (l)
and millilitres (ml) or centilitres (cl).

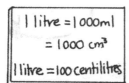

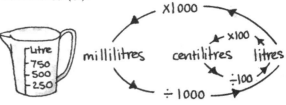

Now test yourself

16 (a) A medicine bottle holds $\frac{1}{2}$ litre of cough medicine:
  (i) How many ml is this?
  (ii) How many 10 ml doses will the bottle hold?
 (b) A barrel of beer holds 8 litres:
  (i) How many ml is this?
  (ii) How many 400 ml glasses can be filled from the barrel?

Weight is measured
using tonnes,
kilograms and grams.

1 kg = 1000 g
1 tonne = 1000 kg

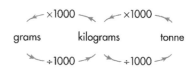

Now test yourself

17 (a) (i) What is the weight in grams of a tub of butter?
  (ii) What is the weight in kg of a pack
   containing four tubs of butter?
 (b) Sue is baking a cake and starts with 2 kg of
  flour and $1\frac{1}{2}$ kg of raisins. She uses $1\frac{1}{4}$ kg of
  flour and 850 g of raisins in the cake.
  What weight is left in grams of:
  (i) flour? (ii) raisins?

IMPERIAL UNITS

Are you aware of imperial units still in use today and know their rough metric
equivalent values?

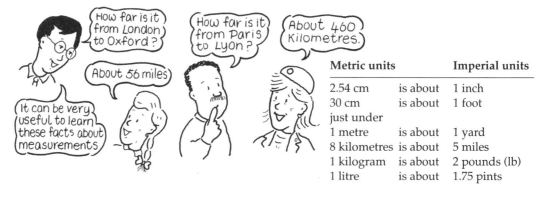

Metric units		Imperial units
2.54 cm	is about	1 inch
30 cm	is about	1 foot
just under		
1 metre	is about	1 yard
8 kilometres	is about	5 miles
1 kilogram	is about	2 pounds (lb)
1 litre	is about	1.75 pints

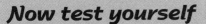
Now test yourself

18 Measure these lines: (i) (ii) (iii) (iv)
(a) in inches
(b) in centimetres
Does the table check
out correctly?
(**Remember:** we are
approximating)

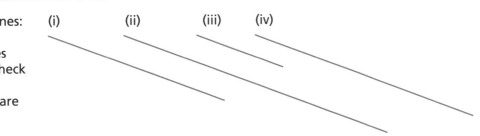

19 How tall are these people approximately in (a) cm; (b) metres; (c) feet?

20 Look at
the scale
for this
map.

Use the scale to work out the approximate distances in (a) miles, (b) kilometres, between
these junctions on the M27:
(i) Junction 1 and Junction 3; (ii) Junction 2 and Junction 8;
(iii) Junction 5 to Junction 11

21 Make these approximate conversions:

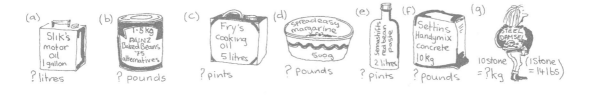

D EGREE OF ACCURACY

Measurement can only be approximate. Choosing the degree of accuracy can be a
problem. Do you have the skill?

Accuracy is essential in some aspects of your work.

If you are making fitted cupboards or steering a ship across the ocean then the
slightest mistake could be costly.

Accuracy depends upon the instrument that you are measuring with.

Now test yourself

22 To what degree of accuracy do you think these instruments will measure?

(a)

(b)

FINISH

(c)

(d)

(e)

(f)

23 What degree of accuracy would be needed if you were involved in the following activities (think about the units used to measure them):

(a) building a wall?
(b) running a marathon?
(c) taking a patient's temperature in hospital?
(d) time-keeping on sports day?
(e) making a fitted cupboard for the kitchen?
(f) measuring the distance between two towns using a car's mileometer?
(g) timing the swimming events at the Olympic Games?
(h) measuring the length of a pencil line in your exercise book?
(i) stating the speed of your car from the speedometer?
(j) giving doses of medicine?

When you use a calculator, be careful not to write down exactly what appears on the display. You have to be sensible and approximate to the degree of accuracy that you are working to, and that you require for the calculation.

For instance, five metres of wood are cut into seven equal pieces.

What is the length of each piece?

This answer is far too accurate.

$5 \div 7 = 0.714285714$

You could not cut a piece of wood to this degree, even if you wanted to do so. The nearest mm would suffice.

ERRORS IN MEASUREMENT

Can you see that a measurement expressed to a given unit has a possible error factor of half a unit?

Rocky's height is given as 185 cm. Since the accuracy is given to the nearest whole number, Rocky's height could be anywhere inside a range of 184.5 cm to 185.499 cm.

Similarly, his weight could be between 127.5 kg and 128.499 kg.

Now test yourself

24 Complete the table for Rocky's statistics:

	Minimum possible value	Maximum possible value	Range
Height	184.5 cm	185.499 cm	185±0.5 cm
Weight	127.5 kg	128.499 kg	
Reach			
Neck			
Biceps			

25 The attendances at recent football games were given to the nearest thousand. Complete the table:

Team	Attendance	Minimum possible attendance	Maximum possible attendance
Aston Villa	27 000		(27 499) → 27 500 would have rounded up to 28 000
Stoke City	11 000		
Port Vale	9 000		
Chesterfield	3 000		

26 A box of drawing pins is said to contain 250 to the nearest ten.
(a) What is the least number there could be in the box?
(b) What is the most there could be in the box?

MORE SIGNIFICANT FIGURES

When working with approximate measures, the general rule for the degree of accuracy of your answer is:

When you multiply or divide, if the question does not tell you the degree of accuracy required, work to one more place of decimals or significant figures in your answer than is the most accurate number in the question.

In many questions you will be told how accurate to be. Make sure you follow these instructions.

Now test yourself

27 Correct each of these answers to the accuracy asked for:
My garden pond has a diameter of 2.85 metres,
measured to 3 significant figures. It is surrounded by
crazy paving.

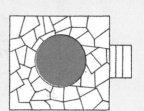

Circumference of pond $= \pi \times$ diameter
$= \pi \times 2.85$
$= 8.9535391$ (by calculator)
$= ?$ (correct to 3 significant figures)

Area of pond $= \pi \times$ (radius)^2
$= \pi \times 1.425 \times 1.425$
$= 6.3793966$ (by calculator)
$= ?$ (correct to 3 significant figures)

FINDING AREAS AND VOLUMES

Can you work out areas by counting squares, and volumes by counting cubes,
using whole numbers?

The area of a flat surface is measured in squares.   1 cm^2 or
1 sq. cm.

You could use square inches (in^2) or square metres (m^2) or square km (km^2)
depending on the size of the surface.

Some surfaces are easy to measure because
squares fit exactly into the shape. It is easy to
count the squares.

Others are not so easy, as the squares don't
fit exactly. Try to make up rectangles to help
you with the count.

Some are really difficult to measure exactly.
Count the whole squares first, then count the
squares that are more than half covered. These
two answers added together give you an
approximate area of the shape.

Area =
6cm^2

Area =
12 ÷ 2 =
6 cm^2

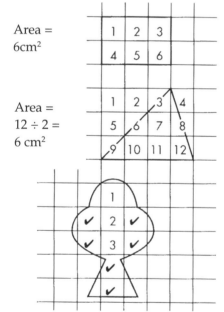

Whole squares	= 3 cm^2
Part squares	= 6 cm^2
Approximate area	= 9 cm^2

Now test yourself

28 Work out the areas of these shapes by counting the squares
(1 square = 1 cm^2).

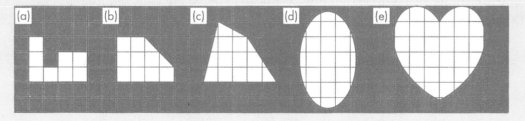

(a)   (b)   (c)   (d)   (e)

The volume of a 3-dimensional shape is measured in cubes.

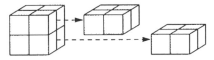

1 cm³ or 1 cubic cm.

Counting cubes in a shape is slightly more difficult because of the ones that cannot be seen.

Now test yourself

29 Work out the volume of the following:

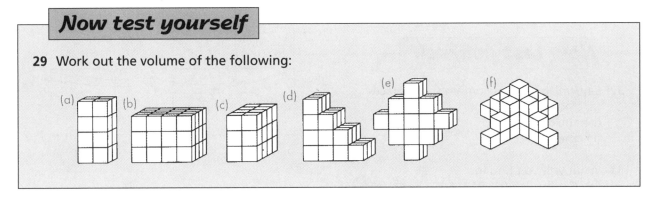

GRID REFERENCES

Can you locate places by means of co-ordinates in the first quadrant?

If you had a large map or grid with lots of places on it, you would need help in finding a certain place quickly. Co-ordinates help you to do just that. They can be used to locate a point accurately or narrow the search down to a small square on the map.

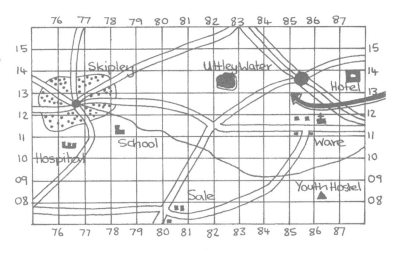

This is a map of a small town. On the map 1 cm stands for 1 km.

Look at the square with the motorway roundabout. The marker points to the bottom left-hand corner corresponding to where vertical line 85 meets horizontal line 13.

We say the **grid reference** of this square is 8513.

Now test yourself

30 Write down the grid references for:
   (a) Skipley High School **L**   (b) the church at Ware **✝**
   (c) the motorway hotel. **☐**

31 What buildings or places are at
   (a) 7610; (b) 8213; (c) 8608?

The square containing the football pitch is called D3. It is above the letter D and in row 3.

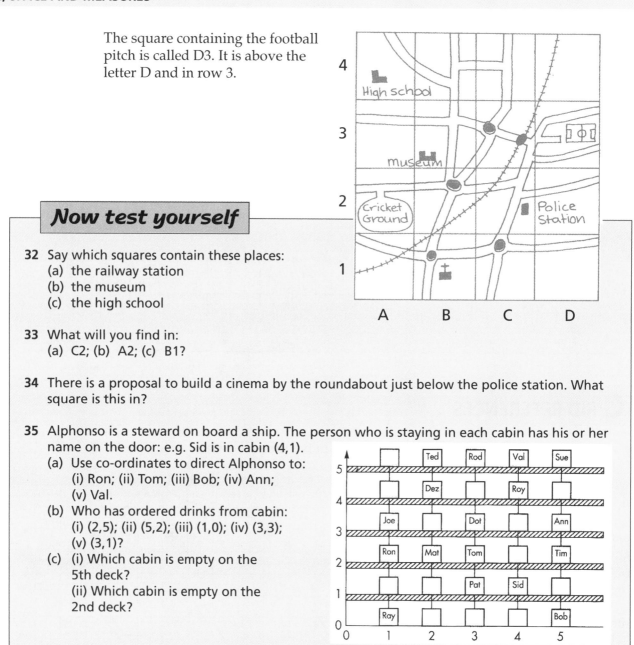

Now test yourself

32 Say which squares contain these places:
   (a) the railway station
   (b) the museum
   (c) the high school

33 What will you find in:
   (a) C2; (b) A2; (c) B1?

34 There is a proposal to build a cinema by the roundabout just below the police station. What square is this in?

35 Alphonso is a steward on board a ship. The person who is staying in each cabin has his or her name on the door: e.g. Sid is in cabin (4,1).
   (a) Use co-ordinates to direct Alphonso to:
      (i) Ron; (ii) Tom; (iii) Bob; (iv) Ann;
      (v) Val.
   (b) Who has ordered drinks from cabin:
      (i) (2,5); (ii) (5,2); (iii) (1,0); (iv) (3,3);
      (v) (3,1)?
   (c) (i) Which cabin is empty on the
      5th deck?
      (ii) Which cabin is empty on the
      2nd deck?

C O-ORDINATE MAPS

Can you pin-point a location by using co-ordinates in four quadrants?

As you can see, the map is only part of a much larger map of Pirate's Island.

To locate a place we use co-ordinates.

e.g. Nook point is at (4,5)
Stack Rocks are at (–4,–3)

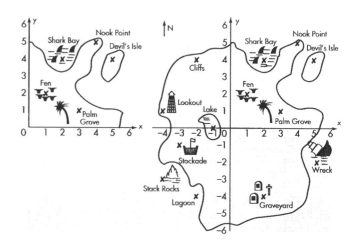

Now test yourself

36 Which places on the map are given by the co-ordinates:
(a) (3, 1); (b) (–4, 1); (c) (5–2); (d) (–2, –4)?

37 Give the set of co-ordinates which locate the following places:
(a) stockade; (b) graveyard; (c) lake; (d) cliffs

38 Give the name and co-ordinates of the following places:
(a) somewhere due west of Palm Grove
(b) somewhere due east of the cliffs

39 ABCD are all rectangles. Write down the co-ordinates of D in each case:
(a) A(2,1) B(2,–3) C(–4,–3); (b) A(–3,3) B(4,3) C(4,0); (c) A(–6,–1), B(–3,2) C(–1,0)

40 Draw a set of axes, both going from –6 to +6, and then plot and join the following points:
(a) Part 1 (4,–6) (–4,–6) (–1,1) (1,1) (4,–6)
(b) Part 2 (0,1) (3,5) (5,3) (1,0) (5,–3) (3,–5) (0,–1) (–3,–5) (–5,–3) (–1,0) (–5,3) (–3,5) (0,1)

A NGLES

Can you measure and draw angles to the nearest degree?

To measure angles you can use a protractor. Most protractors have an **inside** and an **outside scale**. You must be careful and use the correct one. A good idea is to estimate the angle first and to say which type it is.

Remember: acute (less than 90°), obtuse (more than 90°) and reflex (more than 180°).

The **outside scale** can be used to count the number of one degree angles that fit into ∠EFG.

The **inside scale** can be used to count the number of one degree angles that fit into ∠ABC.

∠EFG = 40°

∠ABC = 30°

Now test yourself

41 How many degrees in each of these:

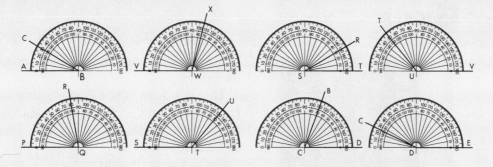

42 For each of the following angles: (a) state the type; (b) estimate the size; (c) measure accurately.

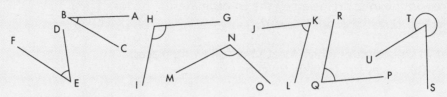

To draw angles accurately you again use a protractor.

Follow this simple flow chart to draw $\angle ABC = 60°$

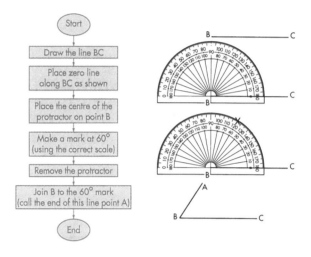

Now test yourself

43 Practise this exercise by drawing angles of:
(a) 75°; (b) 130°; (c) 30°; (d) 160°; (e) 220°
Note: If you use an angle measurer you move the lines to match the angle and read the angle in the direction you moved the arrow.

S CALE

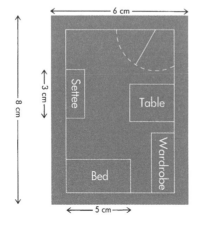

Can you understand scales in maps and drawings?

This is a drawing of Tina's bedroom. Two centimetres on the diagram stands for 1 metre in the real room. We say the scale is: 2 centimetres to 1 metre.

On the scale drawing, the length of the bed is 5 cm.

So the length of the real bed is 2.5 metres.

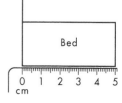

Now test yourself

44 (a) What is the length and width of the bedroom on the plan?
    (b) What are the length and width of the real bedroom, in metres?
    (c) How long is the settee on the plan?
    (d) How long is the real settee?

45 Here are three sketches of the plans of rooms. Draw them accurately to the scale given.

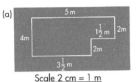

(a)

Scale 2 cm = 1 m

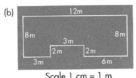

(b)

Scale 1 cm = 1 m

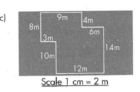

(c)

Scale 1 cm = 2 m

46 On a map, the scale is given as: 1 cm = 5 km.
    (a) What real distance is represented by 3 cm on the map?
    (b) What distance on the map would a length of motorway 30 km long be shown as?

47 On a map, the scale is given as 1:50 000.
    (a) What real distance does a 1cm line represent in km?
    (b) What real distance is represented by a line 8 cm long on the map?
    (c) A road is 15 km long. How long would the line on the map be, representing this road?

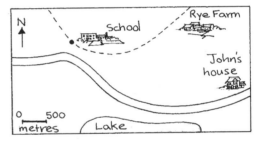

48 (a) Pete lives at Rye Farm. How far approximately does he have to walk to school?
    (b) John catches the bus. How far is this journey?
    (c) How long is the lake in km?

COMBINING MEASUREMENTS

Some measurements can be combined to form new ones.

Speed is a measure that is a combination of two other measures, i.e. distance and time.

Speed is measured in **miles per hour**, for example.

Density is another measure that is a combination of two other measures.

Density is measured in **grams per cm³** (i.e. a combination of mass and volume).

If you have to calculate a compound measurement like speed in metres per second or density in grams per cm³ you can do this by dividing the first measured unit by the second.

Jim walks a total distance of $\boxed{10}$ miles.

He walks at a steady rate for $\boxed{2}$ hours.

This is equivalent to walking at an average speed of 5 miles per hour.

$$\text{average speed} = \frac{\text{total distance}}{\text{total time taken}}$$

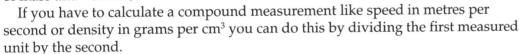

Now test yourself

49 Fill in the missing measures:

(a) The train travels for $\boxed{3}$ hours.

It travels a distance of $\boxed{180}$ miles.

The average speed of the train is $\boxed{?}$ miles per hour.

(b) The sprinter runs $\boxed{100}$ metres.

It takes him $\boxed{10}$ seconds.

His average speed is $\boxed{?}$ metres per second.

(c) The cyclist travels for $\boxed{\frac{1}{2}}$ an hour.

His average speed is $\boxed{20}$ mph

He travels $\boxed{?}$ miles.

(d) Concorde averages $\boxed{2000}$ km/hour.

It travels $\boxed{3000}$ km.

It flies for $\boxed{?}$ hours.

In general:

$$Speed = \frac{Distance}{Time} \qquad Distance = Speed \times Time \qquad Time = \frac{Distance}{Speed}$$

$$S = \frac{D}{T} \qquad D = S \times T \qquad T = \frac{D}{S}$$

Now test yourself

50 Write down the missing units:

(a) **speed** in km/h,
time in hours,
so **distance** in…

(b) **speed** in m/s,
time in seconds,
so **distance** in…

(c) **distance** in miles,
time in hours,
so **speed** in…

(d) **distance** in km,
time in hours,
so **speed** in…

(e) **distance** in m,
speed in m/s,
so **time** in…

(f) **distance** in cm,
speed in cm/s,
so **time** in…

51 How far does a train go in four hours at an average speed of 150 km/h?

52 How long does it take a bird to fly ten miles at an average speed of 30 mph?

53 What is the average speed in km/h of a middle distance runner who covers 10 km in 50 minutes?

$$density = \frac{mass}{volume}$$

For instance, a block of wood has a volume of 100 cm³. Its weight is 600 grams.

What is the density of the wood?

$$density = \frac{mass}{volume} = \frac{600}{100} = 6g/cm^3$$

Now test yourself

54 A litre of liquid weighs 1500 g. What is the density of the liquid?

55 A metal has a density of 40 g/cm³. What will be the weight, in kg, of a piece of metal that has a volume of 500 cm³?

56 What is the density of a piece of wood that weighs $1\frac{1}{2}$ kg and has a volume of 300 cm³?

T HE CIRCLE

Can you calculate the area and circumference of a circle?
 The names of the main parts of a circle are shown below:

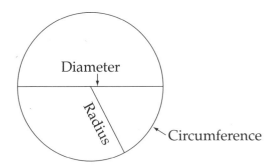

In a circle the value of $\dfrac{\text{circumference}}{\text{diameter}}$ = 3.14159…

It has been proved that the exact value cannot be worked out, but for most problems a value of

$$3.142 \quad \text{or} \quad 3.14 \quad \text{or} \quad \frac{22}{7}$$

is accurate enough.

This ratio of $\dfrac{\text{circumference}}{\text{diameter}}$ is so important that it was given a special

symbol π (the Greek letter pi).

Since $\dfrac{\text{circumference}}{\text{diameter}} = \pi$ it follows that

circumference = $\pi \times$ diameter

or as a formula
$$C = \pi d$$
$$= 2\pi r$$

where C is the circumference, r the radius and d the diameter.

The diameter of a circle is 20 cm. Calculate its circumference.
$$C = \pi d$$
$$= 3.14 \times 20$$
$$= 62.8 \text{ cm}$$

Hence the circumference is 62.8 cm.

Now test yourself

57 Taking π = 3.14, calculate the circumference of these circles:

(a)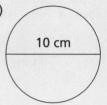
10 cm

(b)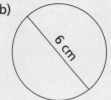
6 cm

(c)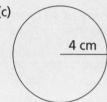
4 cm

(Don't forget that the diameter is twice the radius of a circle!)

It can also be shown that:

$$\text{Area of a circle} = \pi \times \text{radius}^2$$
or
$$A = \pi r^2$$

Find the area of a circle whose radius is 3 cm.

$$
\begin{aligned}
A &= \pi r^2 \\
&= 3.14 \times 3^2 \\
&= 3.14 \times 9 \\
&= 28.26 \text{ cm}^2
\end{aligned}
$$

Now test yourself

58 Taking π = 3.14, calculate the area of these circles:

(a)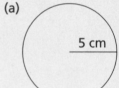
5 cm

(b)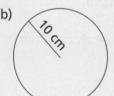
10 cm

(c)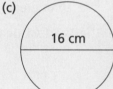
16 cm

PYTHAGORAS' THEOREM

Can you follow Pythagoras' Theorem?

If you draw a square on the longest side of a right-angled triangle, its area is equal to the sum of the areas of the squares drawn on the two shorter sides.

Suppose you let the length of the hypotenuse (the longest side) be h and the lengths of the other sides be a and b, then Pythagoras' Theorem can be expressed as:

$$h^2 = a^2 + b^2$$

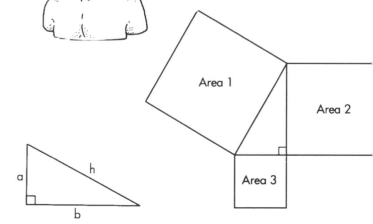

If you draw a square on the longest side of a right angled triangle, its area is equal to the sum of the areas of the squares drawn on the two shorter sides.

Area 1

Area 2

Area 3

Example 1

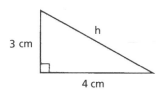

$h^2 = 3^2 + 4^2$
  $= 9 + 16$
  $= 25$
$h = \sqrt{25} = 5\text{cm}.$

Example 2

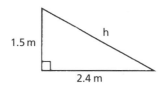

$h^2 = 1.5^2 + 2.4^2$
  $= 2.25 + 5.76$
  $= 8.01$
$h = \sqrt{8.01} = 2.83$ m (to 3 s.f.)

Now test yourself

59 Calculate the length of the side marked by the letter h in these triangles:

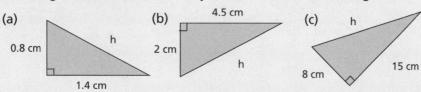

60 A ladder leans against the top of a vertical wall 5 m high. The foot of the ladder is 2.5 m from the base of the wall. How long is the ladder, assuming that it does not project over the top of the wall?
(Give your answer to 2 decimal places.)

Suppose the side that you wanted to calculate was not the longest side but was one of the two smaller sides.

Pythagoras' Theorem:
  $h^2 = a^2 + b^2$

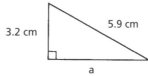

The hypotenuse is given ($h = 5.9$)
Therefore: $5.9^2 = a^2 + 3.2^2$

Now test yourself

61 Calculate the length of the side marked by the letter.

(a)

(b) (c)

62 A wire goes from the top of a vertical pole into the ground at a point 15 m from the base of the pole. If the ground is horizontal and the wire is 20 m long, how high is the pole?

63 A ship sails from port along a bearing of 045° for a distance of 40 km. It then alters course to sail a further 25 km along a bearing of 315°. How far is the ship from port at this point?

64 The diagram shows a tent when erected:
(a) What is the height of the tent?
(b) What is the length of the guy-rope?

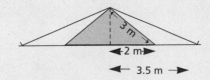

Pythagoras' Theorem can also be used to check that a triangle is right angled. If it is then: $h^2 = a^2 + b^2$

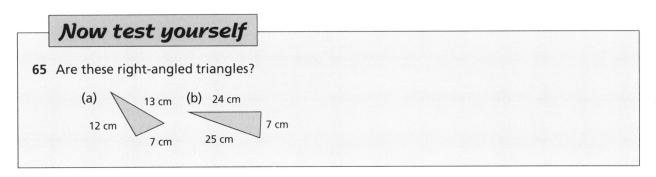

Now test yourself

65 Are these right-angled triangles?

(a) 13 cm

12 cm

7 cm

(b) 24 cm

25 cm

7 cm

CHAPTER 9

*P*roperties of shapes

You should already know how to sort out 2-D and 3-D shapes.

Try sorting these 2-D shapes into different groups such as: three-sided shapes; four-sided shapes; shapes with right-angles; shapes with curved lines; shapes that cannot be folded in half; and so on.

Now try these 3-D shapes. Put them into groups such as: prisms; shapes with a curved surface; pyramids; shapes with a uniform area of cross-section; and so on.

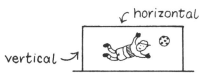

Now you are ready to start this chapter properly!

LINES AND ANGLES

Can you recognize the words associated with lines and angles?

Some special lines are given names.

Two lines that meet at a right angle are called **perpendicular lines**.

Lines that never meet but run in the same direction are called **parallel lines**.

Railway lines are an example of parallel lines.

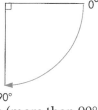

An **angle** is a measure of turn between two lines. Angles are measured in **degrees**.

The diagram is an angle of **90 degrees** and is a special angle called a **right angle**.

It forms the corner of a square.

Angles that are smaller than a right angle are called **acute** angles (less than 90°).

Angles that are larger than a right angle are called **obtuse** angles (more than 90°).

Angles that begin to come back on themselves are called **reflex** angles (more than 180°).

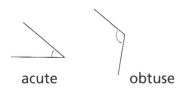 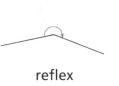

acute   obtuse   reflex

To measure **angles** you can use either:
(a) a **protractor**;   or (b) an **angle measurer**.

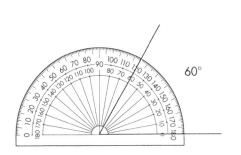

60°

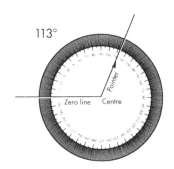

113°

Now test yourself

1 How would you describe the hulls of these boats?
Are they acute, obtuse or right-angled?

(a)   (b)   (c)   (d)

2 (a) List the lines which are parallel.
(b) List the perpendicular lines.
(c) Is there a vertical line?
(d) Which line is horizontal?

3 Measure these angles and state what
kind of angles they are:

(a)   (b)   (c)   (d)

Remember: the point of the angle should be at the centre of the protractor or angle measurer and one side of the angle should be along the zero line.

LINE SYMMETRY: MIRROR IMAGES

Can you reflect simple shapes in a mirror?

You will need a mirror to complete this exercise.

This is half a picture. When you place a mirror along the dotted line you get the complete picture.

Does it have line symmetry?

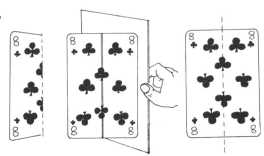

Now test yourself

4 Put a mirror on these dotted lines. What is wrong in each case?

(a) (b) 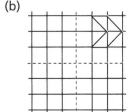 (c)

5 Without using a mirror, draw in the other half of each picture to make it symmetrical.

(a) (b) (c) (d) (e)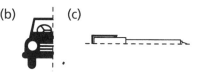

6 Reflect this pattern in the horizontal axis of symmetry and then reflect the whole thing in the vertical axis.

(a) 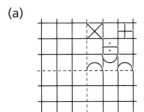 (b)

7 Try some mirror writing (the first name is done for you in each case):

(a)

(b)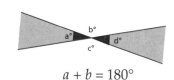

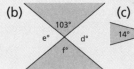 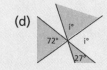

ANGLES ON LINES

Can you understand the language of angles and triangles?

When two straight lines intersect, the two angles that lie opposite each other are called vertically opposite angles (or X angles).

$$a + b = 180°$$

Measure angles $a°$, $b°$, $c°$ and $d°$. What do you notice?

Since they are straight lines that are intersecting, adjacent angles (next door to each other) add up to 180°. We would call $a°$ and $b°$ **supplementary angles**.

Now test yourself

8 What other pairs are supplementary?

9 Calculate the angles marked by the letters. Look for vertically opposite angles and angles that are on a straight line.

(a) (b) (c) (d)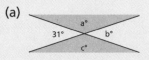

When a straight line is laid across parallel lines not only do we create vertically opposite angles but also **corresponding angles** (or F angles).

These angles marked in the diagram are corresponding angles and they are all equal.

Now test yourself

10 Calculate the angles marked by the letters. Look for vertically opposite angles and corresponding angles.

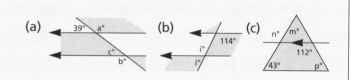

(a) 39° a° c° b° (b) 114° i° i° (c) n° m° 112° 43° p°

When a straight line cuts across parallel lines then the angles marked in the diagram are called **alternate angles** (or Z angles).

Alternate angles are equal.

Cut out any triangle from a piece of paper. Tear off all three corners.
Now place the corners together as shown. What can you say about the sum of the angles of a triangle?

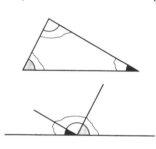

Now test yourself

11 Measure all the angles in these triangles. Is it true, what you found out above?

(a)

(b)

12 Calculate the angles marked by the letter.

(a)  55° 64° a°

(b)  81° 33° b°

(c) 27° c° 112°

13 Now cut out a quadrilateral (any four-sided figure). Tear or cut off the four corners and put them together. What do they add up to?

TRIANGLES

A triangle is a shape with three straight sides. Inside any triangle there are three angles.

There are several types of triangle. The basic triangle is called a **scalene** triangle. This is a triangle with all three sides of different length and all three angles different from one another.

An **isosceles** triangle is one with two sides of equal length and two of its angles equal.

An **equilateral** triangle is one with all three sides equal in length and all three angles equal.

A **right-angled** triangle is one with one of its angles equal to 90°.

Remember: the three angles of a triangle add up to 180°.

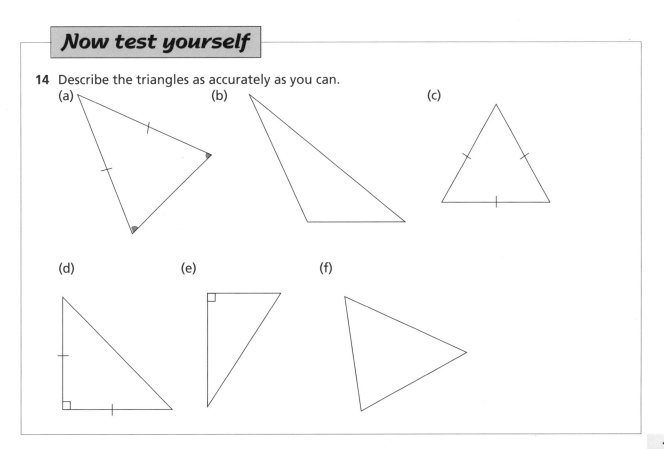

Now test yourself

14 Describe the triangles as accurately as you can.

(a)   (b)   (c)

(d)   (e)   (f)

15 Calculate the missing angle in each of the following triangles.

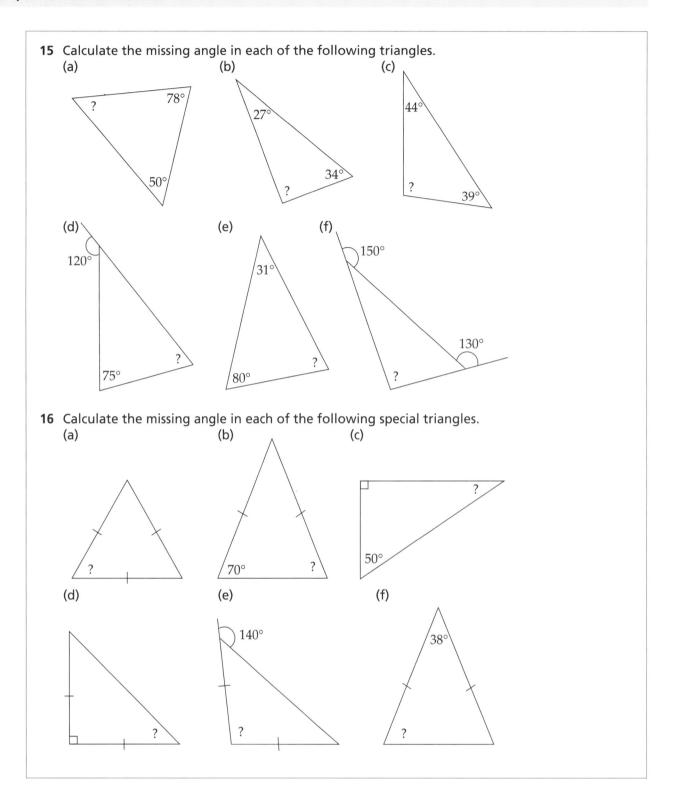

(a)

78°
?
50°

(b)

27°
34°
?

(c)

44°
?
39°

(d)

120°
75°
?

(e)

31°
80°
?

(f)

150°
130°
?

16 Calculate the missing angle in each of the following special triangles.

(a)

?

(b)

70°
?

(c)

?
50°

(d)

?

(e)

140°
?

(f)

38°
?

BEARINGS

Can you follow and use compass bearings?

In an ordinary compass the needle is balanced on a pin so that it can move freely. It will always line itself up pointing **north**.

Bearings are angles measured from the north line in a clockwise direction.

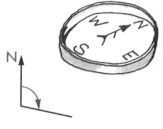

N

For instance:
The picture shows a balloon on a bearing of 050° from a control tower.

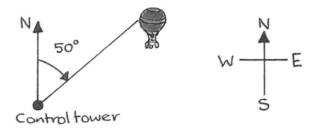

The angle between the north line and the direction of the balloon is 50°, measured in a clockwise direction. Bearings are always given in three figures. We say that the bearing of the balloon **from** the tower is 050°.

Remember, bearings are always:
(a) about the **north** line
(b) in a **clockwise** direction
(c) **from** a given point
(d) given using **three** figures

Now test yourself

17 Write down the bearings of A from the point X in the following:

(a) N 47° ··A X

(b) N 106° X ····A

(c) N A········X

(d) A··· N 50° X

(e) N X 25° A·

(f) N X 15° ·A

(g) N A X 25° E

(h) N 120° X A····

18 Study the map and remember the four important facts about bearings.
Use a protractor to measure:
(a) the bearing of the church from the school;
(b) the bearing of the school from the inn;
(c) the bearing of the inn from the church;
(d) the bearing of the beacon from the school.
(A 360° angle measure would be better. Remember to give your answers using three figures.)

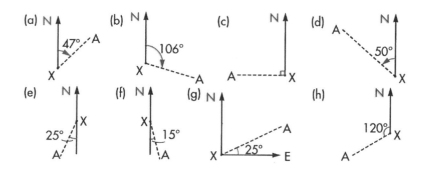

19 A submarine has its radar in operation.
The picture looks like this diagram.
Estimate the bearings of the five ships from the submarine.

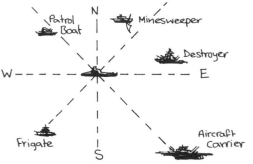

Q UADRILATERALS

Can you identify quadrilaterals?

A **quadrilateral** is a shape with four sides.

Inside any quadrilateral there are four angles. The sum of these four angles totals 360°.

There are several types of quadrilateral.

(a) The **general quadrilateral**: This is a figure which has four sides and four angles.

(b) The **parallelogram**: A parallelogram is a four-sided figure with opposite sides equal in length and parallel to each other and diagonally opposite angles equal to each other.

At this point, we can say that a diagonal line joins opposite corners of a shape and any quadrilateral has two diagonals.

In the case of a parallelogram the diagonals bisect (divide equally) each other, but they are not of the same length.

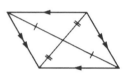

(c) The **rectangle** or **oblong**: A rectangle is a four-sided figure with opposite sides equal in length. The four angles of the rectangle are all right angles. Its diagonals are equal in length and they bisect each other.

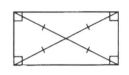

(d) The **rhombus**: A rhombus is a four-sided figure with opposite sides parallel and all sides of equal length. The diagonals bisect each other at right angles and also bisect the corner angles. As with the parallelogram, the rhombus has equal diagonally opposite angles. We sometimes call this shape the diamond.

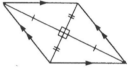

(e) The **square**: The square is a four-sided figure with all sides of equal length. The four angles of the square are all right angles. The diagonals bisect each other at right angles and also bisect the corner angles (45°).

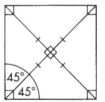

(f) The **kite**: This four-sided shape is basically made up of two different isosceles triangles with the same base lengths. The diagonals do not, in this shape, bisect each other.

(g) The **trapezium**: The trapezium has only two sides parallel. It is like a triangle with its top cut off parallel to its base.

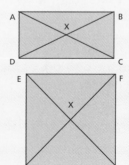

Now test yourself

20 The rectangle:
Copy and complete:
(a) AB = ?
(b) BC = ?
(c) AX = ? = ? = ?
(d) AC = ?
(e) angle AXD = angle ?
(f) angle AXB = angle ?

21 The square:
(a) EF = ? = ? = ?
(b) EX = ? = ? = ?
(c) EG = ?
(d) EG is perpendicular to ?
(e) angle EXF = ?°

22 The **parallelogram**:
   (a) JK = ?   (d) KX = ?
   (b) KL = ?   (e) angle KJX = angle ?
   (c) JX = ?   (f) angle KMJ = angle ?

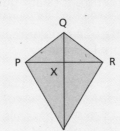

23 The **kite**:
   (a) PQ = ?
   (b) PS = ?
   (c) PX = ?
   (d) angle QXR = ?°
   (e) angle PQX = angle ?
   (f) angle PSX = angle ?

24 On this dot pattern it is possible to draw six full squares.
   Can you find them all?
   (a) How many rectangles can you find?
   (b) How many parallelograms can you find?
   (c) How many trapezia can you find?
   (d) How many kites can you find?
   (e) Are there any other shapes?

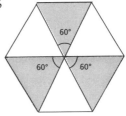

S YMMETRY OF POLYGONS

Can you describe the symmetry of various quadrilaterals and other polygons?
   One way to draw a regular hexagon is to draw lines moving outwards from the centre. Before you can do this you need to calculate the angle between each line.
   360° ÷ 6 equal angles = 60°
   Follow these steps:

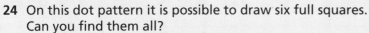

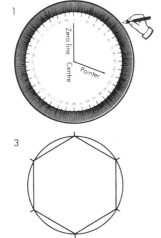

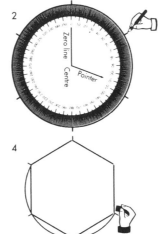

Now test yourself

25 Use this method to draw:
    (a) (i) a regular pentagon (5 sides); (ii) a regular octagon (8 sides).
    (b) What are the angles at the centre for each polygon?

26 The order of rotational symmetry of a regular hexagon is 6.
    (a) What is the order of rotational symmetry for:
        (i) a regular pentagon;
        (ii) a regular octagon.
    (b) Draw the lines of symmetry for each of these.
    (c) If shapes fit together without gaps we say they **tessellate**. Which of the shapes given in
        (a) will tessellate? Can you think of other regular polygons that will tessellate?

27 Here is a set of quadrilaterals.

    (i) Rhombus   (ii) Square   (iii) Parallelogram   (iv) Kite

    (a) State the order of rotational symmetry for each shape.
    (b) Draw in the lines of symmetry (if any).
    (c) Will any of them tessellate?
    (d) Mark equal angles in each shape.

D RAWING SHAPES

Can you draw simple 2-D and 3-D shapes and describe what you have drawn?
    To construct a triangle of side lengths 10 cm, 7 cm and 5 cm:

(a) draw a base line AB 10 cm long
(b) open compasses to 7 cm and
    make an arc from A
(c) open compasses to 5 cm
(d) make another arc from B
(e) join up points A, B to C
(f) describe what you have drawn: 'a 10 cm by 7 cm by 5 cm triangle'.

To construct a rectangle 10 cm by 6 cm:

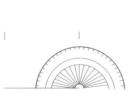

(a) draw base   (b) from each end   (c) draw two   (d) join up open
    line 10 cm   mark two   perpendicular   ends to form a
                right angles   lines 6 cm   rectangle

(e) describe what you have drawn: 'a 10 cm by 6 cm rectangle'.

Now test yourself

28 Draw a circle of radius 5 cm.

29 Construct a square, side length 8 cm.

30 Construct a parallelogram, side lengths 9 cm and 6 cm and an included angle of 60°.

31 Experiment with ruler, protractor and compasses to draw a regular hexagon.
(**Hint:** start with a circle and keep your compasses open to the radius of the circle.)

32 Draw accurately: (a) a kite; (b) a rhombus; (c) an isosceles triangle. Mark in all the angles and side lengths.

ISOMETRIC DRAWINGS

Sometimes you have to draw on 2-D paper a 3-D object. Can you draw the different views?

This is an isometric drawing of a 3-D shape made up of building blocks. Then look at it from:

(a) directly above
(b) the side
(c) the front

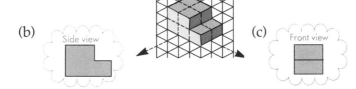

Now test yourself

33 Draw what you would see from the three positions for these shapes:
(a)   (b)

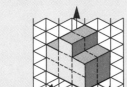

34 Make an isometric drawing of the shape below:

35 Take five cubes and arrange in a 'T-shape'. Make an isometric drawing and then draw the plan, front and side view.

36 Take five cubes and make an 'addition sign'. Make an isometric drawing and then draw the plan, front and side view.

37 Using only four cubes, see how many **different** shapes you can make.

38 Make an isometric drawing of a different shape.

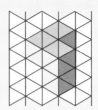

R OTATIONAL SYMMETRY

Can you recognize rotational symmetry?
When the shape is turned upside-down it appears not to have moved. It looks the same. When this happens, the shape is said to have **rotational symmetry**.

Now test yourself

39 Which of these letters of the alphabet can be turned upside down yet still look the same?

H N T S V Z

40 Which of these shapes has rotational symmetry:
(a)   (b)   (c)   (d)

   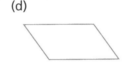

41 Trace each of these diagrams. Then turn them to see if they have rotational symmetry.
(a)   (b)   (c)

42 Sometimes the shape does not have to be rotated through half a turn to look the same. Trace each of these shapes and see how many times the tracings will fit onto the shape before you get back to the start.
(a)   (b)   (c)

43 Each of these diagrams has rotational symmetry of the order given. The order is the number of times a shape can be rotated and still look the same, before it reaches its original position. If *x* marks the centre of rotation, complete the diagrams.
(a)   (b)   (c)

Order 4   Order 3   Order 5

44 Sometimes the shapes are rotated about a point well away from the shape.

By using tracing paper or otherwise, rotate these shapes through 90° clockwise about the origin

90° clockwise about the origin

(a)   (b)   (c)   (d)

IDENTIFYING SYMMETRIES

Can you identify symmetries of other shapes?

Now test yourself

45 (a) Draw in the letters of the alphabet that have a reflective symmetry about a vertical axis. (Capitals only)

A   **Y**

(b) Now draw in the letters that have reflective symmetry about a horizontal axis. Which letters have two axes of symmetry?

B C D

(c) These two letters have rotational symmetry. Do you notice the **point of rotation**? Draw the other letters of the alphabet that have this rotational symmetry. Put in the point of rotation.

H S

Which letters have both reflective and rotational symmetry?

46 All these shapes have symmetry of some kind. Draw in the axes of symmetry and/or the centre of rotation.

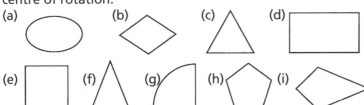

(a)   (b)   (c)   (d)

(e)   (f)   (g)   (h)   (i)

47 3-D shapes have **planes of symmetry**. Imagine the cube cut along the planes shown below. You would have two equal halves. When this happens the shape is said to be symmetrical about a plane.

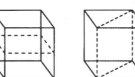

Draw in the planes of symmetry for these shapes. (There may be more than one.)

(a)   (b)   (c)

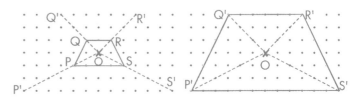

E NLARGEMENTS

Can you enlarge a shape by a whole number scale factor?

If you are enlarging a shape, you need to consider two things:

(a) the centre of enlargement; (b) the scale factor of the enlargement.

The **centre of enlargement** is the point from where you should start all your measurements.

The **scale factor** of the enlargement tells you 'how many times larger' you are to make the new shape:

e.g. scale factor 2 = twice as large

scale factor 3 = three times as large etc.

For instance

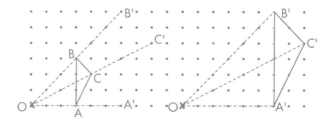

Centre of enlargement is O and the scale factor of enlargement is 2

Measure OA × 2 = OA'. Measure OB × 2 = OB'. Measure OC × 2 = OC'.

Join up the new points A'B'C' to obtain your enlargement.

Now test yourself

48 On squared paper copy the shape and then draw the enlargement:

(a)

centre of enlargement
scale factor 2

(b)

centre of enlargement
scale factor 3

Sometimes the centre of enlargement can be **inside** the shape.

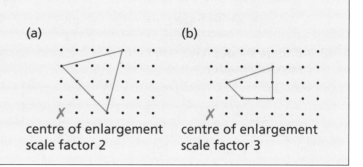

Centre of enlargement is O and the scale factor of enlargement is 3.

Measure OP × 3 = OP'. Measure OQ × 3 = OQ'. Measure OR × 3 = OR'.

Measure OS × 3 = OS'. Join up the new points P'Q'R'S' to obtain your enlargement.

Now test yourself

49 On squared paper, copy the shape and then draw the enlargement:

(a)

(b)

centre of enlargement O
scale factor of enlargement 2

centre of enlargement O
scale factor of enlargement 3

F RACTIONAL ENLARGEMENTS

Can you enlarge a shape by a fractional scale factor?

If you enlarge a shape by a fractional scale factor you are reducing the shape in size. An enlargement may make things smaller if the scale factor is less than 1!

Follow the guide lines used on the previous page about enlargements and remember how the centre of enlargement can be inside or outside the shape.

For instance, plot the points A(1,1) B(3,8) C(7,8) D(5,1).

Join them up to form a parallelogram.

Using A as the centre of enlargement enlarge the parallelogram by a scale factor of $\frac{1}{2}$.

Steps to follow:

(a) halve the distance AB
(b) mark this point B'
(c) halve the distance AC
(d) mark it C'
(e) halve the distance AD
(f) mark it D'
(g) join up AB'C'D' for your new shape.

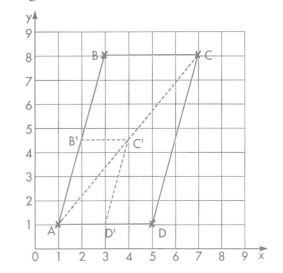

Now test yourself

50 Plot the points P(1,1) Q(5,5) and R(9,1). Join them up to form a triangle PQR. Using the point (5,3) as the centre of enlargement enlarge the triangle PQR by a scale factor of $\frac{1}{2}$.

51 Enlarge the shape in the diagram by a scale factor of $\frac{1}{2}$.

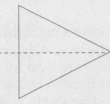

Centre of
enlargement

CONGRUENT SHAPES

Can you understand congruency of simple shapes?
These three are the same shape. They have been rotated or reflected but they are the same shape.

They are **congruent** shapes.

This is **not** congruent to the other three.
Can you see why?
(Trace the shapes if it helps.)

Now test yourself

52 Can you match the **congruent** pairs? Which is the odd one out?

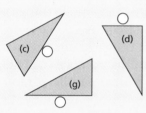

53 Can you see which of the set of triangles are congruent to triangle ABC?

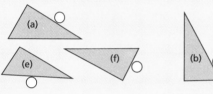
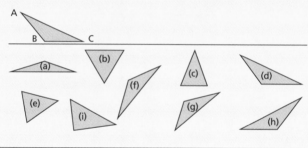

LOCI

Can you work out the path of a moving object?
The **locus** of a point is the path the point traces as it moves in a particular direction obeying a rule. All points along the path must obey the rule.

For instance, draw the locus of a point which moves so that it is always 2 cm from a fixed point, as shown in the first diagram:
Rule: the point stays the same distance from a fixed point.
Locus: a circle with the fixed point as centre and radius the given distance. (This is a model for any rotation about a fixed point.)

Now, draw the locus of a point that is the same distance from a straight line, as in the second diagram:
Rule: the point stays, say, 2 cm from the line.
Locus: two parallel lines on each side of the straight line and the same length with two semicircular ends of radius 2 cm.

Here's another example. Draw the locus of a point that is the same distance from two fixed points:
Rule: the point is the same distance from two fixed points.
Locus: the perpendicular bisector of the line joining the points.

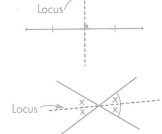

And here is another. Draw the locus of the point that is the same distance from two intersecting lines:
Rule: the point is the same distance from two intersecting lines.
Locus: the bisectors of the angles between the lines.

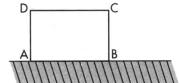

Now test yourself

54 In the drawing, the rectangle ABCD represents a sheet of plastic, standing vertically, on horizontal ground on its edge AB. It is to be rotated in a vertical plane, without slipping, about the point B until it is standing vertically on the edge BC.
(a) Draw the new position of the sheet, labelling clearly the vertices A, C and D.
(b) Draw the locus of the point D for this rotation.

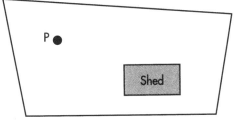

55 In the diagram there is a field with a goat tied to a stake in the ground P. There is also a shed. The length of the rope is 10 metres.
(a) Using a scale of 1 cm = 10 m draw the locus of the limits as to where the goat can graze.
(b) If the farmer wishes to hide from the goat, standing at P, show by shading the area where he must hide using the shed as cover.
(**Hint:** draw sight lines from P to the shed.)

56 The diagram shows the rear of an estate car. The roof of the car is horizontal. The door of the rear end of the car is hinged at C and can be opened until the door makes a 30° angle above the horizontal. Draw accurately the locus of the point A as the door is fully opened from a closed position.

N ETS

Can you see how a 3-D container can be opened out and laid flat?

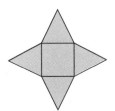

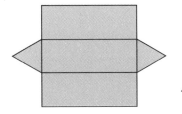

This is the net of a pyramid with a square base

This is the net of a triangular prism.

Now test yourself

57 Draw an accurate net for a cube of side length 5 cm.

58 Draw an accurate net for a cuboid measuring 5 cm by 3 cm by 2 cm.

59 A pyramid is made up of four equilateral triangles. The length of each side is 8 cm. Draw the shape on card. Put on some tabs for gluing purposes and cut out the net. Make up the shape.

Shape, Space and Measures

At the start of Key Stage 3 the majority of pupils will have reached at least Level 4 in Mathematics. By the end of Key Stage 3 most pupils should be within the range of Levels 4–7. Levels 5–6 are the target for 14-year-olds. Level 8 is the standard reached by very able pupils.

Use our checklist to assess the Level reached, by ticking the skills that have been mastered.

Level 4

- [ ] Make 3-D mathematical models by linking given faces or edges.
- [ ] Draw common 2-D shapes in different orientations on grids.
- [ ] Identify congruent shapes and orders of rotational symmetry.
- [ ] Reflect simple shapes in a mirror line.
- [ ] Choose and use appropriate units and instruments, interpreting, with appropriate accuracy, numbers on a range of measuring instruments.
- [ ] Find perimeters of simple shapes, find areas by counting squares, and find volumes by counting cubes.

Level 5

- [ ] When constructing models and when drawing or using shapes, measure and draw angles to the nearest degree, and use language associated with angle.
- [ ] Identify all the symmetries of 2-D shapes.
- [ ] Know the rough metric equivalents of Imperial units still in daily use.
- [ ] Convert one metric unit to another.
- [ ] Make sensible estimates of a range of measures in relation to everyday situations.

Level 6

- [ ] Recognize and use common 2-D representations of 3-D objects.
- [ ] Know and use the properties of quadrilaterals in classifying different types of quadrilateral.
- [ ] Solve problems using angle and symmetry properties of polygons and properties of intersecting and parallel lines, and explain these properties.
- [ ] Devise instructions for a computer to generate and transform shapes and paths.
- [ ] Understand and use appropriate formulae for finding circumferences and areas of circles, areas of plane rectilinear figures and volumes of cuboids when solving problems.
- [ ] Enlarge shapes by a positive whole-number scale factor.

Level 7

- [ ] Understand and apply Pythagoras' theorem when solving problems in two dimensions.
- [ ] Calculate lengths, areas and volumes in plane shapes and right prisms.
- [ ] Enlarge shapes by a fractional scale factor.

☐ Determine the locus of an object moving according to a rule.
☐ Appreciate the continuous nature of measurement and recognize that a measurement given to the nearest whole number may be inaccurate by up to one half in either direction.
☐ Understand and use compound measures, such as speed.

Level 8

☐ Understand and use mathematical similarity.
☐ Use sine, cosine and tangent in right-angled triangles when solving problems in two dimensions.
☐ Distinguish between formulae for perimeter, area and volume, by considering dimensions.

Exceptional performance

☐ Sketch the graphs of sine, cosine and tangent functions for any angle, and generate and interpret graphs based on these functions.
☐ Use sine, cosine and tangent of angles of any size, Pythagoras' theorem, and the conditions for congruent triangles, when solving problems in two and three dimensions.
☐ Calculate lengths of circular arcs and areas of sectors, and calculate the surface area of cylinders and volumes of cones and spheres.

CHAPTER 10

Collecting data

You should already be able to find a piece of information from tables or lists.
Look at this bus timetable. Can you answer the questions?

	BUS A	BUS B	BUS C
Meir park	0900	1100	1330
Meir broadway	0907	1106	1337
Normacot	0912	1110	1342
Longton	0918	1115	1348
Fenton	0925	1120	1354
Hanley	0940	1130	1410

(a) What time does Bus B reach Hanley?
(b) When can you catch Bus A at Longton?
(c) When does Bus C leave Meir Park?

You should also be familiar with form-filling. Can you enter information into a simple database? Can you extract information from one? Many of you will have used computers in this way. Copy and complete the data below about yourself.

Now proceed!

F REQUENCY TABLES

Once you have specified an issue for which data needs to be researched, can you collect and group the data with suitable class intervals?
Can you also make out a frequency table for your data?

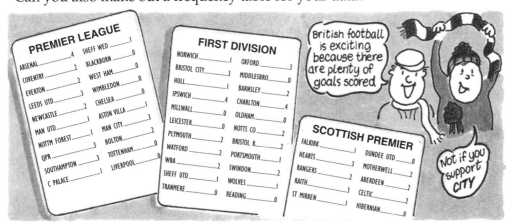

Now test yourself

1 Copy and complete the tally chart for the football results.
Make a mark in the tally column for each score. At the end, count up the number of tally marks in each row. Put this number in the frequency column.

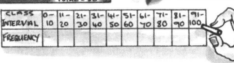

NUMBER OF GOALS SCORED	TALLY	FREQUENCY
O	HHT	
1	HHT I	
2	IIII	
3	II	
4		

2 Imagine you are the teacher. Complete the blackboard work.

YEAR 10 EXAM. RESULTS
37, 26, 51, 76, 32, 40,
28, 59, 71, 32, 91, 66,
32, 46, 81, 76, 79, 61,
52, 39, 21, 44, 37, 90,
9, 17, 66, 42, 23, 66,
91, 81, 66, 72, 55, 50,
48, 29, 33, 21, 37, 55,
62, 61, 55, 72, 31, 49,
59, 70

CLASS INTERVAL	TALLY	FREQUENCY
0 – 10	I	1
11 – 20		
21 – 30	HHT	
31 – 40	HHT III	
41 – 50	HHT I	
51 – 60	HHT II	
61 – 70	HHT III	
71 – 80	HHT I	
81 – 90	HHT I	
91 – 100	II	
	TOTAL = 50	

BAR CHARTS

PIE

$\frac{37}{6} = 5\frac{1}{2}$

CARS
BICYCLES

Now make up the frequency table below.

CLASS INTERVAL	0–10	11–20	21–30	31–40	41–50	51–60	61–70	71–80	81–90	91–100
FREQUENCY										

3 Here are the weights of the pupils in Class 2A:
35kg 43kg 52kg 39kg 62kg 54kg 58kg 37kg 44kg 52kg
43kg 48kg 53kg 42kg 55kg 37kg 45kg 50kg 40kg 46kg
52kg 53kg 49kg 37kg 44kg 54kg 49kg 61kg 59kg 60kg
(a) Choose suitable class intervals to help you group the results.
(b) Group the information on a tally chart.
(c) Create a grouped frequency table.

COLLECTING DATA

Can you design and use observation sheets (survey sheets) for collecting data? Can you also say something about your results?

To reduce the number of cars on the road in a particular city at peak times, people were asked to give each other lifts to work and share transport.

A survey was done between 8.00 a.m. and 9.00 a.m. to find out the number of occupants there were in each car passing a certain point between these times. An observation sheet on which to collect the data might have looked like this.

NAME: J. WILLIAMS
TIME: 8–9am DATE: 1/3/91
PLACE: VICTORIA PLACE

No. of Occupants	Tally	Freq
		40
1		48
2		34
3		18
4		7
5		3

This is a tally chart. When you make your tally marks, put them together in 5's.

From the results it is easy to see that the most common number of occupants (mode) was two. However there were a lot of cars with only the driver in them. The number of cars with more than three occupants was much smaller.

It seems that few people acted on the council's advice to share transport.

Now test yourself

4   Now design and use an observation sheet of your own to collect data about
how many brothers/sisters each child has in your class or year at school.
Comment on your results. (You could make up your own survey if you want to.)

F REQUENCY TABLES: CLASS INTERVALS

Can you collect, group and order continuous data (data which is collected by
measuring things)?

Can you then make out a frequency table for this grouped data using equal class
intervals?

> means 'greater than'
e.g. 9 > 4 means
  '9 is greater than 4'

< means 'less than'
e.g. 5 < 10 means
  '5 is less than 10'

$\geq$ means 'greater than or equal to'
$\leq$ means 'less than or equal to'

$5 < t < 10$ means 't is greater than 5 but less than 10'
$5 \leq t \leq 10$ means 't is greater than or equal to 5 but
less than or equal to 10'

When you have lots of different results it is sometimes better to
try to put them together to help them make more sense.

35 minutes 48 seconds. What group does that time go into?

Runner number 21: he's the first of the over 35 minutes group.

Now test yourself

5   Here are the finishing times for all of the runners in a cross-country race.
Make out a table as in the diagram and put in all the finishing times.

23 minutes 27 seconds	33 minutes 23 seconds	39 minutes 59 seconds
24 minutes 15 seconds	33 minutes 42 seconds	40 minutes 01 seconds
27 minutes 55 seconds	35 minutes 48 seconds	41 minutes 34 seconds
28 minutes 11 seconds	35 minutes 52 seconds	42 minutes 11 seconds
29 minutes 08 seconds	36 minutes 12 seconds	43 minutes 34 seconds
30 minutes 25 seconds	36 minutes 57 seconds	43 minutes 56 seconds
31 minutes 45 seconds	37 minutes 04 seconds	44 minutes 27 seconds
31 minutes 50 seconds	37 minutes 56 seconds	44 minutes 39 seconds
32 minutes 12 seconds	39 minutes 24 seconds	44 minutes 56 seconds

6   A group of children are having a darts competition. They measure how far
    each dart is from the bull's eye. These are the distances:

5.9 cm	1.6 cm	13.6 cm	9.4 cm
11.2 cm	2.9 cm	22.1 cm	10.4 cm
10.7 cm	7.6 cm	16.9 cm	23.5 cm
6.8 cm	5.1 cm	3.7 cm	17.9 cm
5.2 cm	5.0 cm	8.9 cm	21.3 cm
15.4 cm	10.1 cm	11.6 cm	5.3 cm
22.7 cm	9.9 cm	8.5 cm	0.8 cm
17.6 cm	10.0 cm	14.5 cm	7.5 cm
20.5 cm	20.4 cm	16.4 cm	11.6 cm
15.2 cm	11.3 cm	11.7 cm	15.8 cm
23.6 cm	4.8 cm	21.8 cm	4.7 cm

Make out a **frequency table** showing this information using suitable class intervals.

S URVEYS

Decide upon an issue that needs surveying. Can you design and use an observation
sheet to collect data? Once you have collected your data can you make sense of
your results?

   Your school is on a busy road with shops on the opposite side. You are concerned
about the amount of traffic passing by, particularly
at lunch time, and you feel that a pedestrian
crossing is essential. Before you can
make any comments you need
to collect data, collate it and
analyse the results.

   You need to design an
observation sheet and use it to
collect the necessary data.

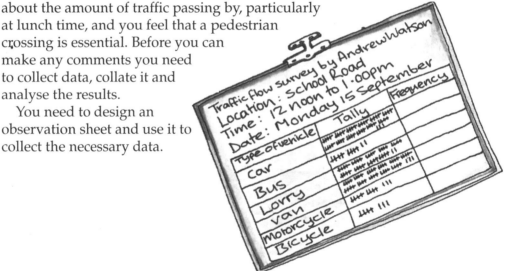

   The results show that in 1 hour during the school lunch time there were 201
vehicles passing the school gates. This meant that some kind of vehicle passed
every 18 seconds.

   Do you think a pedestrian crossing is necessary?

   Does the high number of lorries and vans affect the decision?

   Maybe there is a case for a crossing warden for the busy times instead of a
pedestrian crossing.

Now test yourself

7   Now design and use an observation sheet to
    see if your school library is used effectively.
    What are the most popular sections?
    Collate your data and analyse your results.
    What are the implications for the teacher
    in charge of the library?

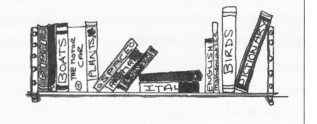

QUESTIONNAIRES

Can you design a questionnaire to collect your data?

Can you then make some sense of your results?

When making up your questionnaire, keep the following points in mind:

(a) A questionnaire should not be too long.
(b) It should contain all the questions needed to cover the purpose of your survey.
(c) Questions should be simple to understand and have only one meaning.
(d) Questions should require a 'Yes/No' answer, a tick in a box or a ringed answer.
(e) Questions should avoid vague words like large, big, small, old, etc.

Try the following questionnaire on your class to survey the wearing of training shoes.

Each question could provide you with data which then needs collating, putting into diagrams and analysing.

Now test yourself

8 Design your own questionnaire to investigate 'television viewing' amongst your classmates.

9 Design a questionnaire to find out what kind of holiday your classmates took this year.

10 Conduct a survey amongst your friends to find out their taste in:
(a) music; (b) literature;
(c) food; (d) drink

MAKING AND TESTING HYPOTHESES

If you state a simple hypothesis can you design and use a questionnaire to test your hypothesis?

Can you state whether your hypothesis was correct as a result of your data gathering?

It is vital that you give a **purpose** to your survey. It is pointless to collect data for no reason.

State what you hope to achieve at the very beginning of your survey. This is usually called a **hypothesis**.

A hypothesis is a statement that is made about two comparable things. For example: 'The weather is hot. We shall sell more cold drinks today.'

Now test yourself

11 Design a questionnaire to test one or more of the following hypotheses:
    (a) The school year should be divided into four terms as opposed to the three terms at present.
    (b) Pupils/parents would prefer the school day to start at 8.00 a.m. and finish at 2.00 p.m. without a lunch break.
    (c) Pupils/parents would prefer to have general school colours as opposed to a rigid school uniform or no uniform at all.
    (d) Pupils would prefer to have mixed physical education lessons rather than separate lessons for boys and girls.
    (e) A single examination at the end of the year is a better method of testing ability and progress rather than a policy of continuous assessment throughout the year.

Once you have designed your questionnaire and collected enough replies then you must analyse the results to see whether the hypothesis is valid or not.

CHAPTER 11

*P*resenting and interpreting data

Once you have collected, recorded and processed your data, you then have to display and understand it!

Bar charts are the most common way of showing your information.

Try answering the questions about this bar chart that shows the number of hours of sunshine for each day of the week.

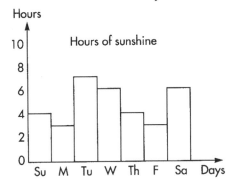

(a) Which day had most hours of sunshine?
(b) Which day had least hours of sunshine?
(c) Between which two days was the difference in sunshine the greatest?

Now make up your own bar chart showing the number of hours of sunshine for the following week:

Another way of showing your information is to draw a pictogram, where a symbol represents a group of units.

For example, this pictogram shows the number of raffle tickets sold by each class in a school.

How many tickets did each class sell?

Now proceed!

= 20 tickets   = less than 20 tickets

Class A
Class B
Class C
Class D

VERTICAL LINE GRAPHS

Can you read and understand a vertical line graph, where the length of the line shows the frequency?

Mary decided to test her die. She rolled it 50 times and recorded her results in a table.

From the results she was able to draw a **vertical line graph**.

Score	1	2	3	4	5	6
Frequency	12	10	9	8	3	8

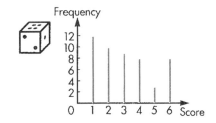

1 She repeated the test with another die, this time rolling it 100 times.
Draw a vertical line graph for these new results.
Do you think this die is a fair one?

Score	1	2	3	4	5	6
Frequency	16	19	7	28	16	14

2 Mr Kool decided to keep a check on the ice-cream sales during one week.
His sales are shown in this vertical line graph.
(a) On which day did he sell most?
(b) Can you suggest why?
(c) On which day did he sell least?
(d) Can you suggest why?
(e) How many ice-creams did he sell on Saturday?
(f) About how many did he sell during the whole week?

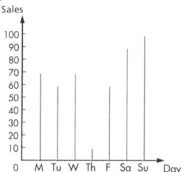

3 Class 1B did a survey on the colour of the cars parked on the staff car park. Draw a vertical line graph from the information they obtained. Can you make observations from the results?

Colour	red	blue	green	white
Frequency	16	12	3	8

4 Ask all your class which is their favourite type of book. Complete a table and draw a vertical line graph.

Type of book	adventure	sci-fi	romance	animal	sport
Frequency					

LINE GRAPHS

Can you read and understand line graphs, knowing that the values in between the plotted points may or may not have any meaning?

5 Freddie is in hospital with tonsillitis. He has his temperature taken every two hours.

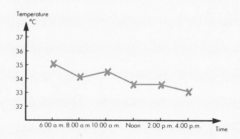

(a) Overall, was his temperature coming down or going up?
(b) Between which hours did it stay the same?
(c) What do you think his temperature was at 11.00 a.m.?

6 Here are some test scores for Sue and Jane.
(a) Would Sue's teacher be pleased?
(b) Would Jane's teacher be pleased?
(c) In which test did they score the same?
(d) Look carefully at the line showing
   Sue's progress. The point marked
   x has no meaning. Why?

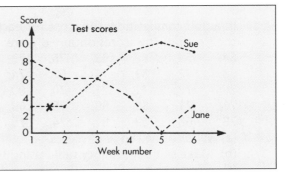

We join points with a dotted line to show trends even when there are no values between the points.

Now test yourself

7 Draw line graphs for the tables in (a) and (b).
(a) the sales for the first six months at a shop are shown. Why do you think the figure is high in January?

Month	January	February	March	April	May	June
Sales (in £1000s)	8	2.5	5	4	3	3

(b) The outside temperature was recorded every four hours one day last week. What do you think the temperature was at 18.00?

Time	00.00	04.00	08.00	12.00	16.00	20.00
Temperature (in °C)	10	12	15	22	22	18

FREQUENCY DIAGRAMS

Can you draw or read frequency diagrams (bar charts), choosing suitable class intervals?

Now test yourself

8 Nassar is in class 3.1 and he scored 45.
(a) How many are there in the class?
(b) Are the results good for the whole class?
(c) What would you say about Nassar's mark?
(d) What do you think the test is out of?

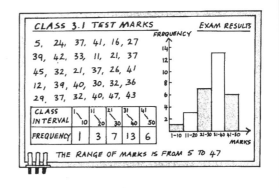

9 Construct frequency diagrams from these tables:
(a) A cricketer's scores in 32 innings:

Runs scored	0–10	11–20	21–30	31–40	41–50	51–60	61–70
Number of innings	3	5	2	6	4	10	2

(b) The ages of the congregation at a church service:

Ages	1–10	11–20	21–30	31–40	41–50	51–60	61–70	71–80
Frequency	1	5	7	4	7	5	9	2

10 In a golf competition, the score for each golfer was noted as they finished their round. The scores obtained were:

64, 69, 82, 85, 76, 73, 71, 74, 76,
68, 72, 83, 75, 67, 74, 67, 83, 78,
76, 72, 71, 71, 70, 80, 76, 74, 73,
71, 71, 83, 80, 78, 69, 72, 72, 76,
78, 68, 69, 81, 74, 75, 85, 67, 80

(a) What is the range of scores?
(b) Make out a frequency table using suitable class intervals.
(c) Construct a frequency diagram and comment on what it shows.

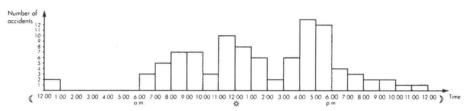

11 This chart shows the times of accidents to children.

(a) How many accidents were there between 5 p.m. and 6 p.m.?
(b) Between which times would you say the 'peak accident period' occurred?
(c) Why do you think there were no accidents between 1 a.m. and 6 a.m.?
(d) Use the bar chart to fill in this table. Then draw a new chart.

	a.m.			p.m.		
Time	12.00–4.00	4.00–8.00	8.00–12.00	12.00–4.00	4.00–8.00	8.00–12.00
Number of accidents						

P IE CHARTS

Can you draw pie charts and read them, especially those published in newspapers?

12 Hi-Fi Music sell records, cassettes, compact discs and videos. This pie chart shows how many of each kind were sold in one hour of a sale. Each small interval represents one item.
(a) How many did they sell of:
  (i) records? (ii) cassettes?
  (iii) videos? (iv) compact discs?
(b) Of the total sales, what **fraction** was:
  (i) records? (ii) cassettes?
  (iii) videos? (iv) compact discs?
(c) In the next hour they sold:
  1 record   3 compact discs
  3 cassettes   5 videos
  (i) Draw a circle of radius 3 cm and mark the circle as shown. Make a pie chart to show these sales.
  (ii) Write each of the sections as **fractions**.

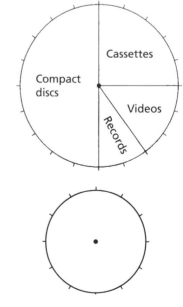

13 This circle has 100 small intervals. Each small interval represents **1 per cent** of the pupils in a school.

(a) What percentage of the pupils go to school by:
  (i) bus; (ii) car; (iii) walking; (iv) cycle?

(b) If there were 500 pupils in the school write down the number of pupils in each group.

(c) Show the information on a bar chart. Which method do you think (pie or bar chart) is better for showing the information?

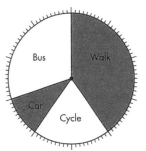

14 Sally decided to see how much of the day she spends doing certain things. An average day worked out like this:

There are 360° in a circle. If we divide 360° by 24 (the hours in a day) it tells us how many degrees for one hour.
360 ÷ 24 = 15°
So 8 hours is 8 × 15 = 120°
Complete the table and chart.

Activity	Number of hours	Angle of sector
sleeping	8	8 × 15 = 120°
school	5	
homework	2	
watching TV	3	
playing	4	
eating	2	
total	24	

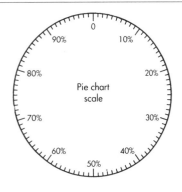

Some schools use a pie chart scale like this one. To use this you have to change your values to a percentage:

$$\frac{8 \text{ hours}}{24 \text{ hours}} = 0.3333\ldots$$

This is approximately 33%

Pie chart scale

CLASS INTERVALS FOR FREQUENCY DIAGRAMS

Sometimes the data you have collected is in the form of a continuous variable, i.e. one that you measure as opposed to counting it.

Can you draw and read frequency diagrams for continuous data, using suitable class intervals?

Inspector Butler times the buses to see how many minutes late they are. During one day his results were as follows:

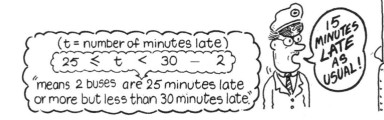

Minutes late	Number of buses
$0 \leq t < 5$	5
$5 \leq t < 10$	9
$10 \leq t < 15$	12
$15 \leq t < 20$	8
$20 \leq t < 25$	4
$25 \leq t < 30$	2

Inspector Butler drew up a frequency diagram to show the drivers. He demanded that buses run on time in future.

Next day his results looked like this:

Minutes late	Number of buses
$0 \leq t < 5$	14
$5 \leq t < 10$	10
$10 \leq t < 15$	8
$15 \leq t < 20$	5
$20 \leq t < 25$	4
$25 \leq t < 30$	1

Now test yourself

15 (a) Draw up a new frequency diagram. Was there an improvement?
(b) Change the length of the interval to 10 minutes (for instance, $0 \leq t < 10$ mins). Draw a new frequency diagram.
(c) Change the length of the interval to 15 minutes (for instance, $0 \leq t < 15$ mins). Draw a new frequency diagram. Why is this one less useful?

16 For a class of thirty children whose heights had been measured we could set out intervals at every 5 cm. Show this information on a frequency diagram.

Class intervals	Frequency
$120 \leq h < 125$	2
$125 \leq h < 130$	4
$130 \leq h < 135$	7
$135 \leq h < 140$	8
$140 \leq h < 145$	5
$145 \leq h < 150$	3
$150 \leq h < 155$	1

F REQUENCY POLYGONS

Here is a grouped frequency table for the results obtained by 120 fifth-formers taking their mock examinations.

Score	0–10	11–20	21–30	31–40	41–50	51–60	61–70	71–80	81–90	91–100
Frequency	2	5	12	19	25	30	16	14	5	2

The table can be shown in the form of a bar chart.

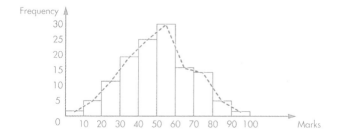

To draw the **frequency polygon**, mark the middle point of the top of each bar and join each successive point up by a series of straight lines.

Now test yourself

17 Draw a frequency polygon to show the weights of 80 boys in the second year at a secondary school:

Mass (kg)	36–40	41–45	46–50	51–55	56–60	61–65	66–70	71–75
Number of boys	2	8	18	26	17	6	2	1

18 In a survey 500 people from Stoke-on-Trent were asked how much they earned in a week. Their results are shown in the table:

Wages (£)	80–100	101–120	121–140	141–160	161–180	181–200
Number of people	20	40	75	200	125	40

A similar survey was carried out in Oxford and their results were as follows:

Wages (£)	80–100	101–120	121–140	141–160	161–180	181–200
Number of people	0	10	60	130	200	100

Draw a frequency polygon for both sets of results and try to draw any comparisons between the two frequency distributions.

It is possible to draw the frequency polygon without drawing the histogram. Simply plot the points where the middle of the tops of the bars of the histogram would be. Join all the points with straight lines.

This method can be used to compare two similar distributions which can be shown on the same diagram.

Now test yourself

19 The frequency polygon represents a comparison between the results of the students in a school, in English and mathematics examinations.
From the frequency polygon, write down the number of students obtaining each grade in each subject.

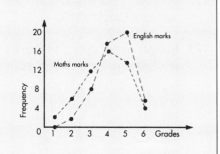

THE MEAN AND RANGE

Can you understand, calculate and use the mean (average) and range for a set of data?

Average contents   When items are packed into boxes loosely like matches, drawing pins, paper clips, etc. it is done by machine. The number in each box may vary slightly but the average contents are usually printed on each box.

Now test yourself

Now test yourself

20 What is the average contents of the box of drawing pins shown?
Would you think it likely for the box to contain:
(a) 102 drawing pins; (b) 96 drawing pins; (c) 120 drawing pins?

21 What is the average contents of the box of safety matches shown?
Would you think it likely for a box to contain:
(a) 37 matches; (b) 51 matches; (c) 31 matches?

Average = **mean**   This is the Evans family.
Grandpa wants to work out their average age.

ROBERT 16 years   SUSAN 14 years   BILL 45 years   JANET 42 years   GRANDPA 68 years

To find the average, he adds up the five ages and then divides by 5.
The **average** age of the family is 185 ÷ 5 = 37 years
This type of average is called the **mean**.

Now test yourself

22 Work out the mean ages of the Jones family
and the Patel family.

23 Robert Evans cycles to work every day.
During one week he times himself. Here are the times:

Mr. Jones 36 years
Mrs. Jones 33 years
Sally 14 years
Tom 1 year

Mrs. Patel 39 years
Mr. Patel 42 years
Mansoor 6 years

Day	Journey to work (minutes)	Journey home (minutes)
Mon.	19	15
Tues.	20	14
Wed.	18	12
Thurs.	23	14
Fri.	20	15

(a) What is his mean time going to work?
(b) What is his mean time returning home?
(c) Can you explain this difference?

Range   Six boys were measuring how far they could throw a cricket ball.
The distances recorded were:
25 m; 37 m; 54 m; 62 m; 44 m; 56 m.
The range of distances were from 25m
(least distance) to 62 m (furthest distance).
To calculate the range we simply take
the smallest number away from the
largest number. **Range** = 62 m – 25 m = 37 m

Now test yourself

24 In the first ten matches of the season the scoring records of two local rival teams went like this:
(a) What was the mean number of goals scored by City?
(b) What was the mean number of goals scored by Vale?
(c) What was the range of goals scored by City?
(d) What was the range of goals scored by Vale?
(e) Try to explain your results and their meaning for City and Vale.

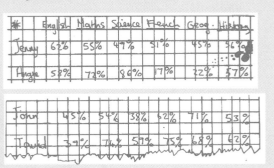

25 Jenny and Angie are comparing examination results:
(a) Work out the mean score for both.
(b) Work out the range for both.
(c) Who do you think has got the better exam results?
(d) Sometimes the mean will not be a whole number. Work out John's and Tavid's average mark.

F INDING THE MEAN FROM DATA PRESENTED IN A FREQUENCY TABLE

Can you calculate the mean from data given to you in a frequency table that uses class intervals?

There were 120 patients in the Mendit Hospital. Their pulse rates over one minute were taken and recorded. The number ranged from 60 to 99 beats/minute. The staff decided to group them in class intervals of five.

Pulse rate beats/min	Mid-value	Frequency	Mid-value × frequency
60–64	62	23	1426
65–69	67	16	1072
70–74	72	15	1080
75–79	77	32	2464
80–84	82	24	1968
85–89	87	6	522
90–94	92	2	184
95–99	97	2	194
	TOTAL	120	8910

Taking the mid-point value to represent each class interval, the medical staff calculated the mean pulse-rate to be:

$$\text{mean} = \frac{\text{total number of beats/minute}}{\text{frequency (of patients)}} = \frac{8910}{120} = 74.25 \text{ beats/minute}$$

Whenever you put data into class intervals you lose **absolute** accuracy but this method gives a reasonable approximation provided that the number of beats/minute is symmetrically distributed within each class interval.

Now test yourself

26 The same 120 patients were asked how old they were. Ages ranged from 25 to 74 years old and they were grouped into class intervals of ten.
Copy and complete the table to calculate the mean age of the patients.

Class interval in years	Mid-value	Frequency	Mid-value × frequency
20–29	24.5	10	
30–39	34.5	15	
40–49	44.5	20	
50–59	54.5	26	
60–69	64.5	30	
70–79	74.5	19	
	TOTAL	120	

27 Fifty of the patients were discharged just before Christmas Day. Before they left they were asked how many days they had spent in hospital. Their answers were as follows:

8, 14, 27, 28, 17, 15, 14, 38, 35, 16,
6, 25, 25, 14, 20, 10, 17, 17, 10, 28,
5, 22, 44, 19, 20, 15, 11, 10, 27, 11,
9, 23, 31, 21, 14, 36, 20, 17, 16, 4,
11, 18, 17, 17, 24, 22, 19, 40, 23, 8

Using class intervals 1–5; 6–10; 11–15; 16–20, etc., make out a frequency table and use it to find the mean length of stay for these 50 patients in the hospital.

MEAN, MEDIAN, MODE AND RANGE

Can you calculate the mean, median, mode and range for a given set of data and can you then interpret the results?

In a very simple experiment, a die was thrown 11 times.

The data is written in order, smallest first. (You need to do this to calculate the median. It is also easier to spot the mode.)

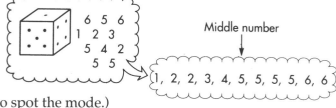

Middle number

6 5 6
1 2 3
5 4 2
5 5

1, 2, 2, 3, 4, 5, 5, 5, 5, 6, 6

For this simple experiment you can calculate the different averages:

mode = number that occurs most frequently = 5
median = the middle number (provided they are in order of size) = 5
mean = $\dfrac{\text{sum of all the numbers}}{\text{number of scores}} = \dfrac{1+2+2+3+4+5+5+5+5+6+6}{11} = \dfrac{44}{11} = 4$

You can also calculate the range:

range = the difference between the highest and the lowest scores
= 6 − 1 = 5

Now test yourself

28 Throw a die twenty times and record your results.
(a) Write them in order, smallest first.
(b) Write down the mode.
(c) Work out the median. **Hint:** There isn't a middle number.
    The median will be half way between the 10th and 11th number.
(d) Calculate the mean.
(e) What is the range of scores?

29 A football team scored the following number of goals in their first ten matches:

2, 3, 2, 0, 2, 1, 5, 2, 0, 1. Find:

(a) the mean score;   (c) the modal score;

(b) the median score;   (d) the range of scores

30 Suzie was in the ice-skating championships. The judges' scores for her performance were:

5.1 5.2 5.1 5.2 5.8 5.4 5.1 4.6 5.3

(a) Calculate the mode, median and mean for this set of scores.

(b) The lowest and highest scores were ignored. Why do you think this was done?

(c) Calculate the mean and range of the remaining scores.

31 (a) Measure the heights of all the girls in your class.

(b) Now do the same for the boys.

(c) Calculate the mode, median, mean and range for each set of heights.

Compare the results for girls and boys. Are there any significant features?

32 (a) Make a table of the shoe sizes of the children in your class.

(b) Work out the mode, median, mean and range for the frequency distribution.

(c) Interpret these results for the benefit of the local shoe shop.

33 In a five-a-side tournament

Team A scored: 0, 0, 0, 1, 5, 6 goals.

Team B scored: 1, 2, 2, 2, 2, 3 goals.

(a) Calculate the mean number of goals for each team.

(b) Which team do you think did better in the tournament?

SCATTERGRAPHS

Can you draw scattergraphs from given information and understand what is meant by correlation?

You should now know how to process data on many variables but you can still only consider them separately. Sometimes it is of much more interest and use to know if there are any relationships between the different variables: for instance, if you are good at French, will you be good at Spanish?

Suppose the following data was collected from a class of pupils after their recent examinations:

Name	Peter	Ali	Phil	Ray	Anna	Sally	Jade	Sue	Jane	Raj	Joy	Lisa	Marie	Jem	Alan
French mark	40	58	22	30	62	76	44	79	61	35	48	72	55	38	60
Spanish mark	38	65	25	34	58	70	50	73	68	40	54	75	65	40	55

From this table a **scatter diagram** can be drawn. This is a graph of one variable against another, where:

(a) one variable is plotted along the horizontal axis

(b) the other variable is plotted along the vertical axis

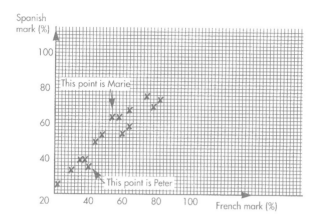

It can be seen from the graph that the plotted points are scattered about.

If there is a pattern to the plotted points there is said to be a **correlation** between the two variables.

If one variable increases in size at the same time as the other variable increases in size then the correlation is **positive**. For instance: the age of a man and the age of his wife; the weight of a child and the height of that child.

If one variable increases in size as the other variable decreases in size, then the correlation between the two variables is **negative**. For instance: the temperature outside and the amount spent on heating.

If the plotted points are scattered all over the graph with no pattern there is **no correlation**. For instance: the size of a boy's shoe compared with his exam marks.

Positive correlation

Negative correlation

No correlation

Now test yourself

34 Draw scatter diagrams for these sets of data. Try to predict any correlation between the two variables before you plot the points. Does your scatter diagram confirm your prediction? What type of correlation is there (if any)?

(a)
Pupil	A	B	C	D	E	F	G	H	I	J
Age (months)	136	140	153	164	177	179	184	186	189	192
Height (cm)	140	138	146	162	152	158	164	162	165	173

(b)
Pupil	Joe	Sid	Ann	Jim	Tim	Sue	Paul	Lisa	Meg	Fay
English %	84	66	78	42	72	48	55	80	64	71
Maths %	54	72	62	80	68	60	70	66	68	60

(c)
Husband's age	55	42	27	38	82	66	42	33	50	26	34	45
Wife's age	52	36	30	38	76	50	40	30	46	22	30	42

LINES OF BEST FIT

Can you draw a line of best fit across your scattergraph to show a relationship between the two variables you are comparing?

The points on a scatter diagram do not usually lie on a straight line but tend to lie within a narrow band. Sometimes it is a good idea to imagine the points as being clustered around some line to show graphically the relationship between the two variables. This is referred to as a **line of best fit**.

Consider the examination marks referred to on the previous page and the appropriate scatter diagram.

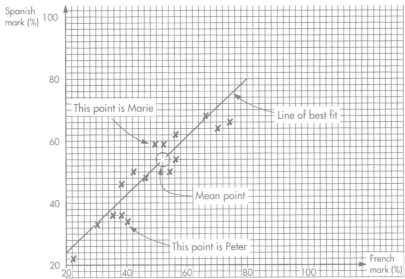

To draw the line of best fit, you must first work out the mean average for each set of marks.

French average $= \dfrac{780}{15} = 52\%$ Spanish average $= \dfrac{810}{15} = 54\%$

Now plot this mean point on the diagram and position your ruler so that it passes centrally through the points and also through this mean point. Your line of best fit should have an equal number of points either side of the line wherever possible. This line suggests a positive link between the French and Spanish marks for this class. So, if a classmember is good at French it is more likely that they are good at Spanish also.

Now test yourself

35 Draw lines of best fit on the scatter diagrams in the questions on the previous page.

CHAPTER 12

*P*robability

You should be able to judge whether or not something is likely to happen.
   Try putting these statements in order of increasing likelihood:

(a) I shall arrive at school on time tomorrow.
(b) I shall become a millionaire one day.
(c) I shall forget to do some homework tonight.

Sometimes there is an equal chance of something happening. Try this example! Which of these events are more likely, less likely or equally likely to happen:

(a) Rolling an odd number on a fair die?
(b) Choosing a club from a pack of playing cards?
(c) Tossing a 'heads' using a fair coin?

If you think about it, you should also be able to decide whether an event is fair or unfair. In which of the following examples have you a fair chance of succeeding:

(a) Tossing a 'tails' on a coin?
(b) Picking a joker from a pack of cards?
(c) Rolling an even number on a die?

You are now ready for the challenge of Chapter Twelve!

THE PROBABILITY SCALE

Can you use the probability scale from 0 to 1?
   You can show probabilities on a probability scale.
   The scale starts at 0 for something that is **impossible** and finishes at 1 for something that is **certain** to happen.

   All other events have a probability between 0 and 1. When you toss a coin, it can land on **heads** or **tails**. Providing it is a fair coin, the probability that it lands on heads is $\frac{1}{2}$.

Now test yourself

Place these events on the probability scale somewhere between 0 and 1. The first one is done for you.

1 Your mum does the ironing.

2 You own a wrist-watch.

3 You have brown eyes.

4 You prefer tea to coffee.

5 The sun will set today.

6 All the oceans will freeze over.

7 You are left-handed.

8 You will have homework tonight.

9 Your dad does the ironing.

Mum does the ironing

You have brown eyes

E STIMATING PROBABILITY

Can you guess the probability of a certain thing happening? For example: what is the chance of it raining today?

If you toss a coin, what are the chances of getting a head?

You are equally likely to get a head or a tail.

Therefore, out of two equally likely outcomes, there is one chance of getting a head.

The probability of 'heads' is 1 out of 2 or $\frac{1}{2}$.

Now test yourself

10 When you roll a fair die there are 6 outcomes.
What is the probability of rolling:
(a) a six; (b) a five; (c) a two?
(Give your answer as a fraction.)

If you were asked, 'What is the chance of it raining today?' you would have to think about a number of things, such as:

(a) What was the weather like recently?
(b) What was the weather forecast?
(c) What time of the year is it?

You might decide that it is **less likely** to rain.

You might decide, taking into account all these circumstances, that:

The probability of it raining would be **about** 1 out of 3 or $\frac{1}{3}$.

Now test yourself

11 Decide an estimate for the probability of the following:
(a) We will have chips for tea tonight.
(b) It will snow on Christmas day.
(c) Owning a pet dog.
Try to give reasons for your decisions.

POSSIBLE OUTCOMES

Can you think of all the possibilities when an event happens?
   If you rolled two dice together and added
the scores together, how many different ways
are there of scoring a total of 7?
The results would be:
(1,6)   (2,5)   (3,4)
(4,3)   (5,2)   (6,1)

Now test yourself

12 A girl has a red skirt, a green skirt and a blue skirt. She also has a red jumper, a green jumper and a blue jumper. List all the different sets of outfits she could wear.

13 Show all the ways in which a man, woman and child can be arranged for a photograph. (Man; woman, child; for example.)

14 Write down the results you could obtain if you tossed a coin and rolled a six-sided die at the same time.

15 How many different ways could you obtain a total score of 5 if you rolled two dice together?

PROBABILITY IN PRACTICE

Did you know that by repeating the same experiment you may not get the same result?
   Toss a coin ten times. How many heads did you get?
   Toss the coin another ten times.
   How many heads this time?
   Keep repeating the experiment.

Now test yourself

16 Will it be possible to get ten heads and zero tails? What is the most likely result?

Cut a pack of 52 cards 20 times.
How many hearts did you get?
Cut the pack another 20 times.
How many hearts this time?
Keep repeating the experiment.

Now test yourself

17 Will it be possible to get 20 hearts? What results would you expect to obtain?

MORE ESTIMATING PROBABILITY

Some probabilities are based on statistical evidence, others on symmetry. Can you say which is which?

If we were to repeat the type of experiment done on the previous page using the following:

  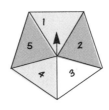

the estimates of probability would be based on the symmetrical properties of the shape.

Other estimates of probability would be based on the results of surveys.

For example, we could only say that the next car to pass our house has a 1 out of 3 chance of being red after conducting a survey on the colour of cars.

Now test yourself

Say whether the following estimates are based on symmetry or survey.

18 A die has a 1 in 6 chance of landing on a three.

19 The next vehicle passing our house has a 1 in 8 chance of being a bicycle.

20 The probability of a pupil in your class owning a cat is $\frac{1}{4}$.

21 The probability of a three-sided spinner landing on the number 2 is $\frac{1}{3}$.

PROBABILITY AS A FRACTION

Can you understand that if there are n equally likely events, then the probability that one event occurs is $\frac{1}{n}$?

When we roll a die and obtain a four, we say:
This can be written more briefly as:

'The probability of rolling a four is $\frac{1}{6}$ because there are 6 possible results.'

$$P(\text{rolling a four}) = \frac{1}{6} \begin{array}{l} \leftarrow \text{one chance} \\ \leftarrow \text{out of 6} \end{array}$$

If we put all the names of the days of the week into a bag and choose one, then we can say:

'The probability of choosing Sunday is $\frac{1}{7}$'

$$\text{or } P(\text{Sunday}) = \frac{1}{7} \begin{array}{l} \leftarrow \text{one chance} \\ \leftarrow \text{out of 7} \end{array}$$

In the following questions assume that all the outcomes are equally likely.

Now test yourself

22 One letter is chosen at random from the letters in the word MATHS.
What is the probability that it is H?

23 In a raffle there are 50 tickets sold. If you have bought one ticket, what is the probability that you will win first prize?

24 What is the probability of choosing the colour red from the colours of the rainbow? (The rainbow has seven colours.)

25 If all the months of the year were put into a hat and one is drawn out at random, what is the chance that it will be April?

26 If you cut a pack of 52 playing cards, what is the probability that you will cut a diamond?

C OMBINED EVENTS

When two events are happening at the same time, can you show all the possible outcomes?

These are two independent events (one does not affect the other).

A list or table of all the possible outcomes from this experiment is called a **sample space**.

Flip a coin twice

The sample space for tossing a coin twice would be:

(head, head)
(head, tail)
(tail, head)
(tail, tail)

The same sample space could be shown using a table or diagram.

		First toss	
		Head	**Tail**
Second toss	**Head**	(h,h)	(t,h)
	Tail	(h,t)	(t,t)

Now test yourself

27 Show a sample space for these **independent** events:
(a) tossing a coin and rolling a die
(b) rolling a red die and a blue die
(c) tossing a coin and choosing an ace from the four aces in a pack of cards.

28 The traffic lights can be on red, amber or green.
A certain stretch of road has 3 sets of lights. Write all possible combinations of colours on the signals as a driver approaches (e.g. red, red, green etc.).

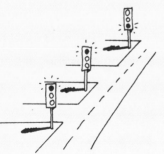

SUM OF PROBABILITIES

Can you see that the sum of all possible outcomes is 1?

If you were asked to cut a pack of playing cards then the probabilities that you would forecast would be:

P(heart) = $\frac{1}{4}$; P(diamond) = $\frac{1}{4}$; P(club) = $\frac{1}{4}$; P(spade) = $\frac{1}{4}$

You will also note that:

P(heart) + P(diamond) + P(club) + P(spade)

= $\frac{1}{4}$ + $\frac{1}{4}$ + $\frac{1}{4}$ + $\frac{1}{4}$ = 1

This applies to other experiments where if the probabilities cover every possible outcome they must add up to 1.

In general, the **sum** of the probabilities of all the outcomes which follow from a given event is 1.

P(head) + P(tail) = $\frac{1}{2}$ + $\frac{1}{2}$ = 1

P(6) + P(5) + P(4) + P(3) + P(2) + P(1) = $\frac{1}{6}$ + $\frac{1}{6}$ + $\frac{1}{6}$ + $\frac{1}{6}$ + $\frac{1}{6}$ + $\frac{1}{6}$ = 1

Suppose you were asked to choose a letter at random from the word FOOTBALLS.

How many ways are there of choosing the letter L?

What is the probability that the letter L will be chosen?

There are two ways of choosing the letter L and there are 9 letters in the word FOOTBALLS.

P(choosing L) = $\frac{2}{9}$

Now test yourself

29 (a) What is the probability of choosing the letter E at random from the letters in the word STEEPLE?

(b) What is the probability of choosing a weekend day if all the days of the week were put into a hat and one was chosen at random?

(c) Four red discs and two blue discs were put into a hat. What is the probability of choosing a red disc at random from the hat?

(d) What is the probability of scoring a number greater than 1 when you roll a six-sided die?

(e) In a class of 20 pupils, 11 are girls. If you choose a pupil at random from the class, what is the probability that you choose a girl?

PROBABILITY OF AN EVENT NOT HAPPENING

Can you see that if the probability of something **happening** is $\frac{1}{5}$ then the probability of it **not happening** is $\frac{4}{5}$, i.e. 1 minus $\frac{1}{5}$?

Some events will either happen or not happen. For instance: will it rain today?

P(rain) + P(not rain) = 1
    so P(not rain) = 1 − P(Rain)

To find the probability of an event **not** happening:

(a) Find the probability that the event will happen
(b) Subtract this probability from 1.

If the probability that it will rain today is $\frac{1}{4}$, then the probability that it will not

rain = $1 - \frac{1}{4} = \frac{3}{4}$

Now test yourself

30 Use this method to work out the following probabilities:
(a) What is the probability of not getting a score of 5 when you roll a six-sided die?
(b) In a raffle, 20 tickets are sold. If you buy two tickets, what is the probability that you will win the first prize? What is the probability that you will not win first prize?
(c) A bag contains four red discs and three blue discs. If you draw out a disc at random what is the probability that it is not a red one?

(d) A bag contains two red discs, three blue discs and four white discs. If you select one disc at random, what is the probability that it will not be white?
(e) A number is chosen at random from the first ten whole numbers. What is the probability that it is not divisible by 3?
(f) The chance of an engine failing is 1/50. What is the probability that the engine does not fail?

RELATIVE FREQUENCY

Can you use frequency tables to help you to estimate probability?
    If you tossed a coin 100 times, how many heads would you expect?
    You may get 45 heads and 55 tails; or perhaps 48 heads and 52 tails; or even 50 heads and 50 tails.
    Since P(heads) = $\frac{1}{2}$ and P(tails) = $\frac{1}{2}$ you would expect approximately half the tosses to land on heads and half the tosses to land on tails.
    The more times you toss the coin then the probabilities will get closer and closer to $\frac{1}{2}$.

When you roll a fair die, you would expect the same number of 3's to appear as say 6's or 4's. This means that if you rolled the die 60 times you would expect:

Score	1	2	3	4	5	6
Frequency	10	10	10	10	10	10

or close to these frequencies.

In other words, each score would appear to be **approximately** $\frac{1}{6}$ of the total number of throws.

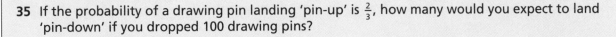

Now test yourself

31 How many 5's would you expect in 150 rolls of a fair die?

32 How many tails would you expect in 50 tosses of the coin?

33 How many hearts would you expect if you cut a pack of cards 100 times?

34 How many times would you have to roll a die for it to land on a 6 say 15 times?

35 If the probability of a drawing pin landing 'pin-up' is $\frac{2}{3}$, how many would you expect to land 'pin-down' if you dropped 100 drawing pins?

Sometimes this will not work. Your own estimates may be more suitable.

Probability estimates

Experiments can be designed to test the probability of an event happening.

You could also apply logical reasoning, based on symmetry, to work out the probability of an event happening **without** doing the investigation yourself.

But there are events that cannot be assessed like this.

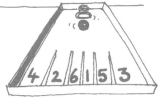

'What is the probability that a cure for a cold will be found in the next five years?'

With probabilities like this you need to take into account other relevant factors and 'weigh them up' in estimating a probability.

Now test yourself

Try to make reasonable estimates for these probabilities. Mention any factors that have influenced your decision.

36 It will rain today.

37 They will find a cure for the 'flu in the next five years.

38 People from outer space will land on earth within the next 50 years.

39 Your next door neighbour will move house in the next two years.

40 You will fall off your bicycle in the next 12 months.

41 An astronaut will land on Mars.

42 England will win the next World Cup at football.

43 Liverpool will win the FA Cup.

44 The next Prime Minister will be a woman.

45 Cliff Richard will have a number one hit in the next 12 months.

Handling Data

At the start of Key Stage 3 the majority of pupils will have reached at least Level 4 in Mathematics. By the end of Key Stage 3 most pupils should be within the range of Levels 4–7. Levels 5–6 are the target for 14-year-olds. Level 8 is the standard reached by very able pupils.

Use our checklist to assess the Level reached, by ticking the skills that have been mastered.

Level 4

- ☐ Collect discrete data and record them using a frequency table.
- ☐ Understand and use the mode and median.
- ☐ Group data, where appropriate, in equal class intervals, represent collected data in frequency diagrams and interpret such diagrams.
- ☐ Construct and interpret simple line graphs.
- ☐ Understand and use simple vocabulary associated with probability, including 'fair', 'certain' and 'likely'.

Level 5

- ☐ Understand and use the mean of discrete data.
- ☐ Compare two simple distributions, using the range and one of the measures of average.
- ☐ Interpret graphs and diagrams, including pie charts, and draw conclusions.
- ☐ Understand and use the probability scale from 0 to 1.
- ☐ Find and justify probabilities, and approximations to these, by selection and using methods based on equally likely outcomes and experimental evidence, as appropriate.
- ☐ Understand that different outcomes may result from repeating an experiment.

Level 6

- ☐ Collect and record continuous data, choosing appropriate equal class intervals over a sensible range to create frequency tables.
- ☐ Construct and interpret frequency diagrams.
- ☐ Construct pie charts.
- ☐ Draw conclusions from scatter diagrams, and have a basic understanding of correlation.
- ☐ When dealing with a combination of two experiments, identify all the outcomes, using diagrammatic, tabular or other forms of communication.
- ☐ In solving problems, use the fact that the total probability of all the mutually exclusive outcomes of an experiment is 1.

Level 7

- ☐ Specify hypotheses and test them by designing and using appropriate methods that take account of bias.
- ☐ Determine the modal class and estimate the mean, median and range of sets of grouped data, selecting the statistic most appropriate to the line of enquiry.

☐ Use measures of average and range, with associated frequency polygons, as appropriate, to compare distributions and make inferences.

☐ Draw a line of best fit on a scatter diagram, by inspection.

☐ Understand relative frequency as an estimate of probability and use this to compare outcomes of experiments.

Level 8

☐ Interpret and construct cumulative frequency tables and diagrams, using the upper boundary of the class interval.

☐ Estimate the median and interquartile range and use these to compare distributions and make inferences.

☐ Understand when to apply the methods for calculating the probability of a compound event, given the probabilities of either independent events or mutually exclusive events; use these methods appropriately in solving problems.

Exceptional performance

☐ Interpret and construct histograms.

☐ Understand how different methods of sampling and different sample sizes may affect the reliability of conclusions drawn.

☐ Select and justify a sample and method to investigate a population.

☐ Recognize when and how to use conditional probability.

F ORMULA SHEET

These are formulae you may need to know in order to answer the following Practice National Test Questions.

$$\text{area of triangle} = \frac{\text{base} \times \text{height}}{2}$$

$$\text{area of rectangle} = \text{length} \times \text{width}$$

$$\text{area of parallelogram} = \text{base} \times \text{height}$$

$$x^2 + y^2 = r^2 \quad \text{(Pythagoras' theorem)}$$

Formulae Sheet

You might need to use these formulae.

Area

Circle

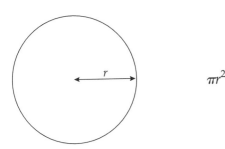

πr^2

Take π as 3.14 or use the π button on your calculator.

Triangle

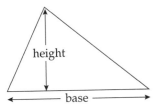

$\dfrac{\text{base} \times \text{height}}{2}$

Parallelogram

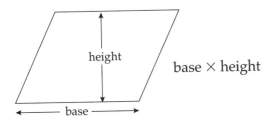

base × height

Trapezium

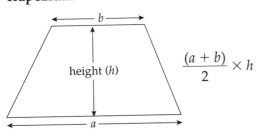

$\dfrac{(a + b)}{2} \times h$

Length

Circle

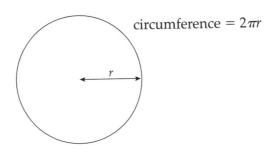

circumference = $2\pi r$

For a right-angled triangle

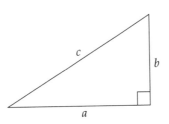

$a^2 + b^2 = c^2$ (Pythagoras' theorem)

Volume

Prism

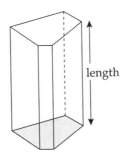

area of cross-section × length

Practice National Test Questions

These are examples of the kind of questions you will meet in your Key Stage 3 National Test papers. Practising these questions will help you prepare for your test and to do as well as you can. So that you can check how well you are doing, the National Curriculum level for each question or part of question is given in brackets.

For some of these questions you may need to refer to the formula sheet on page 159.

When you take your SATs you will be allowed to use a calculator for Test Paper 2 but not for Test Paper 1. Follow the calculator symbol correctly when doing the practice questions.

NUMBER

1 The table shows the distances, in miles, along the M6 motorway from Carlisle to other cities.

Carlisle	0 miles
Kendal	47 miles
Preston	89 miles
Stoke	155 miles
Birmingham	199 miles

(a) What is the distance between Carlisle and Kendal?
(b) What is the distance between Kendal and Stoke?
(c) What is the distance between Preston and Birmingham?   [LEVEL 3]

2 Here are some cards: | 0 | | 1 | | 2 | | 3 | | 4 | | 5 |

Rebecca picked these three cards: | 4 | | 3 | | 2 |

She made the number 243 with her cards.

(a) Make a smaller number with Rebecca's three cards.
(b) Make the biggest number you can from Rebecca's three cards.
(c) What extra card should Rebecca pick to make her number 10 times as big?
(d) What number is 10 times as big as 234?   [LEVEL 4]

(e) Kirsten has these cards: | 0 | | 1 | | 2 | | 3 | | 4 | | 5 | | . |

She makes the number 23.4 with four cards.
(i) Use some of Kirsten's cards to show the number 10 times as big as 23.4.
(ii) Use some of Kirsten's cards to show the number 100 times as big as 23.4.
          [LEVEL 5]

3 (a) The number 24 can be written in other ways. e.g. $4 \times 6 = 24$
Write the number 24 in other ways by filling in the missing numbers.

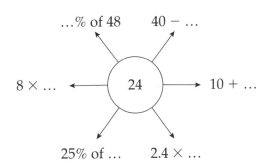

...% of 48 $40 - ...$

$8 \times ...$ 24 $10 + ...$

25% of ... $2.4 \times ...$

(b) Use any of the signs: $+, -, \times, \div$ to make this sum correct.

20 ... 4 ... 19 = 24   [LEVEL 4]

4 Carlos has 40 eggs. He wants to sell them by putting them into boxes of 6.
He thinks he will need 240 boxes!
(a) You can tell he must be wrong before you work out the right answer.
Explain why Carlos must be wrong.
(b) Work out how many boxes of 6 eggs Carlos will have.
(c) How many eggs will Carlos have left over?
(d) Richard wants to buy 22 eggs to paint.
How many boxes must Richard buy?   [LEVEL 4]

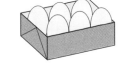

5 Dixco want to buy 35 TVs from the manufacturers at £135 each. If the total order is less than £5000 there is a delivery charge. The manager thought that he had ordered enough TVs so as not to pay a delivery charge.
(a) Work out the actual cost to see if he was right.
(b) How many TVs can he order if he only has £2000 to spend?

Remember to write down enough working to show you have not used a calculator!

[LEVEL 5]

6 Four people share 3 bars of chocolate between them.
(a) What fraction of a whole bar does each person eat?   [LEVEL 4]
(b) Ron and Dora share a bar. Ron is on a diet and only eats $\frac{3}{8}$ of the bar. A whole bar contains 600 calories. How many calories does Ron have?   [LEVEL 5]

7 Value added tax (VAT) is charged at $17\frac{1}{2}\%$.
Here is one way of calculating $17\frac{1}{2}\%$ of £240.

10% of £240   = £24.00
5% of £240   = £12.00
$2\frac{1}{2}\%$ of £240   = £6.00
────────────────
$17\frac{1}{2}\%$ of £240   = £42.00

(a) Show how to work out the VAT on a ring costing £380 by a similar method.
(b) Show how to work out 35% of £60.
(c) Show how to work out $22\frac{1}{2}\%$ of £60.   [LEVEL 5]

8 Look at these number cards   │ 0 │ │ +2 │ │ −4 │ │ +8 │ │ −2 │ │ −8 │

(a) Fill in the missing cards to make the sums correct:

│ −4 │ × │   │ = │ −8 │

│ −4 │ × │   │ = │ +8 │

(b) Choose one of these cards to give the lowest possible answer and state your answer.

│ −4 │ − │   │ = ...

(c) Now do the same to give the highest possible answer.

│ −4 │ − │   │ = ...

[LEVEL 6]

9 Nick says:

an increase from 10 to 20 is a 100% increase.

Rosie says:

so a decrease from 20 to 10 is a 100% decrease.

(a) Nick is right. Rosie is wrong. Say why Rosie is wrong.
(b) Complete the correct statements:
    An increase from 80 to 100 is a ......% increase
    A decrease from 100 to 80 is a ......% decrease.

[LEVEL 6]

10 Mr Blockhead tries to work out the answer to 258 × 96.

He works it out as 3870 but thinks that he may have made a mistake.

(a) Make a rough estimate of 258 × 96 and show the numbers that you use.
(b) Compare your estimate with Mr Blockhead's answer. Do you think he made a mistake? If so, can you spot it?
(c) What is the exact answer to 258 × 96?

[LEVEL 6]

11 A particular cycle is sold in three different shops as shown:

Shop A	Shop B	Shop C
£120	£165	£150
20% off	a third off	£35 off

(a) Which shop is selling the cycle at the cheapest price?
(b) What is the cost of the cheapest cycle?

[LEVEL 6]

162

12 The table shows the results of a survey done in a school.

	Wear spectacles	Do **not** wear spectacles
Boys	3	47
Girls	12	48

(a) How many pupils took part in the survey?
(b) What fraction of the pupils wear spectacles?
(c) What is the ratio of boys to girls who took part in the survey?
   Write your ratio in the form $1 : n$
(d) What percentage of the girls do not wear spectacles?
(e) What is this percentage written as a decimal?   [LEVEL 6]

13

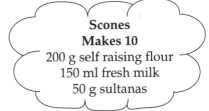

Fill in the missing quantities in the list of ingredients to make 8 scones.
                                                                [LEVEL 6]

14 Which one of these signs would you place on a roadside leading to Leeds?

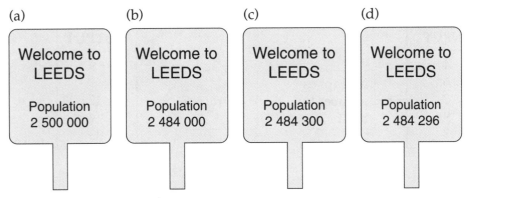

Explain why.   [LEVEL 7]

15 A rocket travels 100 km in 10 minutes, both recorded to the nearest whole number.

(a) What is the least possible distance the rocket could have travelled?
(b) What is the maximum distance it could have travelled?
(c) Calculate its maximum possible speed in km/min.   [LEVEL 7]

16 Study these cards:

3^5 Card A 5×10^2 Card B 5^3 Card C 5^5 Card D 5×10^3 Card E

Write these values as simply as possible:
(a) Card A $\times$ Card C
(b) Card D $\div$ Card C
(c) Card B + Card E
(d) Card B $\times$ Card E (Answer in standard form)
(e) Choose two cards and one operation from $+, -, \times, \div$ to give an answer of $\frac{1}{10}$

$\ldots\ldots = \frac{1}{10}$ [LEVEL 8]

A LGEBRA

1 A video shows Kevin outside his safe door. This is what he does:

Firstly: He unlocks the safe door.
Then: He opens the safe door.
Finally: He takes out the cash.

The video is then run backwards. Think about what you see.
Fill in the gaps to show what you see.

Firstly: Kevin ....the cash.
Then: Kevin ....the safe door.
Finally: Kevin ....the safe door.   [LEVEL 3]

2 Follow these instructions:

(a) If you think of the number 15, what number do you write down?
(b) What number do you first think of if you write down the number 17 at the end?   [LEVEL 3]

3 Fill in the missing numbers in this function machine which:
(i) Inputs a number   (ii) Multiplies it by itself   (iii) Subtracts 7.

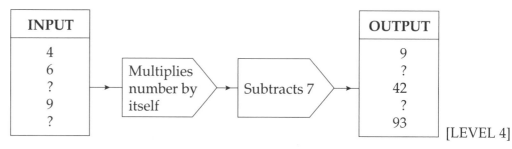

                    [LEVEL 4]

4 A mother has 5 bags of sweets and 2 sweets left over. Each bag has n sweets inside. The four children in her family were asked how many sweets there were altogether. The children said:

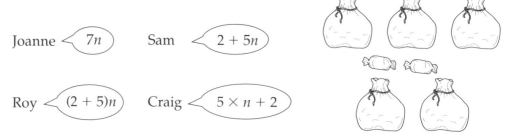

Joanne $7n$ Sam $2 + 5n$

Roy $(2 + 5)n$ Craig $5 \times n + 2$

(a) Name the two children who are right.
(b) Choose one correct answer and explain why it shows the right number of sweets.
(c) There are 42 sweets altogether. Complete the equation to show a correct answer:

.... = 42   [LEVEL 5]

(d) Solve the equation to find n, the number of sweets in a bag.   [LEVEL 6]

5 Examine these algebra cards:

x^2 x^3 $x + x$ $x + 2$ $x + 3$

$3x$ $2 \times x$ $x + x + x$ $2x + x$

    (a) Which of the cards will give the same answer as $x \times x$
    (b) Which **two** cards will give the same answer as $2x$
    (c) **Three** of the cards have the same value. Which three are they?

    (d) Write a new card which is the same as $x + 2$ + $x + 3$ [LEVEL 5]

6 Look at this diagram:

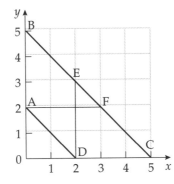

    (a) The line AF has the equation $y = 2$
       Write down the equation of line DE.
    (b) The line AD has the equation $x + y = 2$
       Write down the equation of line BC.
    (c) Write down the co-ordinates of E.   [LEVEL 6]

7 Two moped hire firms advertise their costs for hiring a moped as follows:

    (a) A formula for the total cost, C, of hiring a moped for n days from Moped
       Hire Co. is:
         $C = 5 + 4n$
       What is the cost of hiring a moped for 4 days?
    (b) What would the cost of hiring a moped from Rentaped for 4 days amount to?
    (c) Write down a formula for the total cost of hiring a moped for n days from
       Rentaped.   [LEVEL 5]

8 Solve each equation for x.
    (a) $3x + 5 = x + 17$
    (b) $2(x - 5) = 8 - x$
    (c) $\dfrac{(x + 5)}{2} = x - 1$ [LEVEL 6]

9 By considering the differences between successive numbers, find the next two
  terms for each of the sequences:
    (a) 2, 6, 10, 14, ..., ...
    (b) 2, 3, 5, 8, ..., ...
    (c) 2, 3, 7, 16, ..., ...   [LEVEL 6]

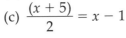

10 Sylvia was investigating straight lines and their equations. She drew these lines:

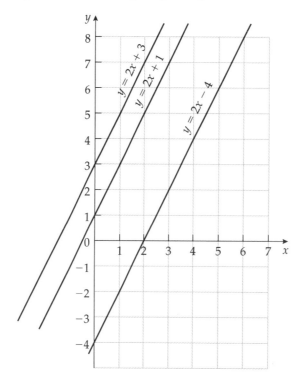

(a) She noticed that $y = 2x$ was in each equation.
 What fact did this tell her about all the lines?
(b) The lines cross the y-axis at $(0, -4)$ $(0, 1)$ $(0, 3)$.
 Which part of each equation helped Sylvia to see where the line crossed the y-axis?
(c) Sylvia decided to investigate more lines so she drew longer axes.
 Where did the line $y = 2x - 7$ cross the y-axis?
(d) Draw another line on the graph which is parallel to $y = 2x$.
 Write the equation of this line. [LEVEL 6]

11 Solve these equations:
(a) $3g - 15 = 42$

(b) $5f + 40 = 10$
(c) $h^2 + 15 = 40$ [LEVEL 6]
(d) Solve these simultaneous equations to find the value of x and y.
$$2x + 5y = 35$$
$$4x - 10y = 10$$ [LEVEL 7]

12 Joan is trying to find a solution to the equation $n^2 - n = 23$

	n	$n^2 - n$
First she finds the nearest whole number root	5	20
	6	30
Then she tries 1 decimal place numbers	5.1	20.91
	5.2	21.84
	5.3	22.79
	5.4	23.76

She finds that 5.3 and 5.4 are the 1 decimal place numbers that are closest to a solution.
Find the 3 decimal place numbers which are closest to a solution.
Show all your trials. [LEVEL 7]

13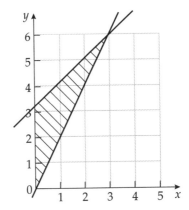

Choose two of the following inequalities that describe the shaded region:

$x > 4$ $x + y < 5$ $y \geqslant 2x$

$y < x$ $y \leqslant x + 3$ $y < 3$ [LEVEL 7]

14 Ray and Linda were using square tiles to make letters of the alphabet.
Ray was exploring 'L's

 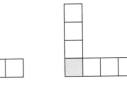

| $2 + 1$ | $4 + 1$ | $6 + 1$ | $2n + 1$ |
| 1st stage | 2nd stage | 3rd stage | nth stage |

(a) Use Ray's method to find how many tiles are needed to make the 8th stage.
Linda was exploring 'T's

| $3 + 1$ | .... | .... | .... |
| 1st stage | 2nd stage | 3rd stage | nth stage |

(b) Fill in the missing number patterns.
(c) Use Linda's method to find how many tiles are needed to make the
10th stage.   [LEVEL 7]

S HAPE, SPACE AND MEASURES

1 Examine these angles:

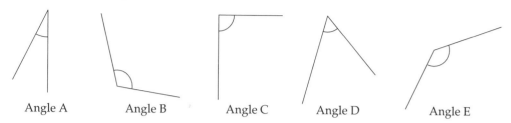

Angle A   Angle B   Angle C   Angle D   Angle E

(a) Which angle is a right angle?
(b) Which **two** angles are bigger than a right angle?
(c) What name do we give to Angle A?   [LEVEL 3]

2

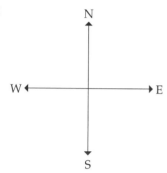

(a) Tom is facing North. He turns through two right angles. Which direction is he facing now?
(b) Rob is facing East. He turns in a clockwise direction to face North. Through how many right angles has he turned?   [LEVEL 3]

3 Examine these designs.

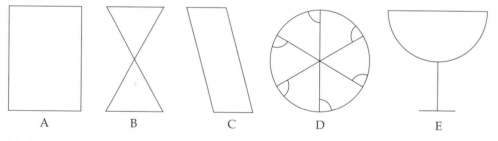

A   B   C   D   E

(a) Draw in any lines of symmetry on shape A.
(b) Which shapes have reflective or line symmetry?
(c) Shape D has rotational symmetry. What is its order of symmetry?   [LEVEL 4]

4 These shapes are made from small cubes.
Write how many small cubes there are in each shape.

(a)   (b)   (c)

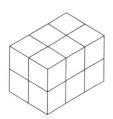
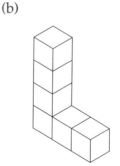
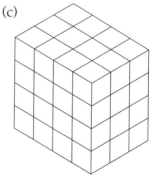

Number of cubes = ...   Number of cubes = ...   Number of cubes = ...

(d)

Number of cubes = ...

(e)

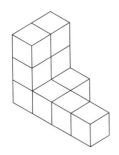

Number of cubes = ...

(f)

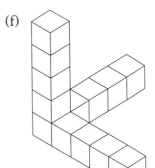

Number of cubes = ...

[LEVEL 4]

5 (a) Draw a net of this 3-D shape.

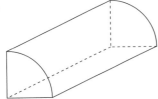

(b) This is a net of another 3-D shape.
Sketch the shape.

(c) Put a tick (✓) under the correct nets of a cube below.

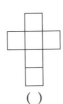 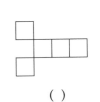 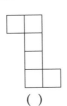

( )   ( )   ( )   [LEVEL 5]

6 Imperial units: inches, feet, miles, pints, gallons, ounces and pounds.
Metric units: centimetre, metre, kilometre, litres, grams, kilograms.
Study these pictures and put in the correct units:

(a)

The length of the insect is:

2 .... or

5.08 ....

(b)

The volume of cola is:

2 .... or

3.521 ....

(c)

The weight of the jam is:

2 .... or

908 ....

[LEVEL 5]

7 Convert these from one metric unit to another:
(a) 35 mm = ...cm   (b) 75 cm = ...m   (c) 2500 m = ...km
(d) 330 ml = ... litres   (e) 2.75 kg = ...g   (f) 4 m = ...mm

[LEVEL 5]

8 These two congruent triangles can be put together to make a rectangle like this:

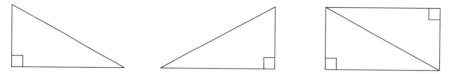

    (a) Can you make a parallelogram using two congruent triangles?
    (b) Can you make a bigger triangle using two congruent triangles?
    (c) This triangle has a special name. What is it?
    (d) Can you make two different **quadrilaterals** using four congruent triangles?
                                                      [LEVEL 5]

9 Majid has timber of different lengths:

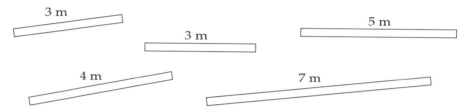

    He wanted to nail three together to make triangles.
    (a) Which 3 lengths will make a right-angled triangle?
    (b) Which 3 lengths will make an isosceles triangle?
    (c) Which 3 lengths will not make a triangle at all?   [LEVEL 5]

10 Here is a grid made up of parallel lines. One 60° angle is marked.

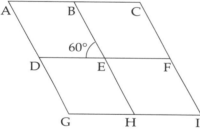

    (a) Name two other 60° angles.
    (b) What is the size of the other angle in the grid?
    (c) How many angles of this size are there in the grid?   [LEVEL 5]

11 (a) Square S is rotated about the origin through an angle of 90° in a clockwise
         direction onto square T. Draw square T.
    (b) Square T is then reflected in the y-axis onto square U. Draw square U.
    (c) Square U is then reflected in the x-axis onto square V. Draw square V.
    (d) What single transformation moves square S onto square V?

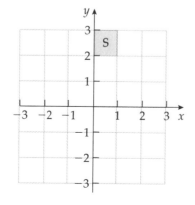

                                                            [LEVEL 6]

12 Four squares join to make an L-shape. The diagram shows the L-shape and the L-shape after a quarter turn in a clockwise direction.

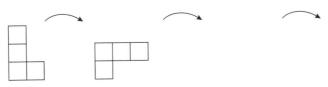

Draw the next two quarter turns. [LEVEL 6]

13 A pencil is in the shape of a hexagonal prism.
The cross-section of the pencil is drawn below.
Each of the 6 triangles is equilateral.

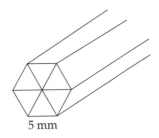

5 mm

(a) Calculate the area of the hexagon.
(b) If the pencil is 200 mm long what is its volume?
(c) Draw 4 cross-sections together to show that the hexagons tessellate. [LEVEL 6]

14 Each of these shapes have an area of 100 cm^2 and vertical height of 10 cm.
Calculate the length of the base in each case.

(a)
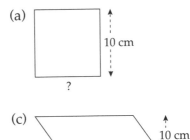
10 cm
?

(b)
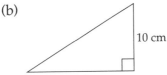
10 cm
?

(c)
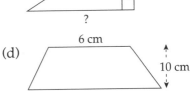
10 cm
?

(d)
6 cm
10 cm
? [LEVEL 6]

15 The diagram shows three legs of a sailing course. The course starts at S, goes South to T, then to R and finally back to S.

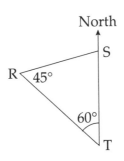

North
S
R 45°
60°
T

(a) Find the bearing of R from S.
(b) Find the bearing of T from R. [LEVEL 6]

16 The shape OAB is enlarged by a scale factor of 3, the centre of enlargement being the origin.

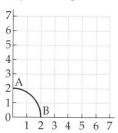

C

(a) Draw and label the enlarged shape OA'B'.
(b) Calculate the length of the arc AB.
(c) Calculate the area OA'B'. (Take π = 3.14)   [LEVEL 6]

17 Raj and Sally each measure the length of a different pencil.
(a) They both say that their pencil is 10 cm long to the nearest cm.
Does this mean that their pencils are the same length?
(b) Explain your answer.   [LEVEL 7]

C

18 A ship, S, is 54 km west and 65 km north of a lighthouse, L.
(a) Draw an accurate scale drawing of the situation using a scale of 1 cm = 10 km.
(b) Using your scale drawing, work out the distance from the ship to the lighthouse.
(c) Use Pythagoras' theorem to check your answer.
Remember to show your working.

C

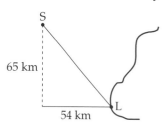

[LEVEL 7]

19 A dog is tied to a tree, T, in the corner of the garden by a lead 2 metres long.

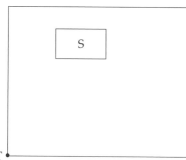

C

(a) Draw and shade in the area he can drop his bone in. Use a scale of 1 cm = 1 m.
(b) Shade in the area of the garden that he cannot see behind the shed, S.   [LEVEL 7]

20 A two-way ladder can be used as a folded ladder or an extended ladder as shown.

C

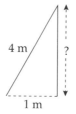

(a) How far apart are the feet of the ladder in the folded position?
(b) How high up the wall will the extended ladder reach if the foot of the ladder is 1 m away from the base of the wall?   [LEVEL 7]

H ANDLING DATA

1   The local Ford garage has the following information stored in its computer:

Model	Colour	Number in stock
Fiesta	Red	10
Fiesta	Blue	8
Escort	Red	16
Escort	Blue	11
Mondeo	Red	–
Mondeo	Blue	6

(a) Which model and colour is the garage out of stock?
(b) How many blue cars do they have in stock?
(c) Which model do they have most of in stock?   [LEVEL 3]

2   The table below shows the number of cars sold by the garage in the first six months of the year.

	Jan	Feb	Mar	Apr	May	June
No. sold	12	6	4	8	2	5

Complete the bar chart to show this information.

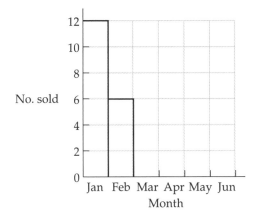

[LEVEL 3]

3   This table shows how many goals Vale and City scored in the first four months of the season.

	Aug	Sept	Oct	Nov
Vale	4	10	12	8
City	2	3	8	10

(a) Complete the pictograms below:

Vale   ⚽ = 4 goals   City

Aug   ⚽

Sep   ⚽ ⚽ ⚽

Oct

Nov

(b) Describe **two** differences between the two teams' scoring records.   [LEVEL 3]

4 Nasser and Naveed are playing a game of cards. Here are their cards:

Nasser

Naveed

Naveed takes one of Nasser's cards without looking and puts it down on the table.
State whether the following statements are true or false.

(a) Naveed is more likely to choose a

(b) Naveed is certain to choose a blue shape.

(c) Naveed is equally likely to choose a

Nasser takes two of Naveed's cards. The first card is a

(d) Complete this sentence: The next card  is less likely than

(e) Which card is it more likely to be? Explain your answer. [LEVEL 4]

5 Examine these ages: 11 years, 15 years, 14 years, 20 years
   (a) Calculate the mean age.
   (b) Calculate the range of ages.
   (c) Write down a different set of four ages with the same mean and range as the original set. [LEVEL 4]

6 In the first five matches of the season, Rangers and Rovers had the following record of goals scored.

   Rangers   2, 0, 2, 3, 3
   Rovers   0, 0, 1, 4, 5

   (a) Calculate the mean for each team.
   (b) Explain who you think had the better start to the season and why. [LEVEL 4]

7 Everyone in Linda's class chose something to do a survey about. Linda did a survey to find out which TV programmes were popular and her results showed:

   Sports programmes were the most popular.
   A very few did not watch TV at all.
   Peak viewing was between 7.00 pm and 10.00 pm.

   Alma surveyed newspapers. Write **four** facts that might emerge from her survey. [LEVEL 4]

8 Andy spins this spinner.
   (a) Which colour is he **most** likely to get and why?
   (b) Which colour is he **least** likely to get?
   (c) He thinks he has an equal chance to land on blue or red. Explain to him why he is wrong.
   (d) He also thinks that the probability of landing on yellow is $\frac{1}{4}$ because there are four colours. Explain to him why he is wrong again.
   (e) Estimate the probability of landing on green as a percentage.
   (f) Estimate the probability of landing on blue as a decimal. [LEVEL 4]

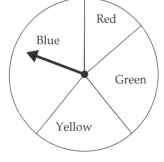

9 These pie charts show how the Taylor family and the Green family spend their weekly wage. The Taylor family earn £800 per week and the Green family £400 per week.

Taylor family   **Green family**

(a) What percentage of their weekly wage did the Green family spend on clothes?
(b) Did the Taylor family spend the same amount? Explain your answer.
(c) Who spent the most on entertainment? Explain your answer.
(d) This table shows how the Wright family spend their wages:

Food	Clothes	Entertainment	Savings	Rent
35%	20%	25%	10%	10%

Show this information on a pie chart.   [LEVEL 5]

10 You are asked to do a survey outside a cinema complex to find out about its popularity.
(a) One of the questions is: How old are you?

Under 20 ☐   20–30 ☐   30–40 ☐   Over 40 ☐

Explain the mistake in this question.
(b) Another question is: How often do you visit the cinema?

Very often ☐   Quite a lot ☐   Sometimes ☐   Rarely ☐

What is wrong with this question?
(c) Write better response boxes to this question.
(d) You decide to ask the first 100 people who arrive for the 8.00 pm showing of a film. State **two** disadvantages of this survey.   [LEVEL 5]

11 Sunjet decided to do a survey of the number of empty seats on their planes one day. The number of empty seats was recorded as follows:

11, 3, 17, 12, 8, 2, 16, 5, 23, 17, 24, 1, 9, 5, 2, 16, 27, 13, 8, 11, 14, 2, 21, 14, 6, 3, 21, 4, 14, 12, 12, 0, 6, 3, 5, 23, 15, 16, 2, 14.

(a) Complete the frequency table below:

Interval	Frequency
0–4	
5–9	
10–14	
15–19	
20–24	
25–29	

(b) Show this information on a histogram.   [LEVEL 5]

12 The diagram below shows a spinner.

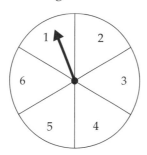

(a) What is the probability of obtaining a 5?
(b) What is the probabilty of obtaining a number less than 5?
(c) What is the probability of obtaining a number more than 6?
(d) The spinner is spun 100 times. Estimate how many times it will land on 6.

[LEVEL 5]

13 Rose and Josh have three number cards each:

Rose

| 2 | 4 | 5 |

Josh

| 20 | 40 | 60 |

They paired each card and started to create a sample space by multiplying the two cards together.

(a) Complete the sample space:

Josh

×	20	40	60
2	40	80	120
4	80	160	?
5	100	?	?

(Rose labels the rows)

(b) What is the probability of their answer being a multiple of 10 in the sample space?
(c) Another sample space is created by dividing Josh's cards by Rose's cards. Draw this sample space.
(d) What is the probability of their answer being a multiple of 5 in the sample space?

[LEVEL 5]

14 Sam rolls two fair dice

The probability that Sam will throw a double 6 is $\frac{1}{36}$

(a) What is the probability that Sam will throw a double 5?

The probability that he throws any double is $\frac{1}{6}$

(b) What is the probability that Sam does **not** throw a double?
(c) What is the probability that Sam will throw one 6 and one 5 together?

[LEVEL 6]

15 The ages of four of the five children in the Williams family are:

Pete	Liz	Joe	Sid
2 years	6 years	9 years	3 years

(a) What is the mean age of these four children?
When John joins the group their mean age goes up to 6 years.
(b) How old is John?

The Brown family have five boys. They have triplets aged 10.
(c) If the mean age of the five boys is 10 years and the range is 6 years, how old are the other two boys?

[LEVEL 6]

16 Examine these three scattergraphs:

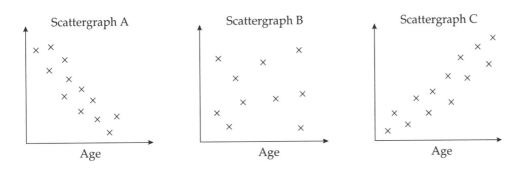

Use each scattergraph only once and say which best describes the relationship between:
(a) The age of a man and the age of his wife.
(b) The age of a car and the value of the car.
(c) The age of a house and the number of rooms. [LEVEL 6]

17 The motorway patrol make the following statements to highlight road safety:

(a) 25% of all motorists break the 70 mph speed limit.
(b) 10% of drivers do not wear their seat belts.
(c) 20% of front seat passengers do not wear their seat belts.

Assuming that you have a speed gun to help you, design an observation sheet to collect the information to prove or disprove the statements made by the motorway patrol. [LEVEL 7]

18 Ten children sat a maths test and an IQ test. Their results are shown in the table.

Maths score	30	47	52	65	40	55	35	60	85	70
IQ score	75	90	95	110	90	105	75	105	130	125

Show this information on a scattergraph.

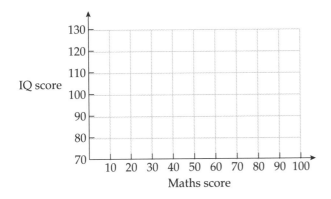

C

(a) Make a hypothesis about the group's maths and IQ scores.
(b) How would you describe the correlation?
(c) Calculate the mean maths score and the mean IQ score.
(d) Draw a line of best fit.
(e) Use this line to estimate the maths score of someone with an IQ of 100. [LEVEL 7]

19 These two pentagonal spinners are spun at the same time by John.

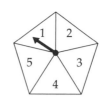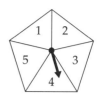

He recorded his results in a table.

Number of throws	Both odd	Both even	One odd and one even
25	11	6	8

Sarah then had a go at spinning them. She spun them 75 times and her results were:

Number of throws	Both odd	Both even	One odd and one even
75	24	13	38

When Andrew had a go his results were as follows:

Number of throws	Both odd	Both even	One odd and one even
100	35	18	47

(a) Whose results do you think will give the best estimate of the different probabilities? Explain your choice.
(b) Combine all three sets of results and make one large table.
(c) Use these results to estimate the probability of the spinners landing on **both odd**.
(d) If the theoretical probabilities are:
P(both odd) = $\frac{9}{25}$ P(both even) = $\frac{4}{25}$ P(one odd, one even) = $\frac{12}{25}$
write out a table of theoretical results you would expect to get after 500 spins.
(e) Explain why you would not expect to get these exact results.   [LEVEL 7]

20 A garden centre examined 100 flowering shrubs to see how many flowers each shrub contained. The centre manager recorded the results.

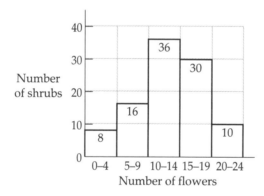

(a) Complete the table below:

Number of flowers	Mid-point (x)	Number of shrubs (f)	fx
0–4	2	8	16
5–9	7	16	…
10–14	12	36	…
15–19	…	30	…
20–24	…	10	…

(b) Calculate an estimate of the mean number of flowers per shrub. Show your working.
(c) What is the modal class?
(d) Can you estimate a median?
(e) What is the probability that a shrub chosen at random will contain less than 15 flowers?   [LEVEL 7]

Answers

CHAPTER ONE

1–4

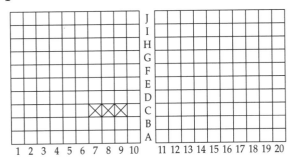

5 G17 and G18

6 There are many different answers to describe Sally's journey.

E.g. Catch the 06.25 train from Milton to Flymouth arriving at 07.05. Wait 40 minutes, then board the 07.45 ferry to Stowe arriving at 08.40. If she stayed with her grannie for just under 5 hours she could catch the 13.30 ferry from Stowe arriving in Flymouth at 14.20. She would then have to wait 30 minutes before she caught the 14.50 train from Flymouth to Milton arriving home at 15.30.

7 Last digits of the multiples of 2 are:
  2 4 6 8 0
Last digits of the multiples of 3 are:
  3 6 9 2 5 8 1 4 7 0
Last digits of the multiples of 4 are:
  4 8 2 6 0
Last digits of the multiples of 5 are:
  5 0
Last digits of the multiples of 6 are:
  6 2 8 4 0
Last digits of the multiples of 7 are:
  7 4 1 8 5 2 9 6 3 0
Last digits of the multiples of 8 are:
  8 6 4 2 0
Last digits of the multiples of 9 are:
  9 8 7 6 5 4 3 2 1 0
Last digits of the multiples of 10 are:
  0

8 Multiples of EVEN numbers have EVEN last digits.
Multiples of ODD numbers have alternate EVEN and ODD last digits.

9 No finite answer. Various patterns.

10 Multiples of 2, 4, 6 and 8 have the same last digits although in a different order.

Multiples of 3, 7 and 9 have the same last digits although in a different order. (Those for 3 and 7 are reversed.)

11–12
$1 + 3 + 5 = 9 = 3 \times 3$ and 9 is a multiple of 3
$3 + 5 + 7 = 15 = 5 \times 3$ and 15 is a multiple of 3
$7 + 9 + 11 = 27 = 9 \times 3$ and 27 is a multiple of 3
The statement is true.

13
$2 + 4 + 6 = 12 = 4 \times 3$ and 12 is a multiple of 3
$4 + 6 + 8 = 18 = 6 \times 3$ and 18 is a multiple of 3
$6 + 8 + 10 = 24 = 8 \times 3$ and 24 is a multiple of 3
The statement remains true.

14
$1 + 2 + 3 = 2 \times 3$ and 6 is a multiple of 3
$7 + 8 + 9 = 24 = 8 \times 3$ and 24 is a multiple of 3
The statement is true because the average of 3 consecutive numbers is always the middle number.

15 $6 \times 8 = 48$
  $10 \times 12 = 120$
  $15 \times 17 = 255$
  $21 \times 23 = 483$
  $101 \times 103 = 10403$ etc.

16–17 EVEN house numbers multiplied together give an EVEN answer. ODD house numbers multiplied together give an ODD answer.

18 Apart from $1 \times 3 = 3$ there can be no other PRIME numbers as answers.

19 I started the journey with 30 litres of petrol in my tank. I travelled 200 km using 20 litres of petrol before refuelling. I put 40 litres of petrol in and then travelled another 300 km. At the end of the journey I had 15 litres of petrol left.

20 Most CDs were sold in December and January. People bought CDs as Christmas presents in December or spent their gift vouchers in January.

21 Sales rose steadily up to a peak in March. As the summer approached sales started to decline.

22 Most goals were scored in the final quarter of the match. This may be because the players get tired. Fewer goals were scored in the first quarter when players are fresh and are concentrating.

23 $6^2 - 4^2 = 36 - 16 = 20$ $6 + 4 = 10$
    $6^2 - 3^2 = 36 - 9 = 27$ $6 + 3 = 9$
    $5^2 - 2^2 = 25 - 4 = 21$ $5 + 2 = 7$
The rule is wrong.
New rule: The difference between 2 squares is equal to the 2 numbers added together multiplied by the difference between the 2 numbers.
E.g. $6^2 - 4^2 = 36 - 16 = 20$
     $(6 + 4) \times (6 - 4) = 10 \times 2 = 20$

24 Typical hypothesis: 'Taller children are heavier.'

25 Typical hypothesis: 'Most children living in our street are girls.'

26 (a) 20   (b) 20   (c) 25

27 (a) 3000   (b) 100

28 (a) 60   (b) 30

29 (a) 45   (b) 45

30 (a) 2011   (b) 2045

31 (a) £286.80   (b) 7 years   (c) 14 years

32 Approximately 10 heads

33 Approximately 5 sixes

34 Approximately 8 scores of 2

35 Approximately 15 spades

CHAPTER TWO

1

Port Vale	7 549	Seven thousand five hundred and forty-nine
Stoke City	12 475	Twelve thousand four hundred and seventy-five
Man. Utd	37 111	Thirty-seven thousand one hundred and eleven
Leek Town	1 092	One thousand and ninety-two
Leeds Utd	26 907	Twenty-six thousand nine hundred and seven
Halifax Town	2 765	Two thousand seven hundred and sixty-five
Enfield	855	Eight hundred and fifty-five
Man. City	30 461	Thirty thousand four hundred and sixty-one

2

Ainslie	2 640 150	Two million six hundred and forty thousand one hundred and fifty
Bramble	3 245 625	Three million two hundred and forty-five thousand six hundred and twenty-five
Chire	1 765 857	One million seven hundred and sixty-five thousand eight hundred and fifty-seven
Dodds	487 650	Four hundred and eighty-seven thousand six hundred and fifty
Efflick	943 450	Nine hundred and forty-three thousand four hundred and fifty
Fromhead	350 000	Three hundred and fifty thousand
Gatcombe	217 900	Two hundred and seventeen thousand nine hundred

3 (a) Seven hundred and fifty thousand pounds
(b) £1 200 000; (c) Ninety-nine thousand nine hundred and ninety-nine pounds
(b) (a) (c) in order of size

4 (a) Two thousands (2000)
(b) Twenty thousands (20 000)
(c) Four hundreds (400)
(d) Four tens (40)

5 (a) 495; (b) 4995; (c) 499 500; (d) 450

6 (a) 3000 is (b) 7000 is
    30 hundreds   7 thousands
    300 tens   70 hundreds
    3000 units   700 tens
                  7000 units

7

8 ten thousands	80 thousands	800 hundreds	8000 tens	80000 units

80 000

8

6 hundred thousands	60 ten thousands	600 thousands	6000 hundreds	60000 tens	600000 units

600 000

9

6 thousands	60 hundreds	600 tens	6000 units

6000

(a)

4 thousands	40 hundreds	400 tens	4000 units

4000

(b)

10 (a) 70; (b) 160; (c) 250; (d) 980; (e) £130;
(f) 220 cm

11 (a) 36; (b) 317; (c) 95; (d)(i) 120;
    ✓✓   ✓✓✓   ✓✓
    3600   31700   9500   (ii) 1200
(e) 2500m

12

13

14 63 days	**18** £5
15 6 sweets	**19** 81 chairs
16 28 pints	**20** 30 cans
17 £21	**21** 49 minutes

Mental test A	Mental test B
1 67	**1** 89
2 23	**2** 44
3 37	**3** 56
4 121	**4** 124
5 20	**5** 16
6 53	**6** 93 mm
7 55	**7** 58p
8 24p	**8** 18

22 247 mm	**26** £216
23 1201 m	**27** £330
24 £151	**28** 26 sweets
25 £19	**29** 14 cm

30 (a) 2205; (b) 5428; (c) 5056; (d) 16 290; (e) 31 350

31 £14 456

32 £6120

33 £7020

34 (a) 27; (b) 24; (c) 38; (d) 55

35 £37

36 14km

37 (a) 2400 (e) 140 000
(b) 2400 (f) 320 000
(c) 45 000 (g) 2 100 000
(d) 210 000 (h) 15 000 000

38 (a) 200; (b) 50; (c) 50; (d) 20; (e) 300; (f) 30; (g) 200; (h) 400

39 (a) 1200; (b) 120; (c) 12; (d) 1.2

40 (a) 3; (b) 30; (c) 300; (d) 3000

41 (a) 2800; (b) 280; (c) 28; (d) 2.8

42 (a) 3; (b) 30; (c) 300; (d) 3000

43 (a) 20; (b) 7.2

44 (a) 200; (b) 128

45 (a) 800; (b) 200	
46 (a) 200; (b) 32	
47 £23 877	**57** £4.25
48 312 000 km	**58** 1.3125 m^2
49 £23 437.50	**59** 95
50 (a) £184.20 (b) £4605	**60** 435
51 £82.50	**61** 158 boxes, 8 tins left over
52 108 000 words	**62** £13.93
53 £1243.20	**63** 28 tins
54 60 480°	**64** 273 000
55 225	**65** 54 000
56 87 235	**66** 9.1875

67 (a) (i) −5°C −2°C 2°C; (b) (i) 7°C; (ii) 17°C
(ii) −10°C −7°C −4°C (iii) 12°C; (iv) 8°C

68 (a) 4°C; (b) −3°C; (c) 7°C; (d) 5°C; (e) 12°C

69 (a) −4°C; (b) −8°C; (c) 7.5°C; (d) 3.00 p.m.; (e) 10°C

70 (a) 0, −5, −10; (b) −1, −5, −9

71 −30	**75** −4
72 −35	**76** +5
73 +15	**77** −3
74 +70	**78** +5

79 (a) 3^2; (b) 5^4; (c) 7^3; (d) 10^6; (e) 2^3; (f) 4^3

80 (a) $6^3 = 6 \times 6 \times 6 = 218$;
(b) $5^2 = 5 \times 5 = 25$;
(c) $8^3 = 8 \times 8 \times 8 = 512$;
(d) $10^4 = 10 \times 10 \times 10 \times 10 = 10\,000$;
(e) $2^5 = 2 \times 2 \times 2 \times 2 \times 2 = 32$;
(f) $12^2 = 12 \times 12 = 144$

81 (a) $5^3 = 125$ $3^5 = 243$ (larger)
(b) $2^5 = 32$ $5^2 = 25$; (larger)
(c) $5^4 = 625$ $4^5 = 1024$ (larger)

CHAPTER THREE

1 (a) 1.59 m; (b) 1.52 m; (c) 1.45 m; (d) 1.39 m

2 (a) 4.45 m; (b) 3.22 m; (c) 10.38 m; (d) 25.75 m

3   (a) 325 cm; (b) 924 cm; (c) 3288 cm; (d) 83 cm

4   (a) 1.48 m; (b) 3.64 m; (c) 4.12 m

5   (a) 1.10 m; (b) 0.98 m; (c) 1.91 m; (d) 1.05 m

6   Arrow B → 1.06 m
    Arrow C → 1.10 m
    Arrow D → 1.12 m

7   (a) Four pounds ninety-five
    (b) Four point nine five metres
    (c) Seven point six four kilometres
    (d) Nought point nought four five kilometres
    (e) One point three nine seconds
    (f) One pound thirty-nine
    (g) Two point two three hours
    (h) Eleven point one one miles per hour

8   (a) $\frac{3}{10}$; (b) $\frac{5}{100}$; (c) $\frac{62}{100}$; (d) $\frac{43}{1000}$; (e) $\frac{5}{1000}$

9   (a) 4.95; (b) 0.594; (c) 199.8

10 A → 0.99   B → 1.04   C → 1.08
    D → 1.14   E → 1.16   F → 1.21

11 (a) 0.25 2.05 2.55 2.70
    (b) 1.05 1.10 1.11 10.50
    (c) 3.80 3.89 3.90 3.98
    (d) 0.05 0.10 0.15 0.50

12 (a) 4.35; (b) 13.04; (c) 96.79;
    (d) 5.7; (e) 11.27; (f) 1.06

13 (a) 6.07 m; (b) 1.93 m

14 (a) £36.92; (b) £13.08

15 0.13 m

16 (a) 24.75; (b) 4.24; (c) 225.6; (d) 4.5; (e) 5.18;
    (f) 0.27

17 9.9 kg

18 1.2 cm   21 26 stamps with 6p change

19 0.25 kg   22 15 boxes with 2 eggs left

20 14.8 m   23 13 journeys with 2 spaces

24 (a) $\frac{1}{3}$; (b) $\frac{3}{4}$; (c) $\frac{1}{4}$; (d) $\frac{3}{5}$

25 (a) $\frac{3}{7}$; (b) $\frac{4}{7}$; (c) $\frac{2}{7}$; (d) $\frac{1}{7}$; (e) $\frac{1}{2}$

26 (a) $\frac{1}{3}$ = 20 minutes; (c) $\frac{1}{5}$ = 12 minutes;
    (b) $\frac{2}{3}$ = 40 minutes; (d) $\frac{1}{6}$ = 10 minutes

27 (a) $\frac{1}{4}$″ quarters;   (c) $\frac{1}{8}$″ eighths;
    (b) $\frac{1}{10}$″ tenths;   (d) $\frac{1}{16}$″ sixteenths

28 (a) $\frac{1}{3}$; (b) $\frac{2}{5}$; (c) $\frac{1}{2}$ ($\frac{2}{4}$); (d) $\frac{5}{12}$

29 (a) £2.25   (b) £0.75
       £2.00   £0.60
       £1.80+   £1.20+
       £6.05   £2.55

30 (a) £334; (b) (i) £233; (ii) £151; (c) £97;
    (d) £233

31 (a) Hi-fi discount £100; TV discount £40;
       video discount £25
    (b) Sale price £200; sale price £160; sale
       price £225

32 (a) 70%; (b) 46%; (c) 92%

33 (a) 84%; (b) 72%; (c) 80%; (d) 70%

34 (a) 50%; (b) 25%; (c) 75%; (d) 20%

35 (a) 75%; (b) 75%; (c) 25%; (d) 60%

36 (a) 60 l; (b) 30 l; (c) 90 l

37 (a) £2.50; (b) £7.50

38 (a) 15; (b) 5; (c) 25%

39 (a) 20; (b) 15; (c) 30

40 Mrs Khan   Mr Smith
    eggs   10%   apple   35%
    flour   25%   flour   30%
    raisins 50%   blackcurrants 25%
    nuts   15%   eggs   10%

41 (a) Clock discount £4; dartboard discount
       £3; table discount £110
    (b) Sale price £12; sale price £27;
       sale price £220

42 (a) £49.50; (b) £13.50; (c) £40.50

43 (a) £313.60; (b) £226.80; (c) £212.55

44 (a) wallpaper   £1.65
       carpets   £30.00
       paint   £2.50
       curtains   £3.30
    (b) three piece suite £440.00
       wardrobe   £162.00
       dressing table   £62.50
       chest of drawers   £34.00

45
$\frac{1}{2}$	0.5	50%
$\frac{1}{10}$	0.1	10%
$\frac{3}{10}$	0.3	30%
$\frac{1}{4}$	0.25	25%
$\frac{3}{4}$	0.75	75%
$\frac{1}{5}$	0.2	20%
$\frac{3}{5}$	0.6	60%

$\frac{4}{5}$	0.8	80%
$\frac{9}{10}$	0.9	90%
$\frac{1}{3}$	0.33...	$33\frac{1}{3}\%$
$\frac{2}{3}$	0.66...	$66\frac{2}{3}\%$

46 (a) The ratio of line C to line D is 3:5
     Line C is 60% of line D
     Line C is $\frac{3}{5}$ of line D

    (b) The ratio of line E to line F is 7:10
     Line E is 70% of line F
     Line E is $\frac{7}{10}$ of line F

    (c) The ratio of line G to line H is 2:5
     Line G is 40% of line H
     Line G is $\frac{2}{5}$ of line H

47 (a) $\frac{3}{4}$ 0.75   75%
    (b) $\frac{1}{5}$ 0.20   20%
    (c) $\frac{9}{25}$ 0.36   36%
    (d) $\frac{7}{20}$ 0.35   35%
    (e) $1\frac{1}{10}$ 1.10   110%
    (f) $1\frac{7}{10}$ 1.70   170%
    (g) $2\frac{1}{2}$ 2.50   250%

48 (b) £50 profit; (b) $\frac{1}{4}$; (c) 25%

49 (a) £800 loss; (b) 40%

50 $6\frac{2}{3}\%$

51 (a) 9; (b) 22; (c) £8; (d) £25; (e) £8

52 (a) £72; (b) £400; (c) £8; (d) £90; (e) £49

53 (a) £9; (b) 11 cm; (c) 90 kg; (d) £4.18; (e) £16; (f) 450; (g) 4p; (h) 96p

54 (a) £2.55; (b) £3.84; (c) £2; (d) £6

55 (a) 1:5; (b) 2 ounces

56 £6

57 (a) 1:5; (b) 5:1

58 11 years old

59 (a) 10 people
     200 g margarine
     400 g flour
     5 tablespoons of water
     3 kg of apples
     150 g sugar
    (b) 5 people
     100 g margarine
     200 g flour
     $2\frac{1}{2}$ tablespoons of water
     $1\frac{1}{2}$ kg of apples
     75 g sugar

60 (a) 7:3; (b) 3:2; (c) 13:7; (d) 9:11

61 (a) 4 parts; (b) (i) $\frac{3}{4}$; (c) 6 m³ sand; (d) 5 m³
          (ii) $\frac{1}{4}$ 2 m³ cement

62 (a) (i) $\frac{1}{3}$; (ii) $\frac{1}{2}$; (iii) $\frac{1}{6}$;
    (b) 4 cubic metres (m³);
    (c) 6 cubic metres (m³)

63 (a) 4.4 m wide; (b) 10.5 m long

64 Miss Jones £19 200 Mrs Cooper £12 800

65 (a) £40 000; (b) £24 000

66 (a) 45 pints of milk
     3 kg rice
     2250 g sugar
    (b) 3 pints
    (c) 300 g sugar

67 (a) 15 tins of white paint;   (d) Pale Pink;
    (b) 6 tins of red paint: (e) 6 extra tins
    (c) 15 tins of white paint;

68 (a) 5:3; (b) 4:5; (c) 2:3; (d) 6:5; (e) 5:4:3

69 (a) 1.8 m; (b) 16 cm

70 (a) 4.5 m; (b) 6 cm

71 (a) 14 cm by 11 cm
    (c) Width = 1.55 m; Length = 1.75 m

CHAPTER FOUR

1 (a) 5800   (f) 1200
  (b) 6100   (g) 1700
  (c) 1500   (h) 5100
  (d) 3500   (i) 100
  (e) 200   (j) 2600

2 (a) 260; (b) 4000; (c) 500; (d) 21 000; (e) 93 000

3 (a) √; (b) x; (c) √; (d) x; (e) x

4 1800 g; 1710 g   **9** b

5 £2.00; £1.98   **10** b

6 20 cm; 22 cm   **11** c

7 6000 g; 6355 g   **12** c

8 100; 105   **13** a

14 (a) (i) 4250; (ii) 4200; (b) (i) 86 500;
   (ii) 87 000; (c) (i) 1720; (ii) 1700; (d) (i) 23.8;
   (ii) 24; (e) (i) 15.5; (ii) 15

15 (a) 20 200; (b) 0.00458; (c) 0.108; (d) 11 000

16 (a) 37; (b) 47; (c) 40; (d) 123; (e) 28

17 (a) 38; (b) 190; (c) 5; (d) 5

18 (a) 60 miles per hour; (b) 48 matches per box

19 (a) 6.9999999 corrected to 7
   (b) 15, because (15 ÷ 4) has a finite answer
   (c) 15, because (15 ÷ 3) has a finite answer
   (d) 15.999999 corrected to 16

20 No answer required

21 6.2×10^8 = 620 000 000

22 1.7×10^{11} = 170 000 000 000

23 2.5×10^7 = 25 000 000

24 2.25×10^{12} = 2 250 000 000 000

25 [2.8 10] = 28 000 000 000

26 [1.8 10] = 18 000 000 000

27 (a) 6.32 cm; (b) 8.37 cm; (c) 7.35 cm

28 (a) 3.42 cm; (b) 4.38 cm; (c) 5.85 cm

29 (a) (i) 0.6; (ii) 0.57; (b) (i) 0.5; (ii) 0.53;
   (c) (i) 7.6; (ii) 7.63; (d) (i) 23.1; (ii) 23.11;
   (e) (i) 7.6; (ii) 7.60

30 (a) 3 tins; (b) $2\frac{1}{4}$ h

31 £49 000

32 16 h

33 £3000

34 £200

35 50 000

36 All the following answers are approximations:
   (a) 95% have televisions
   (b) 50% have a garage
   (c) 10% wear spectacles
   (d) 5% have swimming pools
   (e) 10% have double glazing

37 £15 000

38 £1000

39 (a) ③ ④ ⑫ ⑮ 22 28 32 35 72 81
   (b) (i) 880; (ii) 55;
       (iii) 1 + 2 + 3 + 4 + 5 + 6 + 7 + 8 + 9 + 10

40 (a) 3
   (b) 3.5
   (c) 1.7
   (d) 4.25

41 (a) [6][−][2][=][X→M][5][+][7][=][÷][RM][=]
   (b) [(][5][+][7][)][÷][(][6][−][2][)][=]

C HAPTER FIVE

1 (a) $15 \times 6 = 30 \times 3 = 90$
   (b) $21 \times 9 = 63 \times 3 = 189$
   (c) $13 \times 12 = 26 \times 6 = 52 \times 3 = 156$
   (d) $72 \div 6 = 36 \div 3 = 12$
   (e) $60 \div 12 = 30 \div 6 = 10 \div 2 = 5$

2 (a) $\frac{1}{2} = \frac{5}{10} = \frac{6}{12} = \frac{7}{14} = \frac{8}{16}$
   (b) $\frac{2}{3} = \frac{8}{12} = \frac{10}{15} = \frac{12}{18} = \frac{14}{21}$
   (c) $\frac{3}{5} = \frac{9}{15} = \frac{12}{20} = \frac{15}{25} = \frac{18}{30} = \frac{21}{35}$

3 (a) $\frac{3}{4} = \frac{6}{8} = \frac{9}{12} = \frac{12}{16} = \frac{15}{20}$
   (b) $\frac{2}{5} = \frac{4}{10} = \frac{6}{15} = \frac{8}{20} = \frac{10}{25}$
   (c) $\frac{3}{8} = \frac{6}{16} = \frac{9}{24} = \frac{12}{32} = \frac{15}{40}$

4 (a) 31 (+4); (b) 9 (−5); (c) 48 (× 2);
   (d) 3 (÷2); (e) 33 (2 × difference); (f) 322
   (3 × difference); (g) 27 (difference + 1);
   (h) 21 (Add two previous nos.)

5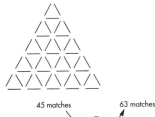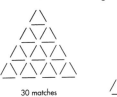

Add on consecutive multiples of 3

6 (a) 36, 49, ... square numbers
   (b) 15, 21, ... triangular numbers

7 (a) 1, 2, 4, 8
   (b) 1, 3, 5, 15
   (c) 1, 2, 3, 5, 6, 10, 15, 30
   (d) 1, 2, 4, 8, 16
   (e) 1, 2, 3, 6, 9, 18, 27, 54

8 (a) 8, 16, 24, 32, 40, 48; (b) 24, 30, 36, 42, 48

9 (a) 19, 23, 29, 31, 37, 41, 43, 47

   (b) See diagram for question 11

10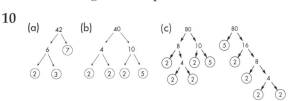

11

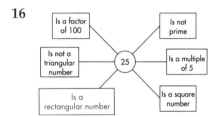

- ○ prime numbers
- □ square numbers
- ▲ triangular numbers

A square number could not be a prime number

12 See question 11 for diagram; 21, 28, 36

13 1, 8, 27, 64, 125, 216, 343, 512, 729, 1000

14
(a) 7
(b) 9
(c) 12
(d) 15
(e) 20
(f) 2.5
(g) 7.5
(h) 25
(i) 40
(j) 99

15 (a) 2; (b) 3; (c) 4; (d) 2.5; (e) 11; (f) 15

16

```
Is a factor          Is not
of 100               prime

Is not a                      Is a multiple
triangular      25            of 5
number

        Is a           Is a square
    rectangular number  number
```

17

```
    21            33            55
   /  \          /  \          /  \
  3 × 7        3 × 11        5 × 11
   (a)           (b)           (c)
```

18 (a) $6 = 2 \times 3$; (b) $77 = 7 \times 11$; (c) $121 = 11 \times 11$

19

```
·
· ·
· · ·   15      10 + 6 = 16
· · · ·          a square number
· · · · ·
```

When you add two successive triangular numbers the result is a square number.
(a) 21 + 15 = 36; (b) 15 + 10 = 25

20

```
· · · · · ·      · · ·      · · · ·
· · · · · · ·    · · ·      · · · ·   Prime numbers
       14        · · ·      · · · ·   are missing.
                 · · ·      · · · ·
                 · · ·          16
                     15
```

All numbers must be prime or rectangular

21 27 unit cubes   64 unit cubes

22
(a) 1, 6, 11, 16, 21, 26, 31
(b) 1, 4, 7, 10, 13, 16, 19
(c) 1, 2, 4, 8, 16, 32, 64
(d) 1, 3, 9, 27, 81, 243, 729
(e) 1, 5, 13, 29, 61, 125, 253
(f) 1, 2, 5, 14, 41, 122, 365
(g) 1, 2, 7, 32, 157, 782, 3907
(h) 128, 64, 32, 16, 8, 4, 2
(i) 5, 6, 8, 12, 20, 36, 68

23 21, 34, 55 (a) 18, 29, 47, 76 (b) 16, 26, 42, 68

24 (a) 22, 29; (b) 49, 64; (c) 47, 62; (d) 41, 55;
(e) 32, 44

25 Examples are:
(a) 1, 2, 3, 4, 5, 6 or 1, 2, 3, 5, 8, 13
(b) 1, 2, 5, 10, 17, 26 or 1, 2, 5, 14, 41, 122
(c) 1, 3, 7, 13, 21, 31 or 1, 3, 7, 15, 31, 63
(d) 1, 4, 10, 19, 31, 46 or 1, 4, 10, 22, 46, 94
(e) 2, 5, 11, 20, 32, 47 or 2, 5, 11, 23, 47, 95
(etc.)

26 (a) $3n$; (b) $2n - 1$; (c) n^2; (d) $3n + 1$; (e) $n/(n + 1)$

27 (a) 5, 7, 9, 11, 13, 15, ...
(b) 3, 8, 13, 18, 23, ...
(c) $\frac{1}{2}$, 2, $4\frac{1}{2}$, 8, $12\frac{1}{2}$, ...
(d) 0, 2, 6, 12, 20, ...
(e) $\frac{2}{3}$, $\frac{4}{4}$, $\frac{6}{5}$, $\frac{8}{6}$, $\frac{10}{7}$, ...

28 (a) $\frac{1}{8}$; (b) 7; (c) $\frac{1}{20}$; (d) 10; (e) $\frac{1}{50}$

29 (a) $\frac{3}{2}$; (b) $\frac{5}{4}$; (c) $\frac{10}{7}$; (d) $\frac{8}{5}$

30 (a) 0.8; (b) 5; (c) 0.16; (d) 0.08; (e) 0.04

C HAPTER SIX

1
(a) Multiply by 4
(b) Multiply by 3 and add 2
(c) Multiply by 2 and add 3

2 (a) 8; (b) 5; (c) 6; (d) 7; (e) 12

3
(a) $7 \times 10 = 70$; $70 \div 7 = 10$; $70 \div 10 = 7$
(b) $8 \times 9 = 72$; $72 \div 9 = 8$; $72 \div 8 = 9$

4 (a) 32; (b) 25

5 270

6 (a) √; (b) x; (c) √; (d) x

7
(a) I have just completed 9 problems and spent 5 minutes on each. That is 45 minutes altogether!
(b) It has just cost me £23.80 for 4 LPs. That is £5.95 each!
(c) Six children each have 11 marbles. That's 66 marbles altogether!

8
(a) (i) 70 cm; (ii) 14 cm; (iii) 320 m
(b) $P = 2(L + B) = 2L + 2B$

9 (a) 60 cm^2; (b) 34 cm

10 (a) $S = D/T$; (b) $D = S \times T$; (c) 50 mph

11 59°F

12 (a) £2; (b) £4 change

13 (a) $c = 20n$; (b) $d = s \times t$

14 (a) $C = 2n + 10$; (b) $C = 3000 + 50m$;
(c) $C = 20n + 150$

15 (a) $x = 2$; (b) $x = 4$; (c) $x = 3$;
(d) $x = 5$; (e) $x = 9$; (f) $x = 7$

16 (a) $x = 2$; (b) $x = 2$; (c) $x = 4$; (d) $x = 6$;
(e) $x = -3$

17 (a) $x = 3$; (b) $x = -10$; (c) $x = 11$
(d) $x = 3$; (e) $x = -4$; (f) $x = -9$

18 (a) $x = 3.464$; (b) $x = 7.746$; (c) $x = 14.142$

19 (a) $x = 2.714$; (b) $x = 3.684$; (c) $x = 4.642$

20 (a) $x = 3.162$; (b) $x = 2.885$; (c) $x = 1.862$

21 (a) $15a^5$; (b) $20a^9$; (c) $21m^7$; (d) $10n^9$

22 (a) $25x^6$; (b) $32a^{10}$; (c) $27x^9$; (d) $256a^8$

23 (a) $12a^3$ (b) $7a^2 + 5a^3$; (c) $4x^3 + 7y^2$

24

(a) number line with arrow pointing left, ending at 6, from −1 to 6

(b) number line with arrow pointing right, starting at −3, from −4 to 3

(c) number line with arrow pointing right, starting at 7, from 4 to 11

(d) number line with arrow pointing left, starting at −1, from −4 to 3

25

(a) arrow pointing right starting at 5, from 0 to 7 : $x > 5$

(b) arrow pointing left ending at 3, from −1 to 5 : $x < 3$

(c) arrow pointing left ending at −7, from −11 to −4 : $x < -7$

(d) arrow pointing right starting at 8, from 5 to 13 : $x > 8$

26

(a) arrow pointing left ending at 4, from −1 to 6 : $x < 4$

(b) arrow pointing right starting at −3, from −5 to 2 : $x > -3$

(c) arrow pointing right starting at 3, from −1 to 5 : $x > 3$

(d) arrow pointing right starting at −1, from −4 to 2 : $x > -1$

27

(a) segment between −2 and 2, from −3 to 2 : $x < 2, -2 < x$

(b) segment between −1 and 3, from −2 to 3 : $x < 3, -1 < x$

28 (a) $n = -4, -3, -2, -1, 0, 1, 2, \ldots 10$
(b) $n = 4, 5, 6, 7, 8, 9, 10$
(c) $n = -4, -3, -2, -1, 0, 1, 2$
(d) $n = -2, -1, 0, 1, 2, 3, 4$

29 (a) $x = 7.589$; (b) $b = 2.702$

30 (a) $x = 2.592$; (b) $x = 3.775$

31 (a) $x = 3.379$; (b) $x = 2.545$

32 (a) $x = 4.264$; (b) $x = 3$

33 (a) $x = 2.089$; (b) $x = 6.116$

34 (a) $x = 5 \ y = 2$ (c) $a = 2 \ b = 5$
(b) $x = 1 \ y = 3$ (d) $x = 2 \ y = 1$

35 (a) $x = 1 \ y = 4$ (c) $x = 5 \ y = 1$
(b) $a = 2 \ b = 2$ (d) $x = 3 \ y = 2$

36 (a) $x = 4 \ y = 1$ (c) $x = 3 \ y = 5$
(b) $a = 2 \ b = 0$ (d) $x = 1 \ y = 1$

37 (a) $x = 8 \ y = 1$ (c) $a = 6 \ b = 2$
(b) $x = 3 \ y = 1$ (d) $x = 10 \ y = 5$

CHAPTER SEVEN

1 HAND ME THAT PEN

2 (a) (1,1) (2,1) (0,0) (1,2) (3,2) (1,1)
(b) (0,2) (0,0) (3,2) (1,1) (3,1)
(c) (1,1) (1,3) (3,0) (0,3) (2,1) (1,0)

3 (a) Bog; (b) Pit; (c) Falls; (d) Lighthouse;
(e) (2,5); (f) (4,4), (g) (8,5); (h) (4,1) (i) Rock
Isle (7,1); (j) Snake Valley (2,3)

4

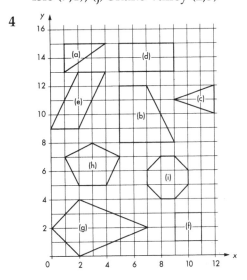

(a) right-angled triangle (b) trapezium
(c) isosceles triangle (d) rectangle
(e) parallelogram (f) square (g) kite
(h) pentagon (i) octagon

5 A (−6,3) E (6,0) I (2,−3)
B (−2,3) F (−5,0) J (5,−4)
C (1,5) G (−1,−2)
D (3,2) H (0,−4)

6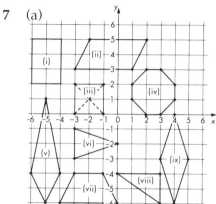

7 (a)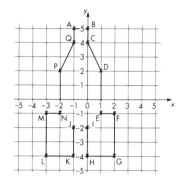

(b) (i) Rectangle (vi) Isosceles triangle
(ii) Parallelogram (vii) Trapezium
(iii) Square (viii) Right-angled
(iv) Octagon   triangle
(v) Kite (ix) Rhombus
(c) (–2,1)
(d) (–5,–4) (4,–3)

8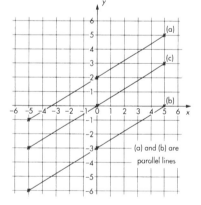

9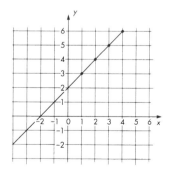

(a) x → x + 2
(b) y = x + 2

10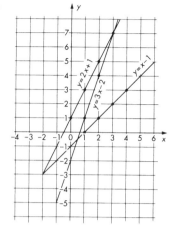

11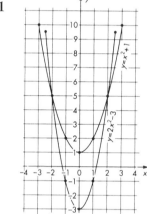

12 (a) $x = 2$ $y = 5$; (b) $x = 2$ $y = 3$

13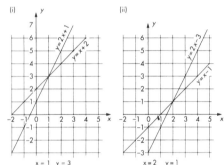

14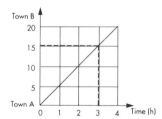

(a) Speed = 5 km/h; (b) 5 km from town B

15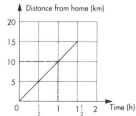

(a) $1\frac{1}{2}$ hours; (b) 5km from work

16 (a) £21; (b) £41; (c) £56

17

(a) £30; (b) £35; (c) £42.50

18 (a) (i) £2.40; (ii) £3.60 (iii) £5.40
(b) (i) $3.30; (ii) $8.40; (iii) $11.80

19 (a) (i) 28.5F; (ii) 38F; (iii) 61.75F
(b) (i) £0.65; (ii) £2.50; (iii) £3.15
(c) (i) 125F; (ii) £3.80; (iii) 25F; (iv) £4.40

20 (a) 10°C; (b) 30°C; (c) 60°C
(d) 59°F; (e) 77°F; (f) 122°F

CHAPTER EIGHT

1 (a) m; (b) mm; (c) cm; (d) l; (e) ml;
(f) kg; (g) t; (h) kg; (i) g

2 (a) mm or cm   (e) mm or cm
(b) cm or m   (f) l or ml or cl
(c) g or kg   (g) m or km
(d) l or ml or cl

3 (a) 4 m; (b) 1.8 m; (c) 60–80 cm; (d) 3 m

4 (a) 5 m; (b) 2 m; (c) 10 m; (d) 14 m

5 Individual answers

6 (a) 3–4 m   (e) 50–70 m
(b) 3–5 m   (f) 2–3 m
(c) 15–20 cm   (g) 3–8 mm
(d) 12–20 cm   (h) 6–10 m

7 Individual answers

8 Individual answers

9 Individual answers

10 (a) 3–4 hours   (d) 2–3 hours
(b) 1 hour   (e) 15–30 minutes
(c) 1 hour

11 (a) 2 hours; (b) $2\frac{1}{4}$–3 hours; (c) 14.40;
(d) 18.07

12 (a) (i) 2.1 cm; (ii) 1.9 cm; (iii) 1.8 cm
(b) (i) 21 mm; (ii) 19 mm; (iii) 18 mm

13 (a) 1.5 cm   (h) 0.25 m   (o) 0.75 km
(b) 9 cm   (i) 1500 cm
(c) 5 mm   (j) 2 m
(d) 110 mm   (k) 3 km
(e) 2.5 m   (l) 1.5 km
(f) 50 cm   (m) 3500 m
(g) 2.75 m   (n) 5250 m

14 (a) 1250 m; (b) (i) 5500 m; (ii) $5\frac{1}{2}$ km

15 (a) 130 cm; (b) 1.3 m

16 (a) (i) 500 ml; (ii) 50; (b) (i) 8000 ml; (ii) 20

17 (a) (i) 1500 g; (ii) 6 kg; (b) (i) 750 g; (ii) 650 g

18 (a) (i) 2″; (ii) 3″; (iii) 1″; (iv) $2\frac{1}{2}$″
(b) (i) 5 cm; (ii) 7.6 cm; (iii) 2.5 cm; (iv) 6.4 cm

19 (a) (i) 180 cm; (ii) 150 cm; (iii) 120 cm
(b) (i) 1.8 m; (ii) 1.5 m; (iii) 1.2 m
(c) (i) 6 ft; (ii) 5 ft; (iii) 4 ft

20 (a) (i) 6 miles; (ii) 12 miles; (iii) 14 miles
(b) (i) 9–10 km; (ii) 18–20 km; (iii) 22–24 km

21 (a) $4\frac{1}{2}$ l   (e) $3\frac{1}{2}$ pints
(b) 3 lb   (f) 20 lb
(c) $8\frac{3}{4}$ pints   (g) 60–70 kg
(d) 1 lb

22 (a) 1 degree   (d) 1 degree
(b) 1 s   (e) 1 s
(c) 5 mph   (f) 1 mm

23 (a) 1 cm   (f) 1 km or 1 mile
(b) 1 s   (g) $\frac{1}{100}$ s
(c) $\frac{1}{10}$ °C   (h) 1 mm
(d) $\frac{1}{10}$ s   (i) 1 mph
(e) 1 mm   (j) 1 ml

24

	Minimum–Maximum	Range
Height	184.5 cm – 185.499 cm	185 ± 0.5 cm
Weight	127.5 kg – 128.499 kg	128 ± 0.5 kg
Reach	64.5 cm – 65.499 cm	65 ± 0.5 cm
Neck	33.5 cm – 34.499 cm	34 ± 0.5 cm
Biceps	25.5 cm – 26.499 cm	26 ± 0.5 cm

25

	Minimum	Maximum
Aston Villa	26 500	27 499
Stoke City	10 500	11 499
Port Vale	8500	9499
Chesterfield	2500	3499

26 (a) 245; (b) 254

27 8.95 m; 6.38 m²

28 (a) 8 cm²   (d) Approx. 17 cm²
(b) 10 cm²   (e) Approx. 30 cm²
(c) 12 cm²

29 (a) 16 cm^3 (d) 30 cm^3
    (b) 48 cm^3 (e) 26 cm^3
    (c) 24 cm^3 (f) 28 cm^3

30 (a) 7811; (b) 8611; (c) 8713

31 (a) Hospital; (b) Uttley Water; (c) Youth Hostel

32 (a) C3; (b) B3; (c) A4

33 (a) Police Station; (b) Cricket ground; (c) Church

34 C1

35 (a) (i) (1,2); (ii) (3,2); (iii) (5,0); (iv) (5,3); (v) (4,5)
    (b) (i) Ted; (ii) Tim; (iii) Ray; (iv) Dot; (v) Pat
    (c) (i) (1,5); (ii) (4,2)

36 (a) Palm Grove; (b) Lookout; (c) Wreck; (d) Lagoon

37 (a) (–3,–1); (b) (2,–4); (c) (–1,0); (d) (–2,4)

38 (a) Lookout (-4,1)
    (b) Shark Bay (2,4) or Devil's Isle (5,4)

39 (a) D (–4,1); (b) D (–3,0); (c) D (–4,-3)

40

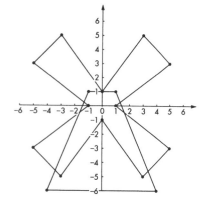

41 ∠ABC = 30° ∠PQR = 80° ∠VWX = 105°
    ∠STU = 130° ∠RST = 30° ∠BCD = 70°
    ∠TUV = 130° ∠CDE = 155°

42 ∠B = 30°, acute   ∠E = 50°, acute
    ∠K = 68°, acute   ∠N = 110°, obtuse
    ∠T = 300°, reflex   ∠H = 105°, obtuse
    ∠Q = 74°, acute

43

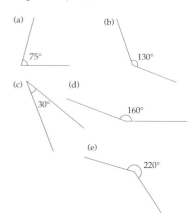

44 (a) 8 cm by 6 cm   (d) $1\frac{1}{2}$ m
    (b) 4 m by 3 m
    (c) 3 cm

45 Individual answers

46 (a) 15 km; (b) 6 cm

47 (a) $\frac{1}{2}$ km; (b) 4 km; (c) 30 cm

48 (a) $2\frac{1}{2}$ km; (b) 4–$4\frac{1}{2}$ km; (c) $2\frac{1}{2}$ km

49 (a) 60 mph; (b) 10 m/s; (c) 10 miles; (d) $1\frac{1}{2}$ h

50 (a) km; (b) m; (c) mph; (d) km/h; (e) s; (f) s

51 600 km

52 20 minutes

53 12 km/h

54 1.5 g/cm^3

55 20 kg

56 5 g/cm^3

57 (a) 31.4 cm; (b) 18.84 cm; (c) 25.12 cm

58 (a) 78.5 cm^2; (b) 314 cm^2;
    (c) 200.96 cm^2

59 (a) 1.61 cm; (b) 4.92 m; (c) 17 cm

60 5.59 m

61 (a) 15 m; (b) 5.13 m; (c) 28.28 cm

62 13.23 m

63 47.17 km

64 (a) 2.24 m (b) 4.15 m

65 (a) No; (b) Yes

CHAPTER NINE

1 (a) Acute; (b) Obtuse; (c) Acute; (d) Right angle

2 (a) KL, IJ; (b) EF and CD; (c) Yes, EF; (d) CD

3 (a) 30°, acute; (b) 100°, obtuse;
    (c) 250°, reflex; (d) 55°, acute

4 (a) There are two handles on the cup
    (b) There are two steering wheels in the car
    (c) There are two clips on the pen top

5   (a)   (b)   (c)

(d)   (e)

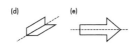
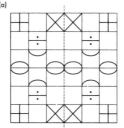

6 (a)   (b)

7 (a)

STAN	ИAT2
John	ndol
FREDA	AGƎЯꟻ
Hajid	bijɒH

(b)
Derek
~~Ɗǝɹǝk~~
Fiona
~~ɒnoᵌꟻ~~

8 (a,c) (c,d) (b,d)

9 (a) a = 149°   b = 31°   c = 149°
(b) d = 77°   e = 77°   f = 103°
(c) g = 166°   h = 14°
(d) i = 81°   j = 72°

10 (a) a = 141°   b = 141°   c = 39°
(b) i = 66°   j = 114°
(c) m = 43°   n = 137°   p = 68°

11 (a) 86°, 44°, 50°; (b) 107°, 29°, 44°

12 (a) a = 61°; (b) b = 66°; (c) c = 41°

13 360°

14 (a) Isosceles; (b) Scalene; (c) equilateral;
(d) Right-angled isosceles; (e) Right-angled;
(f) Scalene

15 (a) 52°; (b) 119°; (c) 97°;
(d) 45°; (e) 69°; (f) 100°

16 (a) 60°; (b) 70°; (c) 40°;
(d) 45°; (e) 100°; (f) 71°

17 (a) 047°; (b) 106°; (c) 270°; (d) 310°; (e) 205°;
(f) 165°; (g) 065°; (h) 240°

18 (a) 047°; (b) 270°; (c) 135°; (d) 342°

19 minesweeper   015°–020°
destroyer   075°–080°
aircraft carrier   135°
frigate   225°
patrol boat   315°

20 (a) AB = CD   (d) AC = BD
(b) BC = AD   (e) ∠AXD = ∠BXC
(c) AX = BX = CX = DX (f) ∠AXB = ∠CXD

21 (a) EF = EH = FG = GH   (d) FH
(b) EX = FX = GX = HX   (e) 90°
(c) EG = FH

22 (a) JK = LM   (d) KX = MX
(b) KL = JM   (e) ∠KJX = ∠MLX
(c) JX = LX   (f) ∠KMJ = ∠MKL

23 (a) PQ = RQ   (d) 90°
(b) PS = RS   (e) ∠PQX = ∠RQX
(c) PX = RX   (f) ∠PSX = ∠RSX

24

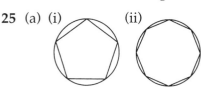

(a) 4   (b) 12
(c) 24
(d) 4
(e) Rhombuses; triangles, hexagons

25 (a) (i)   (ii)

(b) 72°, 45°

26 (a) (i) Order 5;
(ii) Order 8

(b)

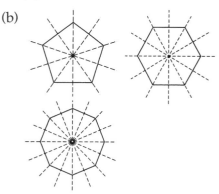

(c) The hexagon will tessellate

27 (i)   (ii)

Order 2
The rhombus will
tessellate

Order 4
The square will
tessellate

(iii)   (iv)

Order 2
The parallelogram will
tessellate

Order 1
The kite will tessellate

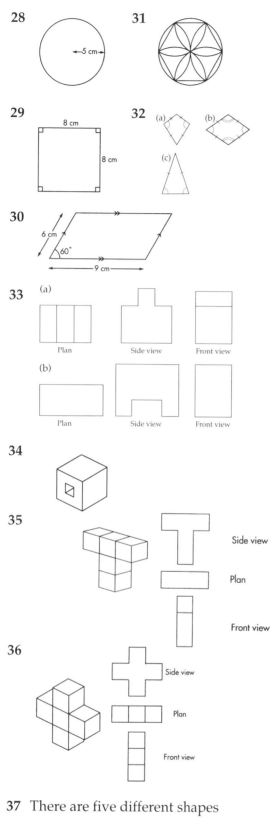

28

31

29

32 (a) (b) (c)

30

33 (a)

Plan   Side view   Front view

(b)

Plan   Side view   Front view

34

35

Side view

Plan

Front view

36

Side view

Plan

Front view

37 There are five different shapes

38 Individual answers

39 H, N, S, Z

40 (a) Yes; (b) Yes; (c) No; (d) Yes

41 (a) No; (b) Yes; (c) No

42 (a) 3; (b) 4; (c) 5

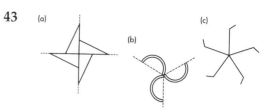

43 (a) (b) (c)

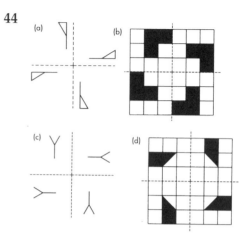

44 (a) (b) (c) (d)

45

(a) A H I M O T U V W X Y

(b) B C D E H I K O X

H, I, O and X have two axes of symmetry

(c) N I O X Z

H, I, O and X have both reflective and rotational symmetry

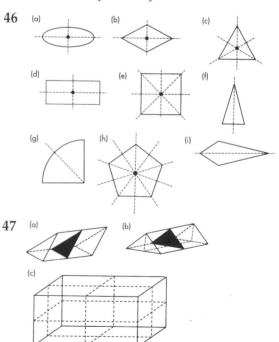

46 (a) (b) (c) (d) (e) (f) (g) (h) (i)

47 (a) (b) (c)

48 (a)

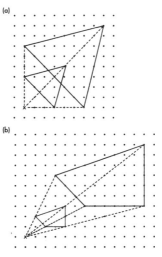

(b)

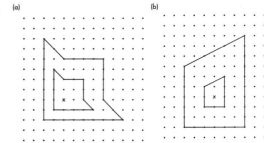

49 (a)   (b)

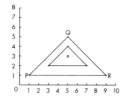

50

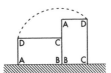

51

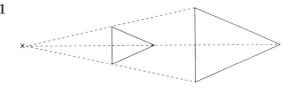

52 (d,f); (a,g); (c,e);
b is the 'odd one out'

53 a, d, f, h

54

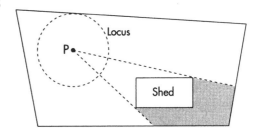

55

56

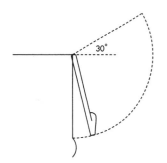

57

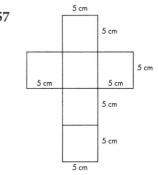

5 cm

5 cm

5 cm

5 cm   5 cm   5 cm

5 cm

5 cm

5 cm

58

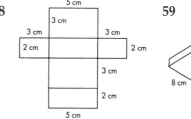

5 cm
3 cm
3 cm   3 cm
2 cm   2 cm
3 cm
2 cm
5 cm

59

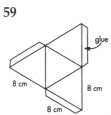

glue

8 cm   8 cm

8 cm

CHAPTER TEN

1

Number of goals scored	Tally	Frequency
0	⦀⦀ ⦀⦀ ⦀⦀⦀⦀	14
1	⦀⦀ ⦀⦀ ⦀⦀	12
2	⦀⦀ ⦀⦀ ⦀⦀	15
3	⦀⦀ ⦀⦀⦀	8
4	⦀⦀⦀	3
Total		52

2 Class interval

0–10	11–20	21–30	31–40	41–50	51–60
Frequency					
1	1	5	8	6	7

Class interval

61–70	71–80	81–90	91–100
Frequency			
8	6	6	2

3

Class interval	Tally	Frequency
35–39 kg	⦀⦀⦀	5
40–44 kg	⦀⦀⦀ ⦀	6
45–49 kg	⦀⦀⦀	5
50–54 kg	⦀⦀⦀ ⦀⦀⦀	8

55–59 kg	‖	3
60–64 kg	‖	3
65–69 kg		0
Total		30

Class interval
35–39 40–44 45–49 50–54 55–59 60–64 65–69
Frequency
    5   6   5   8   3   3   0

4   Individual answers

5
Time in minutes	Tally	Frequency
$15 \le t < 20$		0
$20 \le t < 25$	‖	2
$25 \le t < 30$	‖|	3
$30 \le t < 35$	‖‖		6
$35 \le t < 40$	‖‖ ‖|	8
$40 \le t < 45$	‖‖ ‖|	8
Total		27

6   **Class interval**
$0 \le d < 5\ 5 \le d < 10\ 10 \le d < 15\ 15 \le d < 20\ 20 \le d < 25$
Frequency
    6   12   11   7   8

7–11 Individual answers

CHAPTER ELEVEN

1
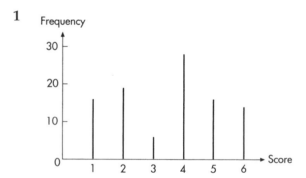

The die is not fair. It is biased towards 4 (with 3 on the reverse face)

2   (a) Sunday; (b) It was a hot day and children are at home; (c) Thursday; (d) The weather was bad; (e) 90; (f) 460

3
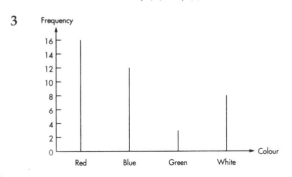

4   Individual answers

5   (a) His temperature was going down
(b) Between noon and 2.00 p.m.
(c) 34°C

6   (a) Yes; (b) No; (c) Week 3;
(d) There is no week $1\frac{1}{2}$ test

7
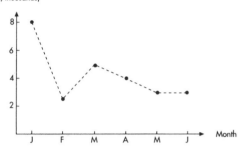

(a) The figure is high for January because of the January sales

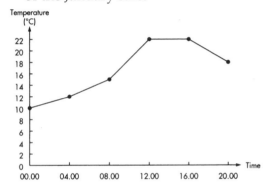

(b) 20°C

8   (a) 30 pupils
(b) The results are good for most of the class but there are a few low scores
(c) It is very good; he is in the top group
(d) The test is 'out of 50'

9
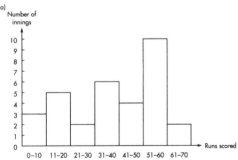

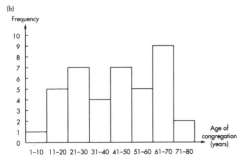

10 (a) Range = 21

(b)

Score

61–65	66–70	71–75	76–80	81–85

Frequency

1	9	17	11	7

(c)

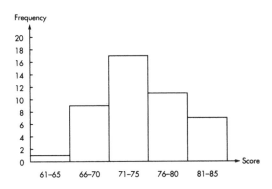

'Par for the course' is probably in the class interval 71–75. There were more golfers over par than under par. This could be due to either poor weather or a poor standard of play.

11 (a) 12

(b) Between 4.00–6.00 p.m. and between 11.00 a.m.–1.00 p.m.

(c) The children were asleep

(d)

Time	midnight–4.00 a.m.	4–8.00 a.m.	8.00 a.m.–noon
Accidents	2	8	27

Time	noon–4.00 p.m.	4–8.00 p.m.	8.00 p.m.–midnight
Accidents	22	32	6

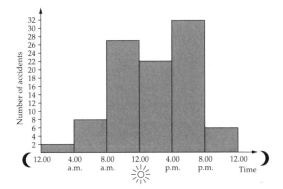

12 (a) (i) 2; (ii) 5; (iii) 3; (iv) 10

(b) (i) $\frac{1}{10}$; (ii) $\frac{1}{4}$; (iii) $\frac{3}{20}$; (iv) $\frac{1}{2}$

(c) (i)

(ii) $\frac{1}{12}$; $\frac{1}{4}$; $\frac{1}{4}$; $\frac{5}{12}$

13 (a) (i) 30%; (ii) 10% (iii) 40%; (iv) 20%

(b) Bus, 150; Car, 50; Walk, 200; Cycle, 100

(c)

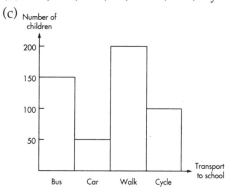

The pie chart shows each section as a fraction of the whole group. Bar charts only compare one section with another.

14

Activity	Number of hours	Angle
Sleeping	8	$8 \times 15 = 120°$
School	5	$5 \times 15 = 75°$
Homework	2	$2 \times 15 = 30°$
TV	3	$3 \times 15 = 45°$
Playing	4	$4 \times 15 = 60°$
Eating	2	$2 \times 15 = 30°$
Total	24	360°

15 (a)

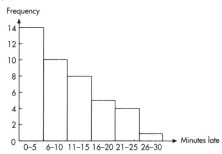

There was a distinct improvement

(b)

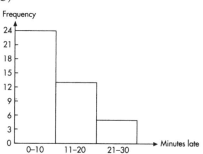

(c)

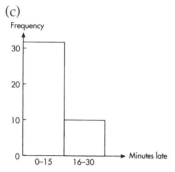

The class intervals are too wide to show an accurate picture of the results

16

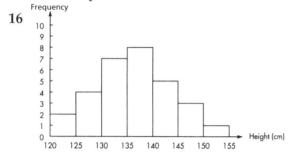

17

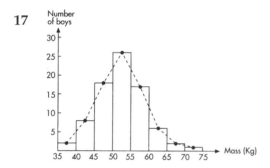

18

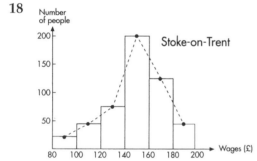

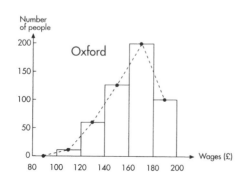

Higher wages are paid to a greater number of workers from Oxford. The cost of living is higher in Oxford so there are not so many low paid workers.

19

Grades	1	2	3	4	5	6
English	0	2	8	18	20	6
Maths	2	6	12	16	14	4

20 100 drawing pins
(a) yes; (b) yes; (c) no

21 40 matches
(a) yes; (b) no; (c) no

22 (a) 21 years; (b) 29 years

23 (a) 20 minutes; (b) 14 minutes;
(c) He cycles downhill on his journey home

24 (a) 2.5 goals; (b) 2.5 goals; (c) 7 goals;
(d) 1 goal; (e) Vale are more consistent than City at scoring goals.

25 (a) Jenny, 53%; Angie, 52%
(b) Jenny, 17%; Angie, 69%
(c) A matter of opinion, although Jenny scores more consistently than Angie
(d) John 53.8%; Tavid, 62.8%

26

Class interval in years	Mid-value	Fre-quency	Mid-value × frequency
20–29	24.5	10	245
30–39	34.5	15	517.5
40–49	44.5	20	890
50–59	54.5	26	1417
60–69	64.5	30	1935
70–79	74.5	19	1415.5
Total		120	6420.0

Mean = 53.5 years of age

27

Class interval in days	Mid-value	Fre-quency	Mid-value × frequency
1–5	3	2	6
6–10	8	7	56
11–15	13	9	117
16–20	18	14	252
21–25	23	8	184
26–30	28	4	112
31–35	33	2	66
36–40	38	3	114
41–45	43	1	43
Total		50	950

Mean = 19 days

28 Individual results

29 (a) Mean = 1.8 goals (b) Median = 2 goals
(c) Modal score = 2 goals (d) Range = 5 goals

30 (a) Mode = 5.1; median = 5.2; mean = 5.2
(b) This procedure removes any bias in the results to give a misleading high or low score (c) Mean = 5.2; range = 0.3

31 Individual results

32 Individual results

33 (a) Team A, mean = 2 goals;
   Team B, mean = 2 goals
   (b) Team B

34 (a)

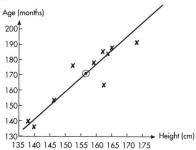

Positive correlation

(b)

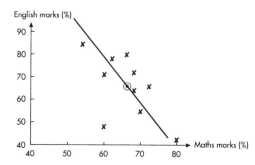

Negative correlation

(c)

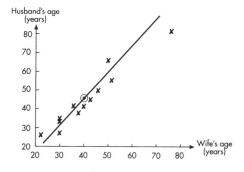

Positive correlation

35 See above diagrams

HAPTER TWELVE

1–9

Statement	Probability
The sun will set today	1
You own a wrist-watch	
Mum does the ironing	
You will have homework tonight	
	$\frac{1}{2}$
You have brown eyes	
You prefer tea to coffee	
Your dad does the ironing	
You are left-handed	
The oceans will freeze over	0

10 (a) $\frac{1}{6}$; (b) $\frac{1}{6}$; (c) $\frac{1}{6}$

11 (a) $\frac{1}{4}$, we have chips twice a week most weeks
   (b) $\frac{1}{50}$, it does not snow on Christmas Day very often
   (c) $\frac{1}{4}$, many people own dogs

12 If red skirt = RS; red jumper = RJ;
   green skirt = GS; green jumper = GJ;
   blue skirt = BS; and blue jumper = BJ
   then the 9 combinations are:
   (RS,RJ) (RS,GJ) (RS,BJ) (GS,GJ) (GS,BJ)
   (GS,RJ) (BS,BJ) (BS,RJ) (BS,GJ)

13 The 6 combinations are:
   (M,W,C) (M,C,W) (W,M,C) (W,C,M)
   (C,M,W) (C,W,M)

14 If heads = H; and tails = T then the
   12 combinations are:
   (H,6) (H,5) (H,4) (H,3) (H,2) (H,1)
   (T,6), (T,5) (T,4) (T,3) (T,2) (T,1)

15 The 4 combinations are:
   (1,4) (4,1) (2,3) (3,2)

16 Individual results

17 Individual results

18 Symmetry

19 Survey

20 Survey

21 Symmetry

22 $\frac{1}{5}$

23 $\frac{1}{50}$

24 $\frac{1}{7}$

25 $\frac{1}{12}$

26 $\frac{13}{52}$ or $\frac{1}{4}$

27 (a)

Dice	1	2	3	4	5	6
Head	H,1	H,2	H,3	H,4	H,5	H,6
Tails	T,1	T,2	T,3	T,4	T,5	T,6

(b)

			Blue			
	1	**2**	**3**	**4**	**5**	**6**
1	1,1	1,2	1,3	1,4	1,5	1,6
2	2,1	2,2	2,3	2,4	2,5	2,6
Red 3	3,1	3,2	3,3	3,4	3,5	3,6
4	4,1	4,2	4,3	4,4	4,5	4,6
5	5,1	5,2	5,3	5,4	5,5	5,6
6	6,1	6,2	6,3	6,4	6,5	6,6

(c)

Ace / Coin	♥	♣	♦	♠
Head	H, ♥	H, ♣	H, ♦	H, ♠
Tail	T, ♥	T, ♣	T, ♦	T, ♠

28 If red = R; amber = A; and green = G, then the 27 combinations are:

(R,R,R)	(R,R,A)	(R,R,G)
(R,G,R)	(R,G,G)	(R,G,A)
(R,A,R)	(R,A,A)	(R,A,G)
(A,R,R)	(A,R,G)	(A,R,A)
(A,G,R)	(A,G,G)	(A,G,A)
(A,A,R)	(A,A,G)	(A,A,A)
(G,R,R)	(G,R,G)	(G,R,A)
(G,G,R)	(G,G,G)	(G,G,A)
(G,A,R)	(G,A,G)	(G,A,A)

29 (a) $\frac{3}{7}$; (b) $\frac{2}{7}$; (c) $\frac{4}{6}$ or $\frac{2}{3}$; (d) $\frac{5}{6}$; (e) $\frac{11}{20}$

30 (a) $\frac{5}{6}$; (b) $\frac{1}{10}$, $\frac{9}{10}$; (c) $\frac{3}{7}$; (d) $\frac{5}{9}$; (e) $\frac{7}{10}$; (f) $\frac{49}{50}$

31 25

32 25

33 25

34 90

35 about 33

36–45 Individual answers

A NSWERS TO PRACTICE NATIONAL TEST QUESTIONS

NUMBER

1 (a) 47 miles   (b) 108 miles   (c) 110 miles

> *Examiner's tip* 1 mark for part (a) correct; 1 mark for **both** (b) and (c) correct.

2 (a) 234   (b) 432   (c) 0   (d) 2340
(e) (i) 234 (ii) 2340

> *Examiner's tip* Putting a nought on the end of a decimal number does not alter its value. You have to move the decimal point.

3 (a) 50% of 48 = 24   40 − 16 = 24
   10 + 14 = 24   2.4 x 10 = 24
   25% of 96 = 24   8 x 3 = 24
(b) 20 ÷ 4 + 19 = 24

> *Examiner's tip* There would be 3 marks for part (a); you would score 1 mark for each **pair** of correct answers.

4 (a) Carlos only has 40 eggs so he could not possibly need 240 boxes.
(b) 6 boxes
(c) 4 eggs left over
(d) 4 boxes

> *Examiner's tip* Try to write sensible explanations using good English. You can use numbers to help you with your explanation.

5 (a)   £135
      ×   35
      ─────
       675
      4050
      ─────
     £4725   – He was
          wrong!

(b)   14 sets
   135)2000
       135↓
       ───
       650
       540
       ───
       110

He can order 14 sets

> *Examiner's tip* A correct answer by itself will not get you the mark. You must show your working out.

6 (a) $\frac{3}{4}$ (b) 225 calories

> *Examiner's tip* Your answer to part (a) should be in its lowest terms but any equivalent fraction will get you the mark, e.g. $\frac{6}{8}$.

7 (a)   10% of £380 = £38.00
       5% of £380 = £19.00
      $2\frac{1}{2}$% of £380 = £9.50
      ────────────────────────
      $17\frac{1}{2}$% of £380 = £66.50

(b)   10% of £60 = £6.00
      20% of £60 = £12.00
       5% of £60 = £3.00
      ────────────────────
      35% of £60 = £21.00

(c)   10% of £60 = £6.00
      10% of £60 = £6.00
      $2\frac{1}{2}$% of £60 = £1.50
      ────────────────────
      $22\frac{1}{2}$% of £60 = £13.50

> *Examiner's tip* Take extra care when working out your initial 10%. You could be halving a wrong answer making everything else wrong!

8 (a) $\boxed{-4} \times \boxed{+2} = \boxed{-8}$

   $\boxed{-4} \times \boxed{-2} = \boxed{+8}$

(b) $\boxed{-4} - \boxed{+8} = -12$

(c) $\boxed{-4} - \boxed{-8} = +4$

> *Examiner's tip* Both the correct card **and** correct answer must be present to get the mark for part (b) and for part (c).

9 (a) 20 to 10 is halving, i.e. a decrease of 50%
(b) 25% increase; 20% decrease

> *Examiner's tip* You must use Rosie's figures and mention '50%' or 'half' in your answer to get the mark.

10 (a) 250 3 100 5 25000
  (b) Mr Blockhead's mistake may have been to forget to put a zero down when multiplying by the tens number.
  (c)
$$
\begin{array}{r}
258 \\
\times \quad 96 \\
\hline
1548 \\
23220 \\
\hline
24768 \\
\hline
\end{array}
$$

> **Examiner's tip** A rough estimate means exactly that. It is better to use 250 than 260 in part (a) i.e. rounding off to the nearest 50 not to the nearest 10.

11 (a) Shop A is the cheapest (b) £96

> **Examiner's tip** Show your working for all **three** shops to get full marks.

12 (a) 110 (b) $\frac{3}{22}$ (c) 1 : 1.2 (d) 80% (e) 0.8

> **Examiner's tip** Make sure that you are using the correct group of people to work out your answers, e.g. what fraction of **pupils** or what percentage of **girls** etc.

13

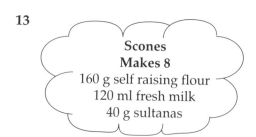

Scones
Makes 8
160 g self raising flour
120 ml fresh milk
40 g sultanas

> **Examiner's tip** You will get 2 marks for all three correct answers. You will only get 1 mark if you only get 1 or 2 of the ingredients correct.

14 The first road sign is the best because the population is never known exactly at any moment. People are always dying or being born or moving in and out of the area.

> **Examiner's tip** There would be 2 marks for this question and you would need to give two reasons for your choice to get both marks.

15 (a) 99.5 km (b) 100.49 km (or 100.5 km)
  (c) 100.5 ÷ 9.5 = 10.58 km/min.

> **Examiner's tip** To get part (c) right you must get the answer to part (b) right. You could get the mark for part (c) for using the correct method even though your answer is wrong.

16 (a) 30375 (b) 25 (c) 5500 (d) 2.5×10^6
  (e) Card B ÷ Card E

> **Examiner's tip** Your answer to part (d) must be in standard form to get the mark.

ALGEBRA

1 Kevin puts in the cash.
  Kevin closes the safe door.
  Kevin locks the safe door.

> **Examiner's tip** There would be 2 marks for all three correct answers. You will only get 1 mark if you only get 1 or 2 correct answers.

2 (a) 35 (b) 6

> **Examiner's tip** Run your answer to part (b) through the machine and check to see that you get 17 at the end.

3

INPUT	OUTPUT
4	9
6	29
7	42
9	74
10	93

> **Examiner's tip** There would be a total of 3 marks for 4 correct answers. You would get 1 mark for 1 correct answer and 2 marks for 2 or 3 correct answers.

4 (a) Sam and Craig
   (b) Both Sam and Craig state that there are
       '5 lots of n sweets plus 2 left over.'
   (c) $2 + 5n = 42$ (d) $n = 8$

Examiner's tip You must get both children in
part (a) right to get the mark.

5 (a) x^2 (b) $x + x$ and $2 \times x$
   (c) $3x$ $x + x + x$ $2x + x$ (d) $2x + 5$

Examiner's tip You must get both cards correct
to get the mark in part (b) and all three correct
in part (c) to get that mark.

6 (a) $x = 2$ (b) $x + y = 5$ (c) $(2, 3)$

Examiner's tip Put the brackets around your
co-ordinates in part (c). You might get
penalised otherwise.

7 (a) £21   (b) £20   (c) $C = 8 + 3n$

Examiner's tip Make sure you write a full
equation in part (c), i.e. use the ' = ' sign.

8 (a) $x = 6$ (b) $x = 6$ (c) $x = 7$

Examiner's tip Try substituting your answers
back into the equations to see if they are
correct.

9 (a) 18, 22   (b) 12, 17   (c) 32, 57

Examiner's tip There would be 2 marks for part
(c) because it is more difficult.

10 (a) All the lines are parallel with a
       gradient of 2.
   (b) The number by itself shows where the
       line crosses the y-axis.
   (c) $(0, -7)$ (d) Individual answers

Examiner's tip There would be 2 marks for part
(d). The equation of the line depends on where
you drew your line.

11 (a) $g = 19$ (b) $f = -6$ (c) $h = 5$ or -5
   (d) $x = 10$ and $y = 3$

Examiner's tip 1 mark for each part. Again
substitute your answers back into the equation
to see if they are correct.

12
n	$n^2 - n$	
5.35	23.2725	too big
5.33	23.0789	too big
5.32	22.9824	too small
5.322	23.001684	too big
5.321	22.992041	too small

   Answer = 5.322 to 3 decimal places

Examiner's tip This is a valuable question
worth 4 marks. Even if you end up with the
wrong answer you could get up to 3 marks by
showing all your trials.

13 $y \geq 2x$ and $y \leq x + 3$

Examiner's tip Check a point inside the region,
say (1, 3), to see if it satisfies the inequalities.

14 (a) 17   (b) 6 + 1 (2nd stage);
       9 + 1 (3rd stage); $3n + 1$ (nth stage)
       – alternatively 5 + 2 (2nd stage);
       7 + 3 (3rd stage); $(2n + 1) + n = 3n + 1$
       (nth stage)
   (c) $3 \times 10 + 1 = 31$

Examiner's tip You must get the expression for
the nth stage in part (b) and use it to answer
part (c) to get full marks.

SHAPE, SPACE AND MEASURES

1 (a) Angle C
   (b) Angle B and Angle E
   (c) Acute angle

Examiner's tip Both angles must be correct to
get the mark in part (b).

2 (a) South   (b) 3

Examiner's tip Part (b) asks for the number of
right angles not degrees.

3 (a)   (b) A, B, and E

(c) order 6

> **Examiner's tip** All lines of symmetry must be drawn, with no extra ones, to get the mark in part (a).

4 (a) 12 (b) 6 (c) 48 (d) 6 (e) 10 (f) 13

> **Examiner's tip** In parts (a), (c) and (d) there are hidden squares. These must be included to get the marks.

5 (a)   (b)

(c) ✓; ✗; ✓

> **Examiner's tip** Use a ruler in part (a).

6 (a) The length of the insect is 2 inches or 5.08 centimetres.
(b) The volume of cola is 2 litres or 3.521 pints.
(c) The weight of the jam is 2 pounds or 908 grams.

> **Examiner's tip** **Both** answers to each part must be correct to get the mark.

7 (a) 3.5 cm (b) 0.75 m (c) 2.5 km
(d) 0.330 litres (e) 2750 g (f) 4000 mm

> **Examiner's tip** Ask yourself whether the number needs to be bigger or smaller before you make the conversion.

8 (a)   (b)

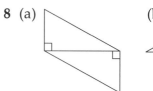

(c) Isosceles triangle
(d)

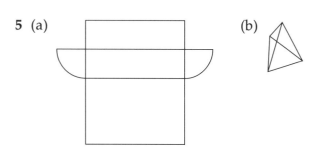

> **Examiner's tip** 2 marks for part (d) but they must be a different shape.

9 (a) 3 m, 4 m and 5 m
(b) 3 m, 3 m and 4 m or 3 m, 3 m and 5 m
(c) 7 m, 4 m and 3 m or 7 m, 3 m and 3 m

> **Examiner's tip** There are alternative answers for parts (b) and (c). Either will do.

10 (a) Any two of $B\hat{A}D$ $E\hat{B}C$ $C\hat{F}E$ $F\hat{E}H$
$E\hat{D}G$ $E\hat{H}G$ $F\hat{I}H$
(b) 120°   (c) 8

> **Examiner's tip** Both angles must be correct to get the mark in part (a).

11 (a)
(b)
(c)

(d) 90° rotation in an anti-clockwise direction about the origin

> **Examiner's tip** There will be two marks for part (d). You will only get both marks for a **full** description.

12

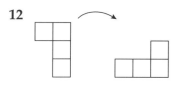
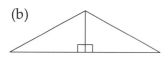

> **Examiner's tip** Use a ruler and put them in the correct order for full marks.

13 (a) 64.95 or 65 mm^2
(b) 12990 or 13000 mm^3
(c)

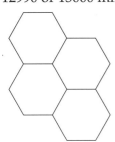

> If you get part (a) wrong you will also get part (b) wrong. You could get the mark for part (b) with a correct method even though your answer is wrong.

14 (a) 10 cm (b) 20 cm (c) 10 cm (d) 14 cm

> Use the information sheet for the correct formulae.

15 (a) 255° (b) 120°

> There will be 2 marks for each part of this question. You will get 1 mark for identifying the other angle in the triangle as 75° even if you get the bearings wrong.

16 (a)

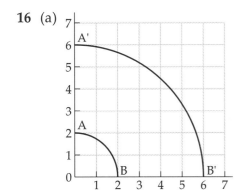

(b) 3.14 cm
(c) 28.26 cm^2

> Use a compass and the correct value for π.

17 (a) No
(b) Either pencil could be between 9.5 and 10.5 cm.

> You must put both upper and lower limits to get the mark in part (b).

18 (a)

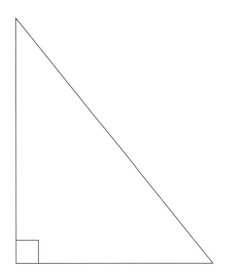

(b) between 83 and 86 km
(c) SL^2 = 65^2 + 54^2
   = 4225 + 2916
   = 7141
SL = 84.5 km

> This is a valuable question. Be accurate in your drawing for 3 marks. Measure the distance in part (b) to the nearest mm. You must show your **full** working out to get all the marks in part (c).

19

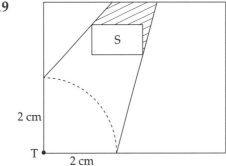

> Use a compass and ruler to get full marks.

20 (a) 2.65 m (b) 3.87 m

> Give a realistic answer to part (b) – not what your calculator says.

HANDLING DATA

1 (a) Mondeo Red   (b) 25   (c) Escort

> **Examiner's tip** 1 mark for each part. Both model and colour must be correct to get the mark in part (a).

2

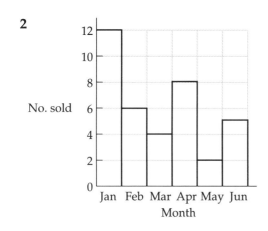

> **Examiner's tip** There would be 1 mark for each correct height of bar.

3 (a)

(b) Vale scored more goals. City steadily improved their scoring record.

> **Examiner's tip** There would be 1 mark for completing the Vale pictogram correctly and 1 mark for each pair of City's pictogram correctly completed. Part (b) would also carry 2 marks.

4 (a) False   (b) False   (c) False

(d)

(e) ▲ There are more blue triangles than white circles.

> **Examiner's tip** There would be 1 mark for each part but part (d) must be in the correct order.

5 (a) 15 years   (b) 20 − 11 = 9 years
(c) 10, 13, 18 and 19 (there are other possibilities)

> **Examiner's tip** The range is a definite number – not from lowest to highest. The correct answer is 9 **not** 11 to 20.

6 (a) Rangers: 2 goals   Rovers: 2 goals
(b) Rangers had the better start because they scored in 4 out of the 5 matches which means they could have won these matches.
or
Rovers had the better start because they could have won their last 2 games and drawn all the others.
Rangers could have drawn or lost more games.

> **Examiner's tip** In part (b) there would be 1 mark for the correct team and 1 mark for a good explanation.

7 Not everybody had a daily paper.
Some people only had a Sunday paper.
Morning papers were more popular than evening papers.
Some papers carried too many adverts.
Most people don't read the supplements .... plus many more!

> **Examiner's tip** There would be 1 mark for each sensible fact.

8 (a) Blue because it has the largest sector/area.
(b) Red because it has the smallest sector/area.
(c) The blue area is much bigger than the red area.
(d) The probability depends on the area and not the number of colours.
(e) 25%   (f) 0.4

> **Examiner's tip** You must get both answers in part (a) to get the mark.

9 (a) 25%

(b) No. The Taylors spent 25% of £800 which is £200.
The Greens spent 25% of £400 which is £100.

(c) The Taylor family spent most on entertainment because their sector is just under 25% of £800.
The Green family spent just under 25% of £400.

(d) **Wright family**

10 (a) You could put a person age 30 in two of the boxes. The age limits are not accurate enough.

(b) The question is too vague. All the descriptions have different meanings to different people.

(c) More than once a month ☐

Monthly ☐

Less than once a month ☐

Never ☐

(d) Fewer children will be at the 8.00 pm showing of any film.
The film might be very popular and attract people who normally don't go to the cinema.
The sample is not randomly selected .... plus more!

11 (a)

Interval	Frequency
0–4	10
5–9	8
10–14	10
15–19	6
20–24	5
25–29	1

(b)

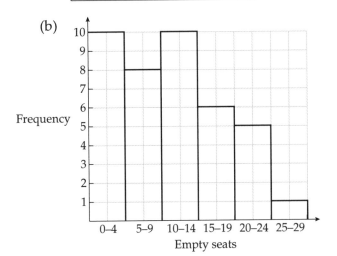

12 (a) $\frac{1}{6}$ (b) $\frac{4}{6}$ or $\frac{2}{3}$ (c) 0 (impossible)
(d) about 16

13 (a)

Josh

×	20	40	60
2	40	80	120
4	80	160	240
5	100	200	300

Rose

(b) 1 (certain)

(c)

Josh

÷	20	40	60
2	10	20	30
4	5	10	15
5	4	8	12

Rose

(d) $\frac{6}{9}$ or $\frac{2}{3}$

14 (a) $\frac{1}{36}$ (b) $\frac{5}{6}$ (c) $\frac{2}{36}$ or $\frac{1}{18}$

Examiner's tip There will be 2 marks for part (c). Show your working as you could get a mark for multiplying the wrong probabilities.

15 (a) 5 years   (b) 10 years
(c) 7 years and 13 years

Examiner's tip Parts (b) and (c) will carry 2 marks each. Show working for a possible method mark even if the answer is wrong.

16 (a) C   (b) A   (c) B

Examiner's tip There would be 1 mark for each part.

17

	Tally	Frequency
Speed **over** 70 mph		
Speed 70 mph or under		
Driver wearing seat belt		
Driver **not** wearing seat belt		
Front seat passenger wearing seat belt		
Front seat passenger **not** wearing seat belt		

Examiner's tip There would be 1 mark for each part of the question but you must have two sections in your chart relating to each hypothesis.

18 (a)

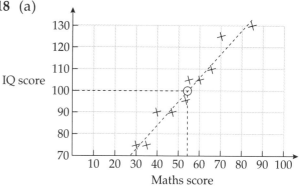

(b) The better you are at maths the higher your IQ score.
(c) Positive correlation
(c) Mean maths score 53.9; mean IQ score 100.
(d) See line drawn in part (a).
(e) 54

Examiner's tip Very valuable question. There would be 3 marks for plotting each point accurately. Plot the mean values (part (c)) as a point before you draw your line of best fit in part (d). Draw lines on your graph to show how you arrived at your answer to part (e).

19 (a) Andrew because he had more spins, i.e. the biggest experiment.
(b)

Number of throws	Both odd	Both even	One odd and one even
200	70	37	93

(c) P (both odd) $= \frac{70}{200}$ or $\frac{7}{20}$
(d)

Number of throws	Both odd	Both even	One odd and one even
500	180	80	240

(e) Perfect results are rare. The results would be round about these numbers but rarely exactly.

Examiner's tip Another valuable question. Use the results given and not what you think should happen.

20 (a)

Number of flowers	Mid-point (x)	Number (f) of shrubs	fx
0–4	2	8	16
5–9	7	16	112
10–14	12	36	432
15–19	17	30	510
20–24	22	10	220

(b) Mean $= \dfrac{16 + 112 + 432 + 510 + 220}{100}$

$= \dfrac{1290}{100} = 12.9$ flowers per shrub

(c) 10–14 flowers   (d) 12–13 flowers

(e) $\frac{60}{100}$ or $\frac{3}{5}$

Examiner's tip Check to see that your answers are sensible.

Glossary

acute angle An angle of less than 90°.
angle A measure of turn (rotation).
approximation A number which is accepted as an estimate of another number.
area The size of a surface (measured in square units).
arithmetic mean The average of a set of numbers, worked out by adding the numbers and dividing the total by the number of numbers in the set.
average A measure of centralness. This could be the arithmetic mean, mode or median.
average speed The total distance travelled divided by the total time taken.

bar graph A diagram using a set of bars, equal in width, whose lengths are proportional to a set of frequencies.
bearing An angle measured in a clockwise direction starting from North.
bias Unfair influence, e.g. weighted die.
bisect To cut in half.
brackets Symbols used to show those terms that are to be treated together.

capacity The amount of space enclosed; the internal volume.
Cartesian graph A pair of axes that intersect at right angles.
circumference The perimeter or boundary of a circle.
class interval The width of the class; the difference between the upper and lower class limits.
class limits The points at which one set of data is separated from the next set.
collate Collect together and put in order.
complementary angles A pair of angles, side by side, that make a 90° angle together.
composite shape A shape made up of two or more basic shapes.
congruent shapes Shapes identical in every respect but may be arranged in different positions.
continuous data Information gained by measurements.
co-ordinates An ordered pair of numbers (x, y) which determine the precise location of a point on a graph, map or plan.
cube A symmetrical block with all side lengths equal and made up of six square faces.
cubic number The third power of a number, e.g. $8 = 2^3$.
cuboid A rectangular-shaped block made up of six rectangular faces.
cumulative frequency A frequency distribution rewritten as a running total of previous frequencies.
cylinder A shape with uniform area of cross-section and circular ends, e.g. tin can, cigarette.

data Facts, figures or information which has been collected or given.
decimal notation Use of a decimal point to separate whole numbers from fractions, e.g. 2.35 m.
degree A unit of measurement for angles; usually denoted by the symbol °.
denominator The term on the bottom line of a common fraction.
density The mass per unit volume of an object.
diagonal A line joining any two corners of a shape which are not next to each other.
diameter A straight line passing through the centre of a circle from one side to the other.
difference The answer obtained when one number is subtracted from another.
dimensions Measurements such as length, width, height, thickness, etc.
directed numbers Numbers which have a positive (+) or negative sign (−) in front of them.
discrete data Information obtained by counting.
dispersion Variation in a set of data.

enlargement A transformation (change) which increases or decreases the size of a figure.
equation A statement of equality, written to show that two things are equal.
equilateral triangle A triangle with all three sides equal in length and all three angles equal to 60°.
equivalent fraction Fractions that have equal value but different numerator and denominator, e.g. $\frac{1}{2} = \frac{2}{4} = \frac{4}{8}$.
estimation A judgement of an approximate value or amount.
even number An integer that can be divided by 2 exactly. Even numbers end in 0, 2, 4, 6 or 8.

exterior angle An angle at a vertex of a polygon formed outside the shape by two adjacent sides, one of which has been extended outside the shape.

factorization The process by which any number or expression is broken down into its factors.
factors A number or expression by which a larger number can be divided exactly.
formula A mathematical rule or statement expressed in algebraic symbols.
frequency distribution A table of results showing how many times something occurs.
frequency polygon The shape formed by joining successive points in a frequency distribution with straight lines.

gradient The slope of a line in relation to the positive direction of the x axis.
grouped data Statistical data put into class intervals.

hexagon A six-sided polygon.
histogram A type of bar graph in which the *area* of the bars and not the lengths represents the data.
horizontal A flat line parallel to the earth's surface.
hypotenuse The longest side of a right-angled triangle.
hypothesis A guessed statement to be proved or disproved by further investigation.

imperial units Units of measure used in the UK; yards, miles, feet, inches, ounces, etc.
improper fraction One in which the top number (numerator) is bigger than the bottom number (denominator).
independent events Events which do not affect each other in any way.
indices Positive, negative or fractional numbers used to express the power to which the quantity is to be raised.
inequality A statement that one quantity is greater than or less than another.
integer A positive or negative whole number.
intercept The point at which two lines meet.
interior angle One of the inside angles of a closed shape made up of straight lines.
inverse operation The exact opposite function that gets you back to where you started, e.g. $5 \times 4 = 20$, $20 \div 4 = 5$.
isosceles triangle A triangle with two equal sides and two equal angles.

kite A quadrilateral with two pairs of adjacent sides equal in length.

like terms Algebraic terms that can be added or subtracted because they have the same letters to the same power.
linear expressions Algebraic expressions not involving powers of the unknown variable, e.g. x, y.
locus The path of a moving object.
lowest common multiple The smallest common multiple of two or more numbers.
lowest terms Used to describe a fraction that has been cancelled down to its simplest form.

mapping A description of how one set of numbers can be linked to another.
mass The quantity of matter that a body contains.
mean *See* arithmetic mean.
median The middle member of a set which has been arranged in order of size.
metric units Units of measure that are based on the decimal system.
mixed number A number that contains a whole number with a fraction, e.g. $\frac{3}{4}$.
mode The most frequently occurring number in a set.
multiple A number that has another number as one of its factors, e.g. 30 is a multiple of 10.
mutually exclusive events Events which cannot happen at the same time.

natural numbers Positive, whole numbers (integers).
negative numbers Numbers, with a minus sign in front of them, to signify a negative quantity.
net A flat shape that can be folded to make a solid geometric shape.
network An arrangement of points with lines connecting them.
numerator The term on the top line of a fraction.

obtuse angle An angle between 90° and 180°.
octagon An eight-sided polygon.
odd number An integer which has a remainder when divided by 2. Odd numbers end with 1, 3, 5, 7 or 9.
origin The point of intersection of the x axis and the y axis. The origin has co-ordinates (0,0).

parallel lines Lines which run in exactly the same direction and never meet.
parallelogram A quadrilateral with opposite sides parallel and equal in length.
pentagon A five-sided polygon.

percentage A number expressed as part of 100. 50% stands for 50 out of every 100.

perimeter The distance around the boundary of a shape.

perpendicular A line which is at right angles to another.

pictogram A statistical diagram that uses symbols or drawings to represent frequencies.

pie chart A circular diagram in which the sectors (slices) represent frequencies.

place value The value of a single digit according to where it appears in the number line, e.g. 5, 50, 500, 5000, etc.

polygon The general name given to a closed shape made up of straight lines.

polynomial equations Equations involving x^2 or x^3, etc.

positive numbers Numbers with a plus (+) sign in front of them. Ordinary numbers without the plus sign are also considered as positive numbers.

power The product of a number multiplied by itself a given number of times, e.g. the third power of $2 = 2 \times 2 \times 2 = 8$.

prime factors Factors which are prime numbers.

prime numbers Any integer which has only itself and 1 as its factors; 2, 3, 5, 7, 11, etc.

prism Any geometric shape that has a uniform area of cross-section.

probability A numerical measure (usually a fraction) of the likelihood of an event taking place.

product The result of multiplication.

proportion A statement of the equality of two ratios.

protractor An instrument used for measuring the size of angles.

pyramid A solid shape with a flat base and sides meeting at a vertex.

Pythagoras' Theorem Applied to the lengths of a right-angled triangle. It takes the form $a^2 + b^2 = c^2$.

quadrant A quarter of a circle.

quadratic equation An algebraic equation involving x and taking the form $ax^2 + bx + c = 0$.

quadrilateral Any four-sided straight line figure.

questionnaire Collection of data by means of a series of questions.

radius A straight line joining the centre of a circle to any point on its circumference. A radius is half of a diameter.

range The difference between the highest and lowest numbers in a set of data.

ratio The relationship between two or more quantities of the same kind.

reciprocal Mathematical expression in which $\frac{3}{4}$ is related to $\frac{4}{3}$, i.e. the reciprocal of 2 is $\frac{1}{2}$.

rectangle A quadrilateral with: opposite sides, equal in length and parallel; and four right angles.

reflection A geometric transformation resulting in a mirror image of the original figure.

reflex angle An angle between 180° and 360°.

regular polygon A polygon that has sides of equal length and equal interior angles, e.g. a square.

rhombus A quadrilateral with opposite sides parallel and equal in length.

right angle An angle of 90°.

rotation A geometric transformation (change) in which a shape turns about a fixed point to another position.

rounding off The process of approximating numbers to a given degree of accuracy.

sample space A list, or table, of all the possible outcomes of an event or events.

sampling A technique of choosing a few so that they represent the total population fairly.

scalar A number that has a size but no specific direction, e.g. length, speed.

scale (a) an ordered series of units or degrees for the purpose of measurement.
(b) The ratio of the actual measurements and those of the lines representing them on a map or scale model.

scalene triangle A triangle with all sides and angles different.

sector A slice of a circle radiating out from its centre.

segment Part of a circle cut off by a line that does not pass through its centre.

semicircle Half of a full circle.

sequence (series) A set of numbers with a pattern.

set A collection of things or numbers.

significant figures The specified number of figures in any number, expressed as an integer or decimal, which serves as an approximation.

simultaneous equations A pair of equations with two unknowns which are satisfied by the same values of the unknown quantities involved.

sphere A perfectly rounded 3-D geometric solid.

square A quadrilateral with four equal sides and four right angles.

square numbers The answers obtained by multiplying any number by itself, e.g. $4 = 2 \times 2$.

square root A number of which the given number is the square, e.g. 3 is the square root of 9 or $3 = \sqrt{9}$.

square unit A measurement of area, e.g. square metre.

standard form A way of expressing a number as a power of 10, i.e. $A \times 10^n$ where $1 \leq A < 10$ and n is the power of 10.

statistics The study of information.

straight angle An angle of 180°.

substitution Replacing a given letter by its numerical value.

sum The result of adding numbers together.

supplementary angles A pair of angles side by side that make up a straight angle.

surface area The area of the surface of a solid shape.

symmetrical Used to describe a shape that can be divided into parts that are: the same in size and shape; and similar in position – on either side of a dividing line or around a central point.

tally A method of counting frequencies as they happen, i.e. keeping 'tally'.

tangent A line that touches the circumference of a circle but does not cut it.

translation A transformation (change) that simply moves a shape from one position to another.

trapezium A quadrilateral with just one pair of opposite parallel sides.

trial and improvement method Guess a solution. Then make a more accurate guess after substituting your original guess into the unknown situation.

triangle A polygon with three straight sides and three included angles which add up to 180°.

triangular numbers Numbers that can be represented by a triangle of dots; 1, 3, 6, 10, 15, etc.

variable An unknown quantity whose value may change.

vector A quantity that has both size and direction, e.g. displacement, velocity.

vertical line A line that moves upwards away from the centre of the earth (at right angles to the horizontal).

volume The measure of space occupied by a solid shape.

x axis The horizontal axis of a Cartesian graph.

y axis The vertical axis of a Cartesian graph.

*I*ndex